UX BEST PRACTICES:

How To Achieve More Impact With User Experience

UX BEST PRACTICES:
How To Achieve More Impact With User Experience

Helmut Degen and Xiaowei Yuan

With support of Nan Guo

New York Chicago San Francisco Lisbon
London Madrid Mexico City Milan New Delhi
San Juan Seoul Singapore Sydney Toronto

The McGraw·Hill Companies

Cataloging-in-Publication Data is on file with the Library of Congress

McGraw-Hill books are available at special quantity discounts to use as premiums and sales promotions, or for use in corporate training programs. To contact a representative, please e-mail us at bulksales@mcgraw-hill.com.

UX Best Practices: How to Achieve More Impact with User Experience

1234567890   QFR QFR   10987654321

ISBN   978-0-07-175251-0
MHID   0-07-175251-X

Editorial Director	Wendy Rinaldi	**Indexer**	Karin Arrigoni
Editorial Supervisor	Patty Mon	**Production Supervisor**	James Kussow
Project Editor	LeeAnn Pickrell	**Composition**	Cenveo Publisher Services
Acquisitions Coordinator	Joya Anthony	**Illustration**	Cenveo Publisher Services
Technical Editor	Nan Gao	**Art Director, Cover**	Jeff Weeks
Copy Editor	LeeAnn Pickrell	**Cover Designer**	Pehrsson Design
Proofreader	Susie Elkind		

To Britta, Jakob, and Julius.
—Helmut

To my daughter, Kristina Yueyue.
—Xiaowei

About the Authors

Helmut Degen works as a team lead and program manager for Siemens Corporate Research (SCR) in Princeton, New Jersey. Before Helmut joined SCR, he worked for Vodafone Holding in Düsseldorf, Germany, and for Siemens AG in Munich, both in the area of User Experience. Helmut received a Ph.D. in information science from the Freie Universität Berlin and a Diplom (comparable to a master's degree) in computer science from the Universität of Karlsruhe, both in Germany. He is married and the father of two boys. Since 2007, Helmut and his family have lived in New Jersey, USA. E-mail: helmut@degen.com.

Dr. Xiaowei Yuan is an expert commissioner of the Standardization Administration of the People's Republic of China and the founder of ISAR User Interface Design. Dr. Yuan used to work at Siemens to localize the User Experience of products for the East Asian market. In 2000, Dr. Yuan returned to China dedicated to undertaking the promotion of the User Experience concept. He worked with many well-known Chinese companies, including Lenovo, Haier, China Telecom, and Ping An, to launch their first step of UCD workflow. He is also an adjunct professor and graduate student tutor for multiple universities, and has fostered many professionals in the field of User Experience in China. Xiaowei received his Ph.D. from the Tübingen University in Germany. E-mail: xiaowei_yuan@isaruid.com.

About the Contributors

Aline Baeck, currently Head of Design at Causata, has worked in interaction design for nearly 20 years. As an Experience Design Architect/Manager at Intuit, she became a passionate advocate for design thinking. She has applied design thinking in many industries, such as national defense (SRI, International), knowledge (Dialog Information Services), medical devices (Acuson), telecommunications (Nortel), B2B Internet (Centegy), and small business (Intuit). Aline received her master's degree from Stanford University and holds several patents. E-mail: alinebaeck@yahoo.com.

Marc Charlier began his career in the hospitality business but soon dived into the marketing field. In 1990, he joined BCT. After working in several customer-related positions, he served as marketing manager for many years. Since 2009, he has served as Manager Corporate Communications at BCT. In the usability project at BCT, Marc was the internal project manager. One of the project results was his successful completion of a degree as a Certified Usability Designer at the Leuven University. Marc writes articles on document management and usability on a frequent basis and was co-author of a textbook about document management. E-mail: marc.charlier@bctsoftware.eu.

Yan Chen, Design Director of the Customer Research & User Experience Design Center, is one of the pioneers of user-centered design at Tencent. Being an expert designer, she has been dedicated to the quality supervision and promotion of User Experience in products. With ten years of usability experience, she led the design of more than ten successful Chinese Internet products, such as QQ, QZone, QQ.COM, and QQMusic. As a pioneer of usability, the theories she advocates and her research results are often shared in this field. E-mail: enya@tencent.com.

Médard Fischer was the head of Swiss Federal Railways' Operations Management Center in Zürich for ten years. Later, he became business project leader for multiple projects such as RCS (Rail Control System) and ALEA (Alert and Incident tool), as well as the head of Requirements Engineering for Operations Management. At the moment, he represents the business for project ADL (adaptive guidance). E-mail: medard.fischer@sbb.ch.

Markus Flückiger is a User Experience expert and requirements engineer. He bridges the gap between developers and users and supports project teams in user-centered software development. Markus has a master's degree in human-computer interaction obtained from Carnegie-Mellon University and a diploma in computer science from ETH in Zürich. E-mail: mdf@zuehlke.com.

Peter Gremett has over 15 years of design and User Experience leadership. He has worked at some of the most well-known companies in the world, including Excite, AOL, PayPal, and Intuit. Working with teams around the globe, he has designed websites, web applications, and software applications that solve business and real customer problems. He is passionate and energetic about designing useful, usable, and engaging consumer products. For him, design is more than a job or a paycheck. He lives in Sunnyvale, California, with his wife and three children. E-mail: designjedi@yahoo.com.

Junius Gunaratne is a user interface developer at Google in New York City. He has been involved with the User Experience community since 2001, specializing in interaction design and front-end development. Prior to Google, Junius worked in various UX roles at Morgan Stanley, Yahoo!, Microsoft, Amazon, and Siemens. His work and published research have been presented at a number of conferences, including CHI, Pervasive Computing, and HCI International. E-mail: junius@google.com.

Andreas Hauser is Vice President of User Experience at SAP AG for OnDemand Solutions, including SAP® Business ByDesign™. He is leading the global User Experience team of approximately 50 people with locations in Germany, the United States, Israel, India, and China. His team is responsible for defining the UI Guidelines, designing the business solutions, as well as conducting extensive user research activities with users globally. Andreas has more than ten years of experience as a UX manager and has gained a great deal of experience in setting up large global User Experience organizations. Previously, he worked as Development Manager in the area of SAP Product Lifecycle Management (PLM), Product Manager for SAP PLM, and Project Manager for Computer Aided Design (CAD) integrations with SAP. Andreas studied business information technology at the University of Cooperative Education in Mannheim and has worked at SAP since 1991. E-mail: andreas.hauser@sap.com.

Hong Ji is Deputy Chief Engineer at the Shanghai Research Institute of China Telecom Corporation, Ltd. As the founder of China Telecom User Experience usability laboratory, she leads the user-centered product development and design team. Over the past ten years, Ms. Ji has been dedicated to developing new products and expanding the market for China Telecom products. She conducted the user experience and usability testing of China Telecom's E-Surfing products and organized the design and development of a special mobile phone for the blind, which won the 2009 China Red Star Design Award, the national leading industrial design award. E-mail: jihong@sttri.com.cn.

Lixian Huang has a master's in applied mathematics and works in the Customer Research & User Experience Design Center at Tencent. He has one year of experience in software development and four years in user research. He is a senior user research engineer and the principal for the project on establishing and optimizing a User Experience evaluation system. He has been engaged in the research and development of UI design tools allowing high-fidelity prototypes. He also has accumulated a great deal of experience in eye tracking studies in HCI. E-mail: henryhuang@tencent.com.

Ming Li is General Manager of the e-commerce website belonging to Ping An Group. She has over ten years of e-commerce experience and five years of usability experience. Ping An's e-commerce website is the largest insurance website in China. Ping An is one of the largest financial groups in China. E-mail: liming@pingan.com.cn.

Qi Luo, Master of Art, works on HCI and user research in the Customer Research & User Experience Design Center at Tencent. She led the User Research Group for many projects in instant messaging, e-commerce, social networking, multimedia, among others. She has completed fruitful research in the quantitative evaluation of User Experience and the user relationship chain on social networks. Email: sybil@tencent.com.

Dr. Thomas Memmel manages a business unit at Zühlke, Switzerland. Within the context of Java Enterprise applications, he works with client technology, User Experience design, requirements engineering, and agile methods. Thomas studied information engineering at the University of Konstanz and obtained a doctorate specializing in human-computer interaction. E-mail: thomas.memmel@zuehlke.com.

Peter L. Phillips is an internationally recognized expert in developing corporate design management strategies and programs. He has had more than thirty years of experience as a senior corporate design manager, a consultant, author, and lecturer. Mr. Phillips is the author of *Creating the Perfect Design Brief: How to Manage Design for Strategic Advantage* (Allworth Press 2004). He also serves on the advisory board and is an adjunct professor in design management for the Suffolk University Executive MBA Program in Innovation and Design Management. E-mail: peterp4@comcast.net.

Anke Richter (Siemens AG) studied information and communication science and psychology in Berlin, Germany. From 1997–2003, she worked as a freelancer in graphic design and layout, public relations, and web and user interface design. Since 2003, she has worked as a usability expert at the Competence Center for User Interface Design at Siemens Corporate Technology. Her main focus is on domain energy, especially Smart Grid–related topics. She has been involved in Siemens user interface pattern activities from the very beginning in 2000. She supported the setup of the pattern library at Siemens Energy Automation and is currently consulting on content extensions and usage of the library. E-mail: a.richter@siemens.com.

Sonja Sander (Siemens AG) studied psychology and computer science with a focus on human factors and usability. Sonja also holds an MBA in strengthening business focus. From 2002 to 2006, she worked as a senior consultant at Siemens Corporate Technology. In 2003, she set up the first user interface pattern library at Siemens for exchanging patterns within the company. Since 2006, she does strategic usability engineering and product management at Siemens Energy Automation. User interface patterns support her major task of achieving consistent and high-quality user interfaces despite organizational and technological challenges. E-mail: sonja.sander@siemens.com.

Shiwei Shui is in charge of User Experience work for the e-commerce website at Ping An. Having focused on User Experience project management and website User Experience solution delivery for several years, he has accumulated abundant experience with online sales and promotions for financial and insurance products as well as credit cards. E-mail: eshui5568@gmail.com.

Sigrid Vandenweghe graduated as an Organizational Psychologist and is a Senior Project Manager at Human Interface Group. She worked on several projects covering User Experience design, information architecture, and design. Her extensive experience covers a wide range of domains, from e-government projects, banking and insurance applications, broadcast software, temp work, and accountancy software, to highly specialized websites for specific target audiences and consumer products. E-mail: sigrid.vandenweghe@higroup.com.

Kris Vanstappen is co-founder and CEO of Human Interface Group, a Belgium-based User Experience consultancy. Kris has worked for more than 25 years on User Experience design projects. Human Interface Group is one of the largest independent usability consultancies in Europe with almost 20 years of experience in optimizing the User Experience of technological solutions. E-mail: kris.vanstappen@higroup.com.

Jian Wu, head of Haier Innovation Design Center, leads the design team in delivering world-class design service, both for this appliance giant and another independent manufacturer in China. During his ten years at Haier, Mr. Wu has developed a brand-new workflow for user-centered design combined with several design assessment methods that ensure all output attracts target consumers and meets their demands. All his efforts have greatly supported Haier in its quest to be the No. 1 major-appliance manufacturer globally and one of the most famous brands in Asia. E-mail: wuj@haier.com.

Contents at a Glance

Contents

Forewords

Foreword by Dan Rosenberg (USA)

There are so many UX books on the market today that it is natural to ask with a degree of skepticism, Why should I read this one? What unique value does it bring to me as a practitioner? This book, edited by Helmut Degen and Xiaowei Yuan, is likely to become a classic because it updates a universally relevant topic in our profession regarding the impact that UX can have on transforming corporate culture and thereby consistently creating successful products and services.

When Helmut and Xiaowei first proposed the idea I was reminded of Mike Wiklund's 1994 *Usability in Practice* book, which contained a collection of successful UI case studies. I had the opportunity to be a chapter co-author for this book. Then the next question that popped into my head was to ask why had it been almost 20 years since this facet of UX was revisited in book format. A lot has changed in 20 years—from a technical perspective with a focus on mobility, from a development process perspective with the rise of Agile development methods, and from a management perspective with globalization. All this is new; therefore, a new book is required. Even the core leadership and communication issues that challenge UX management have changed recently with the emergence of products like the iPhone and iPad that awoke all CEO's to the revenue-generating power of good experience.

I have led several corporate UX teams over the last 25 years, and I can assure you that no company builds a great product solely on the contribution of their UX team. UX teams must effectively collaborate with the primary and secondary stakeholders like product management, development, and marketing for product success to be achieved and their impact felt. For UX to function as a catalyst for change, we must always work to make the entire organization successful. This book—*UX Best Practices: How to Achieve More Impact with User Experience*—will provide you with insights regarding how a group of leading practitioners are achieving this goal today. That is why I believe you should read it.

—*Daniel Rosenberg, Senior Vice President*
SAP User Experience

Daniel Rosenberg is Senior Vice President for User Experience at SAP, the world's largest Enterprise Applications Software company. The SAP global UX team is located in eight different countries. Prior to joining SAP, he was Vice President of R&D for UI Design at Oracle Corporation. He has authored or co-authored many well-known publications in the HCI field and is one of the founding editors of ACM's *NetWorker* magazine.

Foreword by Jiangming Dong (China)

Over the past few decades, the recognition of the importance of User Experience (UX) has grown tremendously. It started with supporting tactical product improvement, such as detecting design flaws and optimizing human performance, and has grown into a full discipline to enhance overall user satisfaction of products and solutions. More and more companies have realized the importance of UX and are exploring ways to integrate its process into their product life cycle.

How do we increase the impact of UX on products? This is a question typically asked by inexperienced UX practitioners who want to establish credibility for their initial work. Interestingly, as their UX skills mature and the UX teams expand, they still face the very same question, but raised more often by their stakeholders, including product management, marketing, and even company executives. Clearly, even solid UX research and designs do not necessarily impact products sufficiently.

From a business perspective, UX practitioners are mostly hired to support product design and development. Whether they work in a separate organization or are blended into product development teams, their roles are always unique when compared to mainstream product teams. Products teams typically focus on delivery goals and technical constraints. UX is often just one of their considerations. In many cases, UX has to yield to other conflicting requirements, and this undermines its impact.

The reasons behind these issues mostly fall into two categories: On the one hand, most product teams lack an in-depth understanding of the processes and the values of UX, thereby misjudging the UX work. On the other hand, many UX practitioners lack the competencies to interpret their work from a product perspective, creating a gap between products and UX.

During the past two decades, I have had the opportunity to work extensively in the area of UX with leading companies in the United States, China, and other countries. This work involves establishing UX teams, managing and conducting UX projects, and training UX practitioners and managers. Although the challenges are the same, the approaches to address these challenges are very different across companies and teams. Generally, leading Chinese companies have acknowledged the importance of UX. However, they do not have the right staff, processes, and tools to implement an effective User Experience program. Western companies, on the other hand, generally have systematic theories and utilities. However, these processes cannot be readily used for Chinese companies when the teams face tremendous pressure for fast delivery and proof of results, which are not feasible using a conventional approach.

The success of increasing the impact of UX depends on the appropriate adaptation of these approaches in the context of specific product types, business contexts, and company culture. The contributors to this book, with a wealth of experience, from a variety of industries and regions, have shared their success stories here. *UX Best Practices* will certainly be extremely valuable to all those working on maximizing the impact of UX.

—Jiangming Dong, User Experience Principle, Head of Global Research and Consumer Labs,
Huawei Technologies, Inc.

Jianming Dong, PhD., is widely recognized as a UX thought leader with many years of experience. He has led many mission-critical UX programs at IBM, eBay, and played UX leadership roles at HFI and Huawei Technologies. His unique contributions to the UX field include the pioneering card sorting tool, a bestseller HCI book in Chinese, and numerous patents and publications.

Foreword by Prof. Dr. Heidi Krömker (Germany)

User Experience has achieved a broad acceptance in science and in industry. Many product suppliers intend for their products to have a positive User Experience that goes beyond mere good utility and usability. As products become more and more similar in terms of functionality, User Experience becomes even more relevant.

User Experience experts, as documented in the ISO 9241-210, came to an agreement about the definition of User Experience as being a " person's perceptions and responses that result from the use and/or anticipated use of a product, system or service." However, the term remains ambiguous.

Science has created a number of methods and techniques that help explain the factors that influence User Experience quality. The scientific community agrees that User Experience is related to positive emotions that result from using a product. These emotions should motivate the user to employ the product continuously in the future.

Due to the competitive nature of the market, User Experience needs to be innovatively designed for different products and product releases, which is an additional challenge for the product development process. There are not many published concepts and methods available today, especially with practical evidence from industry, that describe how User Experience can be systematically and successfully integrated into a product development lifecycle.

Considering this, the two editors of this book, *UX Best Practices,* offer an interesting approach. The editors, internationally experienced User Experience experts, have sought the secret of User Experience in different regions of the world in order to collect success stories.

Helmut Degen has applied and validated his outstanding theoretical knowledge over many years in Europe and the United States in different industrial domains that span from telecommunications to mobile phones, e-commerce, and enterprise applications.

Xiaowei Yuan is a User Experience expert and pioneer who transferred the User Experience concept from Europe to China. He introduced User Experience to the Chinese academia and industry more than ten years ago. At that time, there were no words for "Usability" and "User Experience" in the Chinese language. Considering this, you can imagine the effort it took to introduce the User Experience concept into Chinese society and industry. It is astonishing how fast the User Experience concept has penetrated the booming Asian product landscape since then.

The reader can expect many ideas, methods, process elements, tips, and tricks that encourage the expert to approach User Experience from a different perspective with a focus on product and business impact. Decision makers can treat the success stories as benchmarks. The documented UX practices will help the reader to improve his or her product development approach.

I am convinced the reader will enjoy these success stories and be inspired by them.

—Prof. Dr. Heidi Krömker, Chair for Media Production
Technical University Ilmenau

Prof. Dr. Heidi Krömker holds a chair for Media Production at the Technical University Ilmenau. Her research interests include Human Computer Interaction and Media Production Processes. Previously Dr. Heidi Krömker was head of the User Interface Design Center of the central technical department of Siemens AG with Usability Laboratories in China (Beijing), USA (New York/Princeton), and Germany (Munich). After her study of social sciences, she managed development projects, such as introducing usability engineering to Siemens. Dr. Krömker earned her Ph.D. in Human Factors at the University of Bamberg, Germany.

Acknowledgments

There are many people involved in a book project such as this. We want to thank all the authors who patiently accepted the iterations of reviews and our review comments. You helped to lift the quality level of every single chapter with each iteration. Furthermore, we want to thank the people supporting the authors. We actually don't know them by name, but their support was crucial. A big thanks goes to the IP departments from the different companies for their timely response.

We also want to thank the people who sent abstracts and drafts to us that did not make it into the book. We appreciate the time and effort they invested.

We want to thank Sam Zheng for valuable discussions and inspiring ideas on this book. Sam helped to bring the strategic versus tactical perspective into the focus of the book.

Another big thanks goes to Emei Xu. Emei became the interface between Helmut and the Chinese contributors and did a great job in coordinating all the reviews.

We want to thank Wendy Rinaldi from McGraw-Hill. You helped us get this work done in a very professional manner. We enjoyed and appreciated all of your professional support and reliable responses throughout the project—listening to the book idea, pitching the book idea successfully within the McGraw-Hill organization, and producing the book itself. You also accepted delays without it affecting your belief in the book. We want to thank Joya Anthony for coordinating the work and the schedule for authoring the single chapters and Melinda Lytle for her support in making sure the graphics in the chapters would translate into a book of high quality. Last but not least, a big thank goes to LeeAnn Pickrell, who managed the copyediting and the proofreading process. These are the last steps in the process where the editors are involved, and it is the part where the nitty-gritty details count. Thanks for your eye for details, accepting patiently the delays, and your professional work. You all did you a great job, and we would do it all again with you!

Helmut wants to thank his family: my wife Britta and my sons Jakob and Julius. I missed many "gemuetliche Abende" (I guess this German expression can be translated as "cozy evenings") in order to read "just another chapter I received today." I couldn't do it without all of your support and love!

Xiaowei wants to thank Kristina Yueyue: my lovely daughter, you bring me lots of happiness!

Introduction

Why This Book?

Products like the iPad and iPhone have set a new User Experience (UX) quality benchmark for the entire product development industry, even beyond consumer products. More and more product-development professionals recognize the value of UX quality. They consequently start expressing the wish for a similar UX quality for their products.

However, the editors of this book ("we") have experienced and observed that it is still difficult to be as involved as User Experience (UX) professionals as we would like to be: early or "upstream" involvement in the product lifecycle process, applying a user-centered design approach with results that impact product quality and ideally improve the bottom line of a company. The reality is often different: late or "downstream" involvement with little or no impact on product quality. We are referring to situations where UX as a contributor is often not well integrated into the product lifecycle process. Furthermore, we have observed that discussions about UX are generally about UX methods ("how-to" talks), mostly held by UX people themselves. We have also seen that UX people have difficulties explaining the value of the UX contributions to non-UX people or even measuring the achieved UX value. It is interesting that the UX discipline preaches the "use of customer wording" for their work products, but has difficulties preaching the same principle when it comes to pitching and explaining its own discipline to its customers. Also we've often experienced the attitude that only UX knows best how to do it without leveraging the knowledge, experience, and ideas of other stakeholders. We call this a UX island attitude.

Triggered by these perceived gaps, we were looking for a single question at the beginning of this book project that could address them: *How to achieve (more) impact with User Experience?* We then looked at the question ... so what? First, we discussed documenting our personal project experiences and success stories. To get a broader insight, we chose another approach: We came to the conclusion that it would be more beneficial if we collected and published success stories from different people, companies, business types, and even regions. One of the editors is rooted in the Chinese world; the other editor is rooted in the "Western" world. Our plan was to collect success stories from the different worlds.

We hope the success stories in the book provide some time for readers to breathe. Let's see where User Experience has achieved impact. The stories will hopefully inspire the reader to apply some of the techniques or process elements to his or her own organization or customers. If readers can apply at least one of these experiences, creating this book was worthwhile. The vision of this book goes beyond that, however: Readers may change their perspective on the User Experience discipline, moving from a "how-to" perspective to an "impact" perspective and then apply this new perspective to their organization or customers' organizations systematically to achieve greater impact with UX contributions more often.

Why Is This Book Unique?

When we started this book project, we analyzed available publications and books about "impact through User Experience." Most books about UX are "how-to" books (how to run a usability test, how to create wireframes, etc.). The "how-to" books show UX tools, techniques, and methods, but they don't tell you which of the techniques and methods are really successful and in which business context. This book describes UX techniques and process elements that are successfully applied in product lifecycle processes. Since we assume the reader is proficient with User Experience, the book does not describe how to apply these methods in detail. We have not discovered another book that focuses solely on "impact through User Experience." Therefore, we believe this book is unique on the market so far.

The other unique "feature" of this book is its cross-regional coverage. We are very proud that we could collect and publish success stories from the United States, Europe, and China.

Who Should Read This Book?

This book is written for people who have influence on product quality and User Experience contributions in an organization. The book is written for directors and managers of User Experience groups or departments. They are often interested in the question of how to become more influential with User Experience contributions. The stories in this book will help these folks learn from others' success and apply these elements to their own organization.

The book is also written for (senior) vice presidents of product management, product development, and technology divisions who want to understand how User Experience can be leveraged strategically to improve product quality, the company's bottom line, and customer satisfaction. The stories in this book will help them learn from industry practices how UX activities can be integrated into the product development process or how the integration can be optimized.

UX consulting companies are another target audience. They want to understand how to increase the value of User Experience for their customers. A few stories in this book are from joint ventures between a UX consulting company and its customers. UX consulting companies can learn how collaborating with a client can lead to product and business impact.

The book is also written for the UX workforce. The success stories in this book may help them understand which techniques and process elements work well in other organizations. With the experience of daily work, the UX workforce can support senior management in optimizing UX processes and their integration into development processes with the aim of achieving more impact.

Last but not least, the book is written for the UX professors, UX researchers, and UX students. The perspective of the success stories may stimulate augmenting current UX curricula and UX research topics beyond the theory and method development perspective to the "impact" perspective. It would be beneficial for the UX industry if teachers, students, and researchers were equipped with the sensitivity and some knowledge that User Experience is one of many important players in the product development game. It would be great if they understood that UX theories and methods are useful for practitioners if they can be utilized in commercial product development organizations with their many constraints in order to achieve (more) product and business impact.

All of the mentioned target groups can help to increase the effectiveness and recognition of the UX industry as a key contributor to the product lifecycle in order to improve the quality of life.

Some Terms

The word "impact" can have a broad meaning. In creating this book, distinguishing between *product* impact and *business* impact was important. When we talk about product impact, we're referring to a positive influence on the quality of a product. When we talk about business impact, we're referring to a positive influence on the bottom line—cost reduction, revenue increase, or both. This book focuses mainly on *product* impact. There are several reasons to focus on product and not business impact. First of all, a prerequisite for business impact is product impact. In many cases, UX still has difficulties achieving product impact. Furthermore, a portfolio or product manager is usually accountable for deciding to develop a certain product and how the product looks. If the decision was incorrect, the product won't be successful in the market, even if it has a great UX. We make the assumption that UX people are not accountable for a portfolio or a product. A third reason not to focus on the business impact is the fact that development activities in industrial environments are usually interwoven. Therefore, it is difficult to prove that a particular development discipline has a certain impact on the bottom line. Some of the success stories in this book indicate its positive business impact, however.

We use the term *product* in a very broad sense. It refers to software products (PC software, enterprise software, e-commerce websites, mobile applications) and software-intensive products or solutions (mobile phones, alarm systems, home appliances). Products can also target different markets (consumer or investment goods).

We refer to the topics of each contribution as a *UX practice*. A UX practice may be a single technique or a combination of techniques. It also may use techniques that stem from other disciplines but help to achieve product impact.

How We Selected the Contributions

Our role as editors was to ensure that the success stories were compelling. Our intention was not to publish just another how-to perspective of known practices. The key criterion for selecting contributors was having a project or organizational experience where User Experience contributions had a proven and repeated product impact. Another hidden criterion was that they had to be willing to publish these success stories. Interestingly, both criteria reduced the contribution candidates rapidly.

We approached authors from organizations with product ownership (e.g., a software company) and authors from firms that provide UX service to organizations with product ownership (a UX consulting company). For the latter, we asked the authors to partner with their customers. We wanted to make sure the success story covered both sides: the side providing the UX service and the side receiving and processing the UX contributions that led to the impact. This also ensured we got the "impact" part of the success story.

We did not want to enforce a certain chapter structure. However, we wanted to make sure that each success story covered certain points. Therefore, we came up with several questions that each success story should answer:

- What is the business context (e.g., product, customers)?

- Which (business) problems did you address with your UX practice?

- What were constraints and prerequisites?

- In which development context did you apply your UX practice?

- What compelling events supported you in applying your UX practice successfully?

- What was the achieved impact?

- How did you apply the UX practice?

- What recommendations do you have for our readers?

We approached many UX professionals and companies. We are grateful to the authors who were willing to share their UX success stories. We are aware that this book is not a representative collection of success stories across the UX industry, but it provides a view into the UX industry.

Guided Tour Through the Book

The book is a collection of success stories. As you might guess, you don't have to read the entire book. However, if you are looking for ways how to improve the impact of UX in your organization strategically and tactically, you can probably find ideas in all of the stories.

The book starts with a success story from Peter Phillips (U.S.). One of the editors (Helmut) met Peter a couple of years ago when he attended a workshop that Peter held. After Peter's workshop, Helmut completely changed the way he looked at User Experience: away from a "how-to" perspective toward a "why-and-what" perspective. Peter had worked as Director of Global Design Strategy for various corporations and was successful in marketing design discipline internally in each of those corporations. In Chapter 1, Peter introduces the concept of design as problem-solving discipline. Peter also describes the function of a design brief, the concept of a value statement, and the partnership relationship. Peter's chapter deviates from the content of other chapters in that it describes general concepts and techniques. However, Peter's chapter sets a good tone for the entire book and its focus on "impact."

After Peter's success story, we share five stories about entire integrated UX processes.

In Chapter 2, Andreas Hauser (Germany) from SAP® describes a success story about how to institutionalize User Experience in a large organization. Andreas led an effort to set up an entire UX organization for the development of a new SAP product line, called SAP® Business ByDesign™. SAP Business ByDesign is a new on-demand business solution for small and mid-sized enterprises. Andreas gives recommendations on how to set up and execute a user-centered design process in a global organization, how to influence the organization and people to ride the user-centered design wave, and how to impact the UI technology to focus on User Experience requirements. He describes how these practices impacted the product quality and, therefore, also the business success of the solution. What is impressive in Andreas' success story is the evolvement of the UX processes that went along with the product's measured and improved UX qualities. In addition, he describes useful details about techniques for quality checks, how to structure teams, how to use UX patterns and guidelines, and also how to move from a waterfall type of development process to an agile development process.

In Chapter 3, Ming Li and Shiwei Shui describe a UX success story from Ping An® (China). The Ping An Group provides comprehensive products and services in insurance, banking, and investment. This chapter focuses on UX processes for the development of an e-commerce website for selling Ping An's services online. The authors describe the team setup and some parts of the process. What is interesting in this story is that the User Experience team, the IT team, and the sales team worked closely together. Furthermore, website design options were tested on the real website and decisions made based on real user data. This practice lead to a five times increased conversation rate.

Sigrid Vandenweghe, Kris Vanstappen (both from Human Interface Group in Belgium), and Marc Charlier (from BCT in The Netherlands) describe an organizational change process in Chapter 4. This story is the first by a UX consulting company (HIG) in conjunction with its client (BCT). BCT (est. 1985) is one of Europe's major players in Enterprise Content Management (ECM). As a UX service provider, Human Interface Group supported BCT to improve the product "CORSA," document management software. What started with a UX assessment led to a collaboration between both companies, which had a strategic impact on BCT's development process. BCT changed its development process to a user-centered-design approach. This success story introduces into the product history the UX quality of CORSA prior to Human Interface Group's involvement. It describes key elements of the UX quality and the changed development process. The change led not only to higher product quality, mainly as a result of User Experience quality, but also to a higher growth rate of 22 percent revenue in the recession year 2009 as well as cost savings.

Hong Ji from China Telecom® (China) describes a story from the telecommunications industry in Chapter 5. Hong introduces the challenges of the telecommunication market today and the strategy to differentiate products by User Experience qualities. Derived from that, she describes an end-to-end product development process with integrated User Experience activities. This process takes into consideration the complexity of the mobile operator technology. What is compelling in Hong's success story is that the changes made had not only a product impact but also a business impact. She demonstrates the success of the integrated development process with a small case study for music downloads. The number of successful music downloads increased from 2,122 per day (the day before the UX improvement was implemented) to 4,130 per day (the day after the UX improvement was implemented), which is an increase of 94.63 percent. The revenue across all products increased by 60 million RMB in 2010.

In Chapter 6, Thomas Memmel, Markus Flückiger (Zühlke Engineering®, Switzerland), and Médard Fischer (Swiss Federal Railways®, Switzerland) describe a success story about the development of the product ALEA (Alarm and Event Assistant) for the Swiss Federal Railways (SFR). The story focuses on how SCRUM was executed conjointly with product management, IT development, UX practices, and people. The different project stakeholders explain their point of view about the UX involvement in the SCRUM approach, which is unique among all success stories of this book. All of the stakeholders appreciated the UX contributions. They acknowledged that the project team, significantly influenced by UX contributions, achieved not only a high product quality, but also a business impact that included improved customer service quality, shortened time to solving the problem raised by ALEA, and reduced costs.

The following success stories focus on certain process elements that led to more impact with User Experience.

In Chapter 7, Yan Chen, Qi Luo, and Lixian Huang from Tencent® (China) describe an User Experience Evaluation System (UESS). The UESS augments standard product key performance indicators with User Experience–related key performance indicators in order to evaluate and improve product quality strategically. The system is used company wide and is connected to strategic business goals. Tencent introduced the system four years ago and has improved it step-by-step. The UESS includes quantitative, qualitative effectiveness, participation level, and process and specification construction criteria. The UESS is used to compare Tencent's own products against competitors and for long-term monitoring of product improvements. The chapter outlines how Tencent steadily improved user satisfaction and, at the same time, reduced the number of user complaints significantly.

Junius Gunaratne (U.S.) describes how different types of prototyping can be used for product development in Chapter 8. Junius' chapter is based on his working experience at Yahoo!®. He describes the use of prototypes for redesigning My Yahoo!, a personalized start page. The chapter describes how prototyping techniques led to an early and shared understanding among the design team, the engineering team, product management, and user groups. The goal of the redesign was to upgrade the My Yahoo! start page with new features while keeping established features on the start page. The chapter describes three types of prototypes: proof-of-concept prototypes, feature-specific prototypes, and comprehensive prototypes. The three prototypes serve different purposes. Each type of prototype is outlined and described as to how it helped improve the quality of the redesigned My Yahoo! start page. This chapter is a nice example of how a specific technique can help achieve a product impact, eventually leading to a business impact. It also shows how the use of prototypes can make the product development process more efficient.

In Chapter 9, Sonja Sander and Anke Richter (both Siemens© AG, Germany) describe an approach for using user interface (UI) patterns to achieve product and business impact. The authors faced the challenge of reducing development costs. Sonja proposed and introduced a pattern-based UX approach that introduced reusable elements. The pattern-based approach led to an adjustment of the development process involving all relevant key stakeholders. It finally led to the development of a pattern library, which realized the reduction of development costs and increased the product quality. The pattern library and usability process have meanwhile been well established in the organization. The pattern library allows the company to employ only three UX people to support approximately 800 developers. This effort is below the industry effort of 5 percent to 15 percent of the total development effort for User Experience activities. The chapter describes the process of defining and using UI patterns.

In Chapter 10, Jian Wu from Haier® (China) describes a Rapid Testing System (RTS) that is used in a three-step design process. The core idea is to standardize measurement tools that are used at the end of the three steps to check the quality of the results. The measurement tools are established in the Haier organization and measure the achieved quality and indicate where improvements are required. This standardization also allows the company to work with external UX consultants as additional resources without compromising the quality of the work. The chapter outlines how Haier applies this method to the design of refrigerators. The introduction of the RTS led to a more efficient development process, which resulted in a 20 percent to 40 percent shorter development time.

Last, but not least, we close the book in Chapter 11 with a "Design Thinking" story from Peter Gremett (U.S.) and Aline Baeck (Intuit®, U.S.). We put this story last because the practice described in their chapter has, at least from the perspective of the editors, the potential to show how the UX discipline can move forward, not just in terms of processes and practices integration. Peter Gremett and Aline Baeck describe the concept of Design Thinking (DT) and how it has evolved within Intuit. DT is now an essential development philosophy at Intuit and the adoption of DT practices has increased product innovations. The scope of DT is not limited to User Experience; it also includes business problems and product innovations. While typical product innovations are often thought of in terms of features and technologies (static perspective), DT introduces context-, people- and task-oriented thinking (dynamic perspective). In other words, DT means applying User Experience methods to general business problems and product innovations. Peter and Aline outline in their chapter several techniques and examples of how DT is integrated and executed at Intuit. The potential for the industry is to resolve the two often conflicting static and dynamic perspectives. Therefore, practicing DT can lead not only to better User Experience solutions, but also to better business solutions and innovations. The broad adoption of DT would mean a major change to "innovation thinking."

What We Have Learned So Far

As written previously, the shared success stories are not representative of the UX industry. However, some common themes can be derived from the stories:

- User Experience contributions have champions outside the User Experience organization who understand or believe in the value of User Experience contributions and support them. In some cases, a temporary championship turned into an established and trusting partnership between UX people and other product development people.

- User Experience concepts and language have been introduced into the organization. On one hand, stakeholders on different levels understand the language. UX experts, on the other hand, understand and speak the product and business language.

- User Experience addresses business problems and User Experience contributions are quantified by key performance indicators (KPIs). It is transparent which UX targets influence product and business targets. The target settings and the target measurement is established in the organizational process. Results of target settings influence the selection of User Experience practices.

- User Experience activities and other development activities are deeply connected and integrated; communication environments are considered in the process and used in daily work for sharing achievements, plans, and expectations for User Experience work results.

- User Experience results are not only captured in text documents (e.g., style guides), but also implemented in process elements (e.g., patterns libraries), which allows organizations to reuse them at low cost in several applications.

We started the book project in the first half 2009. The question is how much the UX industry has evolved since then. In order to answer this question, one of the editors (Helmut) launched the survey "Global UX Market Impact Study for Product Development Organizations" in October 2011. The topics of the survey were derived from the insights of the UX success stories of this book. So far, 31 participants from all over the world have provided qualified responses.

One question asked what the average achieved UX quality level for the first release of a product is on a scale from 1 (poor UX quality) to 10 (Apple-like UX quality). The average value as selected by 31 participants is 6.0. We were also interested in understanding what the intended target UX quality is (we used the same scale). The participants selected, on average, the value 8.8.

We wanted to understand what hindered product development organizations today to deliver products with a desirable UX quality effectively and efficiently. We offered 12 statements that reflected potential reasons. Out of 31 participants, 30 of them selected at least 1 of the 12 statements or added a new reason. Here is the list of the 6 most-often-selected statements:

- Not having sufficient UX resources available (selected 18 times; 56 percent)

- Development process does not provide sufficient time to define a UX solution with an acceptable UX quality (selected 15 times; 47 percent)

- Lack of understanding what the business value of UX is (selected 15 times; 47 percent)

- Insufficient integration of UX activities with the development process (selected 11 times; 34 percent)

- Lack of understanding which UX quality level the customer really needs (selected 11 times; 34 percent)

- Difficult to find skilled and experienced UX people (selected 10 times; 31 percent)

The survey also asked about whether UX is mentioned in the product or business strategy and whether the achievement of UX objectives is measured systematically. Sixty-eight percent (selected 21 times) of the participants confirmed that User Experience is explicitly mentioned in business or product strategy. However, 61 percent (selected 19 times) confirmed that their organization does not measure systematically whether the UX objective has been met.

The survey results indicate that UX activities are still not properly integrated into the product lifecycle process and in the business value proposition today. The survey results also indicate that the UX success stories published in this book are rather exceptional in the UX industry and can be considered as benchmarks.

The UX industry still has a way to go. One option to move forward is to invest in UX process assessments and improvements' initiatives. These could help to increase the impact of UX contributions systematically. The UX practices described in the success stories in this book can be used as a starting point to improve existing UX processes.

Chapter 1

Collaborative, Innovative Design Briefs:

A Key Tool to Position UX Design as a Credible,
Trusted, Core, Strategic Business Competency
in any Enterprise

By Peter L. Phillips

The term *design* is not always interpreted the same way by everyone who uses it. Design takes many forms and there are many types of designers. There are product designers, graphic designers, packaging designers, UX designers, user interface designers, landscape designers, floral designers, interior designers, architects, engineers who "design" circuitry for microchips, and on and on. The list seems endless. So, when we say we are designers, often people are not really sure just what we are talking about!

What is design? The great designer Paul Rand had the perfect answer, in my opinion. Rand said, "Design is a problem solving discipline." No matter what the design discipline, all designers use specific knowledge and techniques to solve *problems.* For the most part, these problems are related to a business in some manner.

In my 30 plus years as a professional graphic designer and design manager, I have learned that the failure rate for new products runs about 30 to 40 percent. Why do these products fail? There are many variables and probable causes. However, at least anecdotally, I know that a vast number of design projects fail simply because the designer, or the design group, did not fully understand the problem they were trying to solve with design techniques. Most often, this can be attributed to either a complete lack of any kind of design brief or to a very poorly crafted brief that didn't really identify the problem.

Why then do people forego the design brief? The most common excuses I have heard are that developing a brief takes too much time and costs too much. I also suspect it has a lot to do with the fact that most business managers are completely uninformed about how to develop a proper design brief and have no experience with developing briefs.

Another reason, in my experience, that many design solutions fail in the marketplace is that there is little or no strategic collaboration between the commissioners of design projects and the designer(s). Rather design is more often viewed as one of several support functions used to launch a new product.

If design is a problem-solving discipline, and the problem to be solved is not clearly articulated, then the chances of a design solution failing is maximized. In order for the problem to be clearly articulated prior to the beginning of the design process, a highly collaborative and strategic relationship must exist between the commissioners of a design and the designers.

This chapter is not about any one particular UX design project, or problem, but rather it is about techniques to identify and articulate clearly just what the business context (problem) really is. It is a strategic partnership process that will lead to credibility and trust between the business project commissioning group and the UX design function.

The best *tool* to meet this business need and assure a strategic partnership is the collaborative, innovative design brief.

What Is a Design Brief Anyway?

During the course of my career, I have learned that people use a variety of terms for what I am calling a *design brief.* Many people refer to them as a *creative brief.* Others are accustomed to terms such as *marketing brief, project brief, job ticket,* or—actually my favorite—*innovation brief.* Whatever the term used, we are talking about a written description of a project that requires some form of design.

My least favorite term is *job ticket.* A job ticket is usually no more than a one-page summary of the title of the project, the due date, budget, the name of the requesting person, or group, and other, mostly tactical, data. In my opinion, most of these job tickets are more or less useless for the actual process of developing a design solution.

I am, as mentioned previously, quite taken with a term commonly used in Europe, *innovation brief.* I like what that term implies. Unfortunately, most businesses don't regard design as an innovative, or even a strategic, business process; rather, they think of it as a support service.

The Format of a Design Brief

Actually, there is no single correct—or preferred—format for a design brief. I have seen really good design briefs that are totally narrative, written in paragraph form, and others that employ the bulleted list format. Increasingly, I am seeing design briefs that have been developed with a computer program format wherein requestors for design work simply fill in the blanks after a list of key questions. I have also seen some excellent briefs formatted as PowerPoint presentations.

The format you eventually adopt depends largely on the specific type of design work you are involved in and the most useful style for your particular company and business. The format is, of course, critical in that it should be easy to read and track through. Other than that, what is most important is that the brief contain *all* of the information and data necessary for every stakeholder in the process. It must also be available in hard copy, as well as online.

The computer program–generated type of format seems to pose the biggest challenges for designers I have talked with over the years. Ironically, for the most part designers have developed these computer-generated formats! It's not so much that the formats are poorly designed but rather that the design brief format is not used properly. The most common complaint is that many fields are left blank by the requestor, or if they are filled in, the information is incomplete. A typical example is a field titled "Audience." A typical answer in this field is "Customers." For me, that's not a suitable entry!

The importance of finding the best format for your organization should not be overlooked. It will take some time, and experimentation, to develop a format that will meet everyone's real-world needs in your company. At the end of the day, you will have to evolve a format that meets your specific needs. I admit that I have always found the narrative format works best for me. My second choice is the bulleted-list approach.

How Long Should a Design Brief Be?

The quick answer is—as long as necessary. A great many participants in my design brief workshops tell me they have been asked repeatedly to make design briefs as *short* as possible. That should not be the goal. The real goal is to make design briefs as *complete and useful* as possible. The final length is ultimately determined by the requirements of the specific project and its complexity.

When Do You Need a Design Brief?

Does every design project require a design brief? Absolutely not! Many design projects that could be classified as routine, or ongoing, do not require formal design briefs. But major projects, in each of the design disciplines, including UX design, certainly do require a written design brief. Please take note—a design brief is *written,* not verbal. The most common excuse I have heard for not writing a formal design brief for major projects is that the time frame for the project was too short to develop a design brief. The second reason most often given for not writing a design brief is that a written brief limits creativity. I disagree. I believe the kind of design brief I am advocating can actually enhance creativity—not stifle it.

Let me be very clear: verbal-only design briefings for important projects add significantly to the time it takes to complete a project. Verbal briefings almost always lead to unfortunate misunderstandings, hard feelings, angry confrontations, major frustration, and design solutions that are not as great as they could have been.

Over the years, the constant mantra I hear from designers and design managers is "They don't understand," "They don't give me enough time," "They don't give me enough money," "They don't let me be creative," "They don't appreciate UX design process!" If this is true, and I believe it often is, my answer is that it is not *they,* but *we* who are at fault. If the design profession isn't getting the strategic information it needs to identify and solve a business problem, then shame on us. It is our fault that "they" don't understand. We haven't communicated our needs effectively. It's really that simple. It is up to the design profession to learn to become proactive—to take a leadership role—in making people appreciate and value design as a core, strategic, business competency of any enterprise. Before we can even think about creating perfect design briefs, we need to understand how to talk about design as a strategic business resource, not as a support service.

Who Is Accountable for Developing a Design Brief?

Once a valid business need that requires design expertise has been identified, and the design group who will execute the project has been determined, the process of creating a design brief must begin immediately.

The very first step is to identify who will assume "ownership" of the project. Ownership means ultimate accountability. If the project is a success, who takes the praise? And what if the project fails? Who is accountable for its failure?

My strong belief is that projects must be *co-owned*. There must be an owner who represents the group with the business need for the design work and a co-owner from the design group who will meet that need. They must be *equal* partners in the project. It is a strategic business partnership, not a customer-service-provider relationship.

Designers and design managers must change their mindset from being service providers, to a mindset of being strategic, equal, business partners. If things go wrong, designers need to stand up and accept accountability.

Client or Partner?

Most designers and design managers I know, and speak with, use the term *client* (or customer) excessively. "My client wants this or that." "My client is very difficult to work with." "My clients never get me involved early enough." "My client doesn't understand design." Using this term *client* tends to telegraph how we are approaching a project. In effect, we are saying we are not in charge of design. They are. Why not be partners? Why not share the responsibilities—and the accountability?

In my own consulting practice, I make a very sincere effort not to use the word *client*. Rather, I talk about *partnering* with people on a project. By strict definition, of course, these people *are* my clients. I just don't want to think of them that way, and I don't want them to think of me as just a service provider; I want to be their partner.

We in the design profession must become equal partners—and equally accountable—with those people who come to us for our particular expertise, our so-called clients. When we become comfortable with this change in mindset, wonderful, creative things can happen. Great design can happen. Working relationships can become a source of empowerment.

Co-ownership

It makes no sense to me for someone with a genuine business need for design to write a design brief and hand it to me for execution. It also makes no sense for me to write a design brief without considering the wealth of important knowledge my partner has. Therefore, many years ago, I determined a minimum of two people must be involved in developing a design brief: someone representing the business-need side and someone representing design. There are, of course, times when there are more than two equal partners claiming ownership of the design brief. A third partner could be involved; this often occurs in situations where there is a business alliance of some type. But, for the most part, two people are all that is required to own the development of a design brief.

Although I strongly advocate this co-ownership of accountability to develop a design brief, I am not advocating development by committee. Once a committee of people feels they are accountable for the actual development and writing of the brief, and for "playing the role of designer," chaos rules. A number of people are on the design brief team, but only two—possibly three—should be "owners." The design brief team's responsibility is to give *input* to, and *approve,* the design brief, not necessarily actually write it.

What Level Should the Co-owners Be?

The management level of the individuals appointed co-owners of a design brief varies depending upon the scope and importance of the project to the enterprise. A very senior executive and the manager, or director, of design would most likely manage the design of a new, breakthrough product or service. On the other hand, a modification to an existing product might utilize a mid-level marketing specialist and a lead designer as co-owners. The owners' level of management is not really an issue; the process of developing the design brief remains the same.

Finally, there is this issue of account managers, or project managers. Many agencies employ people to be account managers—what we used to call the "suits." Should they be co-owners? I have no problem with an account manager being a co-owner of the design brief process, providing the account manager thoroughly understands design, the design process, and the information a designer needs. Over time I have encountered account managers who are superb salespeople and very good project managers. Unfortunately, they didn't know much about design. In my opinion, by putting such people between the designer and the client/partner, a buffer is formed that is counterproductive to the actual realization of a great design solution. The designer must have direct contact with the person he, or she, is developing a design solution for.

Design Is a Problem-Solving Discipline

Most highly successful designers understand that design is a problem-solving discipline. Design differs from art in that the artist is charged with personal interpretation of a subject, whereas design is concerned with developing a solution to a defined problem. Therefore, the strategy for developing a design solution must be married to a well-articulated business problem. This is another reason that designers and their business partners *must* work in partnership to develop a useful design brief.

For a design solution to be truly effective, it must solve the *problem*. It follows that not only must the problem be clearly stated, but the business objectives of the solution also have to be clearly articulated. Once there is a clear understanding of the actual business problem and its objectives, then—and only then—can a coherent design strategy be developed.

The Collaborative Brief Development Process

The first step in the collaborative brief development process is for the co-owners to meet to identify and describe all the business objectives of the design project. A key question to be answered is, Exactly what business problem(s) are we trying to solve? Just what are we trying to do?

This is followed by a discussion of the business reasons—the actual needs—for the design project. Finally, the co-owners must articulate all of the desired outcomes upon completion of the design activity.

Critical Content of a Design Brief:
A Checklist for Success

Once the co-owners have identified and clearly stated the business context, the need(s) of the marketplace, and the desired results of the project, they may begin developing the rest of the brief.

The contents of the brief include:

- Background and description of the project
- Category/industry review
- Target audience(s) review
- Company portfolio
- Business objectives and UX design strategy

- Project phases: scope, timeline, and budget

- Research data

- Appendix (if required)

The following is a summary of each of these elements.

Background and Description of Project   The first element is the background and description of the business context of the project.

Category/Industry Review   The second element is a section describing the current business category for this project. Usually included in this section is information about the competition, industry trends, brand and subbrand concerns, pricing, and promotion of the product or service, and the marketing strategy for this project.

Target Audience Review   Typically, the third critical element is a comprehensive discussion of the target audiences for the product or service. Specifically who are these people you want to respond to this design solution, and how do you want them to respond?

Company Portfolio   The next section should deal with the commissioning company's complete portfolio of products or services. How does this particular project tie-in with other company products or services? In what ways should the outcome of this design project relate to the company's brand positioning?

Business Objectives and UX Design Strategy   The next element to be addressed is perhaps among the most critical of the brief elements. It has to do with *marrying business objectives to a strategy for developing a design solution.*

A technique that has worked well for many groups is for the brief co-owners to create, in the case of UX design, a three-column table, such as the one shown in Table 1-1. The first column has the heading "Business Problem." Under this heading, the specific business objectives are listed. The second column has the heading "UX-Related Problems." The specific UX problems are listed under this heading. Finally, the third column has the heading "UX Design Strategy." This column is developed by the UX design group and the strategies listed are agreed to by the brief's co-owners.

This approach has many advantages. First and foremost, it helps to speed the whole process up—believe it or not! It also nearly completely eliminates a lot of common misunderstandings throughout the entire process. Using a table or chart format allows all stakeholders to understand just what the problems

Business Problem	UX-Related Problems	UX Design Strategy
Increase revenue by *x%* by enhancing customer perceptions of ease of use of our products.	(1) Users don't find the camera easy (for use case: take a picture and send). (2) It is not clear why people don't write picture messages. (3) Users don't reply to received messages as often as possible (for use case: reply to received message). (4) Users sometimes overlook received messages. (5) Users cannot invite other people to an appointment easily (for use case: make appointment).	(1) Run usability test: design, prototypes, usability tests (2) Focus groups (3) Field studies: design, prototypes, usability tests (4) Home stories: design, prototypes, usability tests
Improve brand awareness by *y%*	(1) The "Operatoreness" is not unique and perceivable enough. (2) Recognizable brand elements should work for advertisement, books, products, and also for interactions (e.g., graphical user interface).	(1) Branding concepts: find brand signature also for interactive elements (e.g., similar to what Apple is doing). (2) Implement branding concept for different channels and media and test it.

TABLE 1-1 UX Example for the Business Perspective from the Mobile Phone World

are that need to be solved and the UX group's strategic approach to finding solutions to these problems. Everyone is on the same page.

Project Phases: Scope, Timeline, Budget Every brief must contain some more tactical information, generally called *Project Phases,* or timeline.

List each phase of the design project process. For each phase, indicate the length of time necessary to complete the phase and the associated costs to complete the phase. For each phase indicate any concept testing that may be required with the target audience. Scope has to do with all of the ancillary elements that may be critical to the final product, i.e., packaging, instruction manuals, trouble shooting guides etc.

This section should also include three very important, yet often overlooked, phases. One is the final approval phase. Here, you must list the details of who is accountable for the final approval of the design project. The second, often-overlooked phase is the implementation phase. Once a design solution is approved, implementing the design solution in the marketplace takes time and money. Finally, the third phase is called "Measurement." How will you determine success? What criteria will you use to measure success or failure? Who will do this measurement? When will it be completed?

Research Data   You may also wish to include a *summary of the key research* used to determine the need for the UX design project in the first place.

Appendix   The appendix usually includes such items as photographs or sketches of competitive products or concepts, research data reports, and color recommendations.

Business Impact of Developing a Collaborative Design Brief

Current ongoing research shows that the most successful product introductions in the last six years all began with a comprehensive briefing process. The obstacle cited of not having enough time to develop a brief just isn't correct. If six or eight hours is spent developing a brief collaboratively, at least ten times that amount of time is saved in executing of the design process. When a comprehensive examination of the business problem to be solved is performed up front, the results are nearly always greater success in the marketplace.

Becoming a Collaborative Strategic Partner

So how do we in the design profession become co-owners, equal partners, in developing a design brief? First, we have to become recognized as a core, strategic *business* competency. I have developed a model that describes an approach to becoming that type of strategic partner.

The Model

Figure 1-1 is meant to be a visual guide to the process I have found works effectively for designers, and design managers, who want to improve the perception of design and the design function, in the corporate world. The design brief is the key tool for making this model work effectively.

Permit me to expand on each part of this model.

The Value You Offer   This is the most critical—and therefore the first—step in my model. If you don't understand why you are valuable, or why design is valuable, then no one else will either. Many of us believe we know why we are valuable, but knowing it and communicating it effectively are two entirely different things. I would also hasten to add that what we believe makes us valuable is not always what others believe is of real value. Being a person who gets work done on time and on very short time

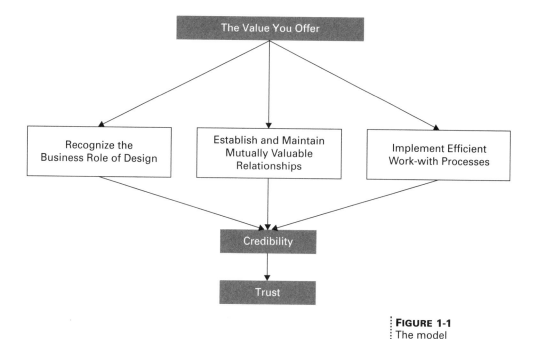

FIGURE 1-1
The model

schedules is a given to them. Staying within budget is also expected. Being very creative? Well that's why they hired you in the first place! Being able to handle multiple projects at the same time? They do the same thing every day. And the list goes on. Designers tend to list the "tactical" things they do every day. Seldom is anything remotely "strategic" on the lists I see.

To be truly valued, an equal partner in the process, a core, strategic business competency, then design and designers must learn to speak the language of business and to relate what they do to business results. If you want to be a co-owner and equal partner in the design brief process, for example, then you must communicate and demonstrate clearly that you are thinking strategically about the effect(s) of design as a solution to the business problem. If your focus is entirely on aesthetics and tactics, you will never be perceived as a full partner. Rather you will be the "decorator," the "design service." Not that aesthetics and tactics do not play a significant role at the end of the day; it just can't be all you talk about.

When I say the value *you* offer, just who do I mean by "you"? In the context of this model, there are two "you's." There is *you,* personally, the individual who will be an equal partner in a process. And then there is the *collective you,* the UX design function as a whole. You want the design function valued and respected as a critical component of the whole organization, and you also want to garner respect and trust as the manager of the design process.

An Exercise to Get You Started

Here is an exercise that works very well at getting to the heart of this value business. You can do this alone to determine your personal added value to the business, and you can do the same exercise with your design staff to come up with the ways in which design as a function adds value to any enterprise. The technique is identical either way.

Make a list of every reason you can think of that either you–or the design function—add value to a business. Write down every single thing that comes into your mind. Don't worry at this point about elegant wording, or even relevance. If it comes to mind, write it down. More than likely, you will create a fairly lengthy list in very short order. That is always gratifying. I have seen people look at the long list they just generated and say, "Wow, look at all the stuff we do so well!" Put this list aside for a while. Maybe a day or two. Then take it out again and work through the list item by item. For each item, ask yourself, "Does this really, really, matter to non-design business people? Do they really care?" If the answer is "No!" then draw a line through the item. I have done this exercise hundreds of times with groups. Let me give you some, admittedly extreme (to make the point), examples of items that had to come off the list: "I am able to keep many details in my head encompassing multiple projects"; "I am friendly and easy to work with"; "I use research data very effectively." All good stuff, but completely meaningless to a business.

I want you to put everything down that came into your head for this first pass, because when you draw a line through those items that are really irrelevant, you will have a visual record of the kinds of things you are saying every day—things that most non-design people really don't react well to.

Now is when the excitement about how long your original list was evaporates. You are going to end up with a much shorter list than you expected.

Next, try to work the list again. But this time do not simply jot down everything that comes into your head. Focus on those items that non-designers would perceive as truly added value. Also, pay more attention to the words you are using to describe each item. This step will take considerably more time than the first go-round. But the results should be equally as exciting. The list will be shorter, but the content will be rich with information about just how design brings added value to a business. Always think in business terms, not aesthetic terms. Just what can design do for a business?

Some of the rather strong items I have seen on this second list include variously worded items such as "We shorten the sales cycle"; "We visually differentiate our company's products, or services, in a cluttered marketplace"; "We create a powerful competitive advantage"; "We clarify the company's business strategy through visual and experiential means."

This is the stuff that will make senior, non-design business managers sit up and take notice. Here is one rather compelling—if also somewhat nonconversational—statement I have seen: "We are responsible for the visual and experiential manifestation of the company's overall business strategy as approved by the board of directors, and the shareholders." That doesn't sound like a simple technical service to me. It sounds more like a statement from a strategic business group—and that's what you want to become.

Once you have discovered just exactly what your added value really is, begin to incorporate these thoughts into everything you do. Some groups actually develop a "design philosophy" from this exercise. Use these powerful strategic business ideas in memos, presentations, meetings, everyday conversation, and in design briefs.

Often chance meetings occur with people in the company who don't know you. Inevitably, they will ask what you do. I try this in class, asking students to tell me what designers do. The first word out of their mouths is almost always, "Umm?" This is followed by something like, "I do design work for UX (or whatever)." Then they stop, not really knowing where to go with the answer to this question. After having done this exercise, you should have a whole arsenal of things firmly implanted in your mind that will capture the attention of the person asking the question. Down deep, what you want is for them to become aware of the importance of design to the business, and you want them to say, "I had no idea; I thought you guys were just technicians. We should talk some more!"

Many human resource professionals describe a technique called the "two-minute drill." These people argue that in an interview situation, the first two minutes are critical to the outcome of the interview. You must be able to communicate, succinctly, and in a compelling way, just what it is you have to offer that is unique. By taking the time to determine the real, added value you offer as a design professional, then you will also be able to learn to communicate this value in two minutes or less. It will take some practice, but it is an important component of changing the perception of design in the business world.

To be truly valued in the business world, you absolutely must know what your value is (and we are all valuable!), and you must be able to articulate it clearly and simply in business terms at the drop of a hat. If you really aren't very clear on just why you're valuable, why you're an asset, no one else will ever get it either. Before moving any further through the model, do this exercise. It makes a wonderful agenda item for a UX design staff meeting. Everyone in your group needs to have the same understanding of your added value. And it beats the hell out of dreary staff meetings where all that happens is an endless list of status reports from each designer!

Recognize the Business Role of UX Design   You could also turn this around to say, "The role of UX design in business." Either way you say it, every designer or design manager doing design projects for a business must understand how design adds value to that business. Remember, design is a problem-solving discipline. If your design activities are in support of a business of some type, then the problem to be solved through design will be a *business* problem. Just how far, and in what ways, can UX design contribute to the solving of a business problem? The answer: "In more ways than most people think!"

I have a very close friend and colleague who told me very bluntly that at the end of the day design really couldn't do very much in terms of solving real business problems. My friend is a brilliant business strategist, particularly in the finance arena. My friend insists that design is necessary only as a vehicle, or environment, to contain information about the company's products or services. His view is not only commonly held, but also, I would say, prevalent in the business world. There are a few companies, of course, whose success depends completely on design, such as Apple, Vodafone, and Electrolux.

It is the design profession's responsibility to change this perception. Frankly, we have done a lousy job of it for years. In order for us to communicate the role of design clearly, as well as its value, we must first understand the role of design in business ourselves.

Just what are the business problems your company (or the client company you are partnering with) faces? Ask yourself, "What is keeping the CEO awake at night? What are the business issues that are most troubling to him or her?" Then ask yourself, "In what ways can effective UX design play a role in solving this problem?"

Mutually Valuable Relationships   Creating mutually valuable relationships all across the enterprise not only for the function of design, but also for the design manager is critical to becoming a strategic partner. It is, however, probably the most neglected aspect of the design function. I encounter this on a regular basis. Designers and design managers seem to have a difficult time in reaching out and being proactive in a business.

Instead the design manager should approach a business department head as an ally. As a partner who offers to help with UX design elements. As an ally who is willing to listen first and then make creative suggestions as to how to assist the department head in meeting his or her business goals. This is a truly mutually valuable relationship.

Often during my corporate career, I would call the manager of a particular function, introduce myself, and offer to attend a future staff meeting to explain how design played a role in their piece of the business. Often, they were not even aware that they required design on a regular basis. They never thought of design in that way. At the staff meeting, I would take perhaps 10 to 15 minutes to point out how design played a part in their work and then offer to consult, if needed, on issues they had that involved design. I didn't offer to do the work, just help them to do it well, and correctly, through other resources. This practice accomplished several things. One, it helped large numbers of people understand that design played a role in their daily lives. Two, it gave my corporate design function wide visibility. Three, it established my design function as a center for expertise. Four, I was able to learn first-hand what business issues each function was most concerned about. Finally, I was able to develop allies all over the company—mutually valuable relationships, if you will, which always served the interests and needs of the design function in future projects. For example, it made the process of listing all stakeholders in the design brief a great deal easier.

In a real sense, these types of interactions are the best way to develop mutually valuable relationships all across a company. As you visit each group, you can focus on developing relationships with one or more individuals in that group who might become real supporters of design later on.

One of the strongest alliances I was able to leverage in my corporate career was with the Law department. Everything we do in design today seems to have a legal perspective. Wouldn't it be better to have a mutually valuable relationship with the Law department, than to face the dreaded "legal review?"

Developing strong and healthy relationships is hard work. And it takes time. It requires tact, listening skills, and the ability to show genuine concern for the other party's needs—not just *your* needs. Above all, it means that a design manager who wants to become a strategic business partner, to be respected and trusted, and become an important corporate asset, rather than a "necessary evil," must take the initiative—and the time—to develop these kinds of relationships. Without *mutually* valuable relationships throughout the organization, you will never really be able to become a core, strategic partner. You will remain a "service provider."

Implementing Efficient Work-with Processes   Please notice how this is phrased: "work-with." This is the opposite of "work-for." We are talking about strategic partnerships, not simply providing a support service. Instead of just driving the taxi and telling your "customer" you'll take them wherever they want to go, become a transportation consultant and offer advice on the best way to get there given their needs, time, and budget.

Working *with* someone is quite different from working *for* him or her. All too often designers and design managers really do believe they are service providers rather than strategic business partners. Believe me, if in your head you think you are a service provider, that's exactly what everyone else will think, too. But in addition to *thinking* you are a service provider, if you also *behave* like one, then that's all you and the design function will ever be in the corporate environment.

All of the stuff covered in the model so far is what makes this change possible. You have learned to understand and clearly articulate the true value of design to the enterprise—in business terms. You have done exercises to appreciate fully, and to understand the role of design in the business as the visual and enabling manifestation of the core business strategy. You have proactively sought out key stakeholders in the company and developed mutually supportive and valuable relationships with them. Now is the time to truly be a partner, not a servant.

Learning to work-with people, to be an effective collaborator and colleague, is easy for some people but can be very difficult for many more. It requires an innate belief in your expertise, knowledge, and added value to a business. Perhaps we are expert UX designers, but are we trusted business colleagues? Just look around at the people who do this well. Lawyers, physicians, CEOs, marketing people, engineers, and nearly every other profession realize they are necessary because of their expertise. Although under strict dictionary definitions they have clients, they don't behave like these people are their "masters." They know the "service" they provide can often make the difference between a business's success or failure. The UX design profession has to get to the same place. If you are simply a service provider, you will never be truly valued in the business environment. However, people who make a significant and recognizable difference are valued.

Of course, this relates directly to the design brief. In the audience section, the needs of *all* audiences—worldwide—need to be articulated. In the business objectives/design strategy section, all geographical business objectives need to be listed, and each of those geographic objectives needs to have specific design strategies associated with them. The only way to be sure you are on the right track is to include representatives of various countries in your key stakeholder list and to be certain you consult with them through the whole design brief development process.

In all circumstances, but particularly in global business situations, design managers need to make a concerted effort to investigate various audiences and to learn how to develop effective design solutions to meet those various audiences' needs. I am a great advocate of design managers, and individual designers, attending such events as national and international sales meetings and trade shows. Even if the theme of these events seems not to be related directly to design, per se, they are opportunities for the design profession to learn, first hand, more about key stakeholders' needs and requirements.

The days of sitting in a design studio and "just doing" design are long over. The design profession must get out into the world and see what is going on. The design profession must actively listen to key internal stakeholders, as well as to members of all of the various target audiences, to create effective design solutions for these groups. You can't create brilliant design solutions by simply sitting in a cubicle somewhere. And it's very hard to work with, and design for, people you have never met, seen, or spoken to.

Credibility and Trust

Once you completely understand the added value you offer to any enterprise (personally and as a design function), once you understand and effectively communicate the role of design in business, once you are able to develop mutually valuable relationships (emphasis on "mutually"), and once you develop the skills to work-with people, not for them, then, and only then, will you begin to have real credibility as a strategic business partner.

Knowledge leads to understanding. Understanding leads to appreciation and credibility. Credibility leads to trust. First, people have to have some real knowledge and understanding of the added value design can offer. Only then will they begin to appreciate great design. Credibility stems from providing solutions that really work to meet the business objectives of the project. Once you have credibility, trust is inevitable.

I have said time and time again, the core reason so many designers complain that they don't have enough time, don't have sufficient budgets, don't get invited into the process early enough, and aren't appreciated or understood is because they aren't *trusted* as business people in the first place. Don't forget, any enterprise, for profit or nonprofit, is in existence solely to make money. A nonprofit business wouldn't be around very long unless it makes enough money to pay the bills. A for-profit company, likewise, would disappear very quickly if it didn't make money.

The purpose of design should be, in the minds of business people, first and foremost to help meet these business objectives. It is up to the design profession to make them understand this is our goal, too. We need to let our business partners know the purpose of design is far greater than just being "pretty or clever."

Non-designers are nearly always the people who ultimately have final approval of design solutions. Think about that for a minute. People who really don't fully understand what they are approving, who have no training or expertise in design, end up being the ones to approve designs! Why? Because designers are not trusted to make business evaluations. For the most part, most non-designers *will* admit a professional designer knows more about the techniques and elements of design than they do. They just don't trust designers to make the final evaluation of whether their design solution meets real business needs. In order for design to become an equal partner, a co-owner of projects, then the design profession must first earn credibility and trust from their non-design partners. Before a design group can be considered as an equal, strategic partner in the design brief process, the design group must earn this trust.

The model I have developed has already helped a great many design groups achieve this goal of credibility and trust. It certainly worked for me. The best way—the best tool, if you will—to realize the tenets of this model is the collaborative design brief. Give it a try!

Summary

- **How can a design brief be used to measure the ROI of a design project?**
  A well-developed design brief will fully describe the problem to be solved with design, the core business objectives to be realized, and the desired outcomes or results desired upon implementation of the design solution. These things will determine the criteria for measuring the monetary investment in the design.

- **How do I determine if a design brief is really needed for a new project?**
  If a design project's scope is very limited, perhaps just a minor fix or two to an existing product, a design brief is probably not necessary. However, if the project entails creating an entirely new design solution, a design brief is critical.

- **Why is it so important for a design brief to be co-developed by both the commissioner of the design project and the designer?**
  Each party brings specialized knowledge and skill sets to the project. By collaborating on the development of a brief, a great deal of time is saved during the execution phase since nearly all questions have already been asked and dealt with efficiently by both parties.

- **We never have time to engage in a lengthy brief development process. Are there any shortcuts?**
  Actually, no. If the project is critical enough to commission in the first place, embarking on a collaborative brief development process is paramount to the eventual success of the effort. The time saved in the execution of a design project will be far greater than the time spent developing a great brief first.

- **Why do we need to test design concepts with the target audience?**
  People who are part of the company developing the design are too close to the project to make a truly objective decision about which design concept works best. Only the people you are designing for—your target audience(s)—can really let you know if your concepts work for them.

- **How long is the design brief used during the execution of the project? When is it no longer required?**
  The design brief is used throughout the entire project. The final three phases include 1) presentation of the design solution for approval; 2) the final design solution implementation plan; and 3) criteria for measuring the results of the design solution in the marketplace. This final phase, measurement, might last for some time after project completion.

Chapter 2

Institutionalizing User Experience to Achieve Business Success

By Andreas Hauser

SAP®

Over the past decade both the nature of customer expectations and the software development process have changed. Many companies have identified the need to better serve their customers, especially end users, because the decision to buy business software is often no longer made by the CIO, but by the departments that use the software. User Experience is becoming more and more important to selling a product successfully. At the same time, the software development process in many companies has not changed. The engineering department continues to decide which features and functions are implemented without real end-user involvement.

Some years ago SAP® decided to build a game-changing business solution. The goal was to extend market penetration significantly in the small and medium enterprises (SME) market. To develop a disruptive and game-changing solution, SAP completely changed the way it built applications from a technological, process, and organizational point of view (see Figure 2-1). User Experience was made a high priority right from the beginning because it was seen as a main differentiator and competitive advantage in the future.

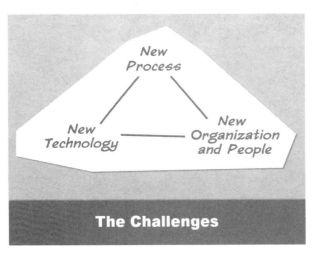

FIGURE 2-1 The challenges

To develop a new breakthrough business solution, we had to create a *new technology platform* that enabled us to develop open and flexible business applications. We developed a pure service-oriented architecture (SOA) and implemented the UI patterns into the development tools.

We also radically changed the *development process.* Superior User Experience was a key goal, and to achieve this, we defined an outside-in driven, iterative development process. User-centered design was mandatory for the entire organization. To measure the achievement of our defined User Experience goals, we developed a user experience key performance indicator (KPI) and presented the achievement with each release to the management team.

In addition to the new technology and the new development process, we set up a completely *new organization* that grew very quickly into a very large and global organization. This was done because the technology as well as the business applications had to be built from scratch. We decided to leverage the talented people in our global organization. People from different locations and cultures worked together as one team.

The new organizational setup was also different than in other SAP organizations. We had a Solution Management organization and a Development organization. Solution Management—other companies call it Product Management—was responsible for defining the market requirements and the detailed product definition. UX designers were responsible for the interaction design and supported the execution of user research activities like site visits or UI validations. Development was responsible for implementing the solution.

The challenge was to apply a scalable user-centered design process in this large and global organization. We had to learn how to collaborate across locations within small teams. Some teams were spread out over more than three locations and had to deal with asynchronous communication, various time zones, and cultural differences. We also learned that "English is not English" and had to learn how to conduct virtual design sessions.

The biggest challenge for us was that the *technology was not available at the time we started designing the solution.* We had to begin with understanding the new market and the user requirements when the technology architecture was still just paper work. We could not wait for one or two years until the technology was available. The time to get the product to market would have been too long.

Within the fast-growing organization, continuously explaining the value of User Experience to non-UX people (developers and solution managers) was a big challenge. Developers are usually happy if they can focus on the implementation of features and functions. Solution managers often have a market research background but are not familiar with user research. Usability professionals understand the value of UX very well, but they are often seen as artists by non-UX people. We had to find ways to change this perception, and we had to make the value of UX visible to our organization. Everybody in the organization had to understand and embrace the value of user-centered design. This chapter will give you some examples of how step-by-step we institutionalized User Experience within the organization.

It was an extraordinary journey for me personally. There were many ups and downs, but we also had a lot of fun, especially within the User Experience team, which was composed of young, dynamic, and creative people. In this chapter, I would like to share my journey over the last few years to achieve more impact with User Experience in the development organization and in the product itself.

It was a challenging time because, to my knowledge, no other software company had done something on this scale before. We could not learn how other companies had mastered the challenges. We had to learn on our own, and sometimes we had to figure out what did and did not work. I learned a lot about how to

- Set up and execute a user-centered design process in a global organization.
- Influence the organization and people to ride the user-centered design wave.
- Achieve impact on the UI technology to focus on User Experience requirements.

Many of the recommended UX practices we used in this project might work for you and your company. Some are more specific to large companies with more complex processes and globally distributed organizations. Take some of the recommendations and try them out in your company. You will discover what works and what needs to be adapted to your circumstances.

Who Is SAP?

SAP is the largest software company in Europe with more than 53,000 employees. Over 109,000 companies in over 120 countries run SAP software. More than 35 million people use SAP software every day. Overall, SAP's reach and breadth make us a leader in our industry.

SAP has built-in industry experience accumulated over 35 years of helping organizations lead their industries. That experience of working with partners and customers around the world has given SAP something that few others can claim: invaluable insight into companies' needs and the expertise to help solve their problems and make their businesses run better.

What Is SAP® Business ByDesign™?

SAP® Business ByDesign™ is SAP's new on-demand business solution for small and medium enterprises. This solution is full of innovation that makes it unique to the market. SAP Business ByDesign is the world's most complete and adaptable on-demand business application. Unlike any other on-demand business software, SAP Business ByDesign, shown in Figure 2-2, delivers transparency and control of the entire business end-to-end—from Customer Relationship Management (CRM) to Supplier Relationship Management (SRM) to Supply Chain Management (SCM) to Financial Management (FIN) to Human Resources (HR). It provides companies an immediate 360-degree view of their business, is easy to use, and adapts quickly to changing business needs.

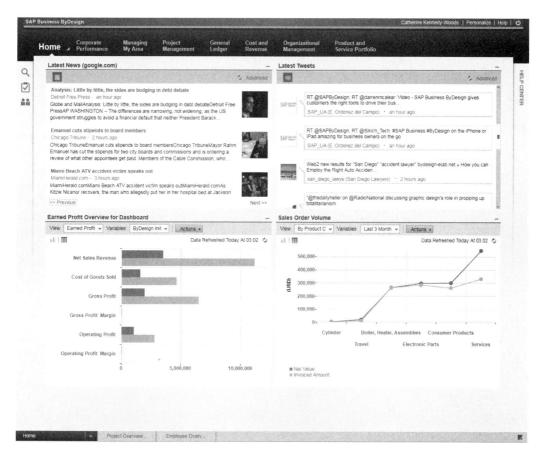

SAP Business ByDesign was built by taking the following key principles into consideration:

- Ensuring market-driven design and development
- Integrating early feedback from end users iteratively into development activities
- Achieving breakthrough User Experience
- Leveraging the benefits of a model-driven and service-oriented architecture

The Project History

Some years ago, SAP decided to start a new research and development project. The project was set up to build a prototype for new business applications, leveraging a service-oriented architecture. Superior User Experience, reducing software complexity, and reducing total cost of ownership (TCO) were the major goals defined.

I participated in the preparation of the solution blueprint, and our team created the first software architecture diagrams. The blueprint was successfully presented to the board, and the research project got the final go. I was asked if I was interested in taking over the challenge to lead the User Interface topic. During the next months, we worked on the UI architecture with the technology team, built first prototypes, and designed a range of new applications to support different user roles. We had the freedom to define the new software architecture, shape a new development process, and design the new business applications.

The research project finished successfully, and the SAP board decided to build a new business solution for small and medium enterprises based on the software architecture defined in the research project. The public launch of the new business solution took place in September 2007. From that time on, the product was called "SAP® Business ByDesign™."

Why Did We Do Something Different with SAP Business ByDesign?

SAP Business ByDesign places user's needs right at the center of its design by addressing the "human" side of business software. This focus is important, because buying decisions for business software are no longer made by the CIO but by the departments that use the software. The goal was to design a solution that met the expectations of users and to ensure that a user could work efficiently and effectively with the system. To achieve this goal, we defined a user-centered design process that was mandatory for the complete organization, as shown in Figure 2-3.

Superior User Experience is important for customers because the expenses associated with a bad UI can end up costing many times more than the cost of the application itself over the course of the application's lifetime. This is due to increased user training time and decreased productivity. In the end, users might even refuse to use the software.

The main objectives of SAP Business ByDesign are

- **Simplicity** It had to be easy to use and easy to learn. Users expect a low learning curve and cannot invest a lot of time in training. Especially in the mid-market, a user typically plays different roles and has many responsibilities. Simplicity and consistency in usage is, therefore, very important. Consistency is achieved by applying a pattern-based approach to all applications, enabling users to perform similar tasks in the same and efficient way.

- **Design for people**   You have to understand the needs of end users to provide an intuitive User Experience. First, we identified the user needs in the beginning of the software development cycle. We observed users in their working environment to gather feedback about their information needs, processes, goals, triggers, communication, and so on. Then we translated the user needs into user requirements and then into system requirements. Finally, use cases were written and wireframes were designed. We tested the use cases and wireframes with end users, and the user feedback was incorporated into the wireframes before handing them over to development.

  We also performed usability tests using the implemented solution, but we did many more tests early in the development process using wireframes. The impact of testing early in the process is greater because changing an already implemented application is much more expensive than doing so at an earlier time when nothing has been implemented. It is very important to have continuous and iterative feedback cycles with end users throughout the whole development process.

- **Provide flexible UI Technology**   The UI Technology has to be flexible to adapt quickly to market, customer, and user needs. We developed the complete solution based on a model-driven and service-oriented architecture. This ensures high flexibility for customers and partners to adapt and extend the solution. It also provides flexibility for end users to personalize the system to individual needs. Implementing the UI patterns into the development environment helped to improve consistency and significantly improved developer productivity.

The Role of the User Experience Team

The ByDesign User Experience team grew in the first two years to a very large UX team located in several countries. It was impossible to hire that many people in such a short timeframe; therefore, we also worked with several contractors.

We hired young and innovative people with an excellent background in interaction design and user research. It was also important that we hired real team players. Why was this important?

The User Experience team plays an important role in the development process, bridging the gap between Solution Management and Development and representing the end-users' requirements. The UX team becomes the user's advocate but, at the same time, may not achieve as deep an understanding of the product domain as needed to fully play this role. Therefore, soft skills are very important to being successful as an interface between developers and solution managers.

There is only one UX team in SAP Business ByDesign, which consists of three subteams:

- **UI Concept and Guidelines** The UI Concept and Guidelines team defines the UI Styleguide for SAP Business ByDesign, provides UI specifications for new UI patterns, and supports the UI Framework team during implementation of the UI patterns. The UI Framework implementation team is part of the Technology team and develops the technological platform to build user interfaces for business applications. UI patterns are implemented within the development tool to ensure consistency. The UI Concept and Guidelines team supports application designers and developers in using the UI Styleguide and collects new UI requirements for future releases. They are also responsible for defining new innovative UI concepts.

- **End-User Involvement Infrastructure** The End-User Involvement Infrastructure team organizes and supports customer, partner, and user activities like site visits, focus groups, use case validations, UI validations, and usability and benchmark tests. They provide and manage a global infrastructure for end-user activities to support application designer and user researcher to conduct activities with users in different countries.

  The End-User Involvement Infrastructure team is also responsible for defining the UCD methodology and conducting UCD trainings for solution managers, developers, and UX people. The team supports the definition and execution of the Product Development Process and ensures that UCD activities are smoothly integrated.

- **Application Design** Interaction designers and user researchers work within application teams (developers and solution managers) to design business applications like Financials, Human Resources, and Customer Relationship Management. They are the user's advocates and drive user-centered design in the application teams. Each application area has one user researcher who is responsible for planning and conducting user research activities for this area. Conclusions derived from user research activities are immediately discussed with developers and solution managers. Either the issues get solved in the current release or the requirements are put on the backlog for the next release. Interaction designers apply the UI Styleguide, are responsible for designing all user interfaces, and support developers during implementation.

"Why Is User Research so Important?"

You can only design a good solution if you know users' needs. Do you discover those needs by asking them? No, of course not. A user may have difficulties articulating how a future software solution should work exactly. If you had asked people during the time when the car was invented what they needed, you probably would have gotten the answer: "faster horses." The art of user research is to observe users and to identify their real needs. This is where the magic comes in. It is the task of the User Experience designer to translate the user's statements and his or her observations into a bigger picture and from there into real needs of users.

More time has to be invested early in the process to improve the design with end users. This saves time in development and ultimately leads to higher user satisfaction and efficiency. It helps you tremendously because you get solid research data that backs up arguments for why features were included or not.

I will tell you a short story about my first experience of the importance of user research. We went to a customer site in Shanghai to do user research. We observed a user who was responsible for entering hundreds of invoices manually into the system. He was not using SAP software. He put the invoice document on the left-hand side of his keyboard and entered the data. After entering ten invoices, he pressed the Save button and waited some time. Afterward, he clicked the Refresh button about ten times to see if the invoices were processed correctly. He told us that he had to check the invoices, and, in case of errors, he had to make the necessary changes immediately. This observation gave us the idea that the system could do this for the user. The user should just enter the invoices and then the system proactively informs the user in case of errors. However, this user said he was very happy with the software solution he was using. You will only have our experience if you go to the user's desk and carefully observe how the user works.

However, spawning innovation through design takes more than just observing the user. You must speak with the partners, the service organization that receives the complaints, analysts, and salespeople—collect all research data and translate the findings into an innovative design together with solution managers, User Experience designers, and developers.

During my business career, I have seen many people come up with amazing and innovative ideas, but most never made it to the product stage. Innovation is about execution and getting the idea to the market. Just having an idea is not sufficient. You have to fight for it and turn it into the solution. If you do not succeed, you do not have impact, in which case, your idea was just another nice idea...

Phases of the Project

The project went through three different phases, as shown in Figure 2-4. In Phase 1, the development process and the UCD process were set apart by intention. Solution Management was responsible for defining the target solution based on outside-in research and the Development team developed, in parallel, the technology platform. From the beginning, the ByDesign

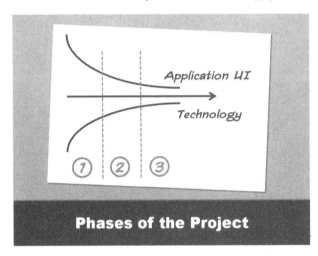

FIGURE 2-4 Phases of the project

User Experience team supported both Solution Management and the UI Framework team that worked on the technology platform. The User Experience designers worked closely with solution managers to define the target design of the applications. We also had to ensure the best possible implementation of the UI patterns within the UI framework, create detailed specifications for the UI patterns, and support the framework developers during implementation. In Phase 2, we had to get the implemented solution closer to the target design, and in Phase 3, we moved to a LEAN and agile development model. The phases were not defined explicitly from the beginning. They evolved through experience. In each phase, we learned a lot about the technology, the process, and the global organization, and with each phase, we improved significantly in all these dimensions.

Phase 1: Design the Solution (Target Design)

We had to start designing the solution although the technology was not available at the time. Our goal was to get into a new market and attract new customers. The solution managers and User Experience designers had to understand the market and user requirements first. They designed the target design for our new solution.

They designed thousands of screens on HTML-based, clickable prototypes that had the look and feel of a real application and for which no code had yet been written. The screens were validated with thousands of users worldwide to improve the solution iteratively. We also went through days of screen reviews using HTML mockups with members of the management team and with the executive board members. It was time-consuming, but a lot less costly to do this exercise early than to wait until the business objects and framework coding were finished. We learned that an HTML mockup tells more than 1000 words. This is a language that developers, solution managers, board members, managers, and people of different cultural backgrounds understand.

We did not want to leverage the existing SAP customer base because we wanted to attract non-SAP customers and users. Therefore, we had to set up our own infrastructure to get access to non-SAP users. Market research companies helped us to get users with the required profile, and we used external usability labs to conduct user feedback activities.

"The Sanity Check"

Designing UI mockups at this time was difficult. The UI Styleguide represented the target design and was based on many technical assumptions. Over time, it turned out that some of the assumptions were technically not possible to implement in the given timeframe. We had to update the UI Styleguide continuously and get it closer and closer to technical feasibility. Keeping everyone involved constantly up to date with the latest changes was a big challenge. We set up a wiki to provide access to the latest information and conducted regular information sessions. Solution managers and the UX designers had to reflect the latest changes in the UI mockups before they handed them over to the application developers. We wanted to ensure the UI mockups were of the highest possible quality. The UI mockups had to describe as precisely as possible what we wanted to achieve as a result. We decided to introduce a "Sanity Check" gate in our development process to ensure compliance of the UI mockups with the Styleguide.

Before solution managers and UX designers gave the UI mockups to development, the mockups went through a formal review meeting with Dan Rosenberg, Senior Vice President of User Experience at SAP, one of our concept experts, and me. We knew the Styleguide by heart along with most technical details. It was important to have such a quality check at this time. The Sanity Check was a gate nobody could get around. It illustrated the importance of consistent UI design. During the Sanity Checks, we assigned each UI mockup a status of "red," "yellow," or "green." "Green" meant the UI mockup was compliant with the Styleguide and development could begin implementation. "Yellow" indicated some smaller changes were required before the UI mockup could be given to development. "Red" indicated a failure; the UI mockup was not compliant at all and had to be reworked and brought back to the Sanity Check again for a final review. It was very painful to execute and document the Sanity Checks. We looked at thousands of screens. During the Sanity Checks, we could not get into too much detail, and we could only identify obvious issues. But it was worth the effort. We got faster and faster in identifying the issues and over time more and more "green" UI mockups were presented in the Sanity Checks.

The overall status of all Sanity Checks was regularly presented to the management team and UX got a lot of visibility. The Sanity Check was the right instrument at this time. We do not need to conduct Sanity Checks anymore because the quality of the UI mockups has improved due to a stable UI Styleguide.

Pattern-based User Interface

It was clear from the beginning we had to *make the UI patterns part of the development environment to enforce consistency* on the developer. This was the right decision because most developers do not want to read the UI Styleguide.

We did a lot of research about common usage patterns in business software and derived the UI pattern out of this research activity. We had already had our first experience with a UI patterns in another SAP product before we started with the SAP Business ByDesign Project. The feedback from customers and users utilizing these UI patterns helped improve the UI pattern library for SAP Business ByDesign.

The UI patterns are designed to fit to user tasks. An example of one UI pattern is the "object work list," shown in Figure 2-5. This pattern supports user tasks of searching for a business object, identifying the object, previewing some data, and triggering an action for the object. Within a UI pattern, all UI elements and the interaction among the elements are pre-defined. A developer does not need to worry about these anymore. The user is automatically presented with a search area that has a basic and an advanced search feature. After a user triggers the search, the result is displayed in a table below the search area. When a user selects an entry in the table, the pattern shows details of the business object in a preview area.

In the beginning, we were unsure how many UIs we could apply the pattern-based approach to and how many would need to be "freestyle" to fit the user's needs. In the beginning, we estimated 70 percent pattern-based and 30 percent freestyle. After designing all the screens, we finally had the answer: 90 percent of the UIs are pattern-based and 10 percent freestyle. You have to be careful with these numbers because the results depend heavily on the number of patterns you provide and the type of applications you are building. The UI pattern "object work list," shown in Figure 2-5, is, for example, used more than 350 times in our solution. This shows the positive return on investment of using a UI pattern.

We were also unsure how much flexibility within one UI pattern a developer should have. If the pattern is very restrictive, you achieve a highly consistent solution, but you will not be able to optimize the UI to support the user's task. We decided to make the pattern a little more flexible for developers. In some cases, it was a little too flexible, and we had to

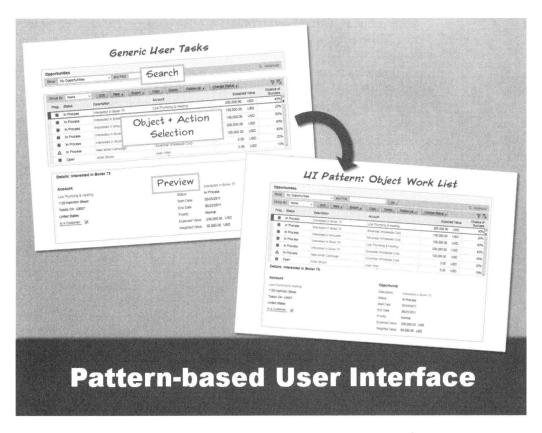

invest a lot of time later in the process to again achieve consistency on the micro-level.

In Phase 1, Solution Management lead the product definition. They were responsible for the detailed requirement definition. The UX designers were responsible for designing the User Experience, but Solution Management was responsible for the overall solution. Solution Management drove the handover process to development and lead the communication with development. The UX designers were involved where necessary. One sign that UX began to be institutionalized was that developers did not start developing without first getting a UI mockup from Solution Management.

Our challenge in Phase 1 was to design a solution without knowing the technical constraints. We created a UI Styleguide based on the UI specifications for the UI framework. The assumption was that the UI specifications would be implemented in the UI framework in less than one year and available in time for our application developers. One year later, the first version of the UI framework was available, and the application developers started building the application UIs. The first version of SAP Business ByDesign was not perfect from a User Experience point of view. The implemented UIs deviated from the target UI mockup because the technology platform team and the application developers could not implement all required features in the available timeframe. We had to improve the next version.

KPIs to Measure Success

At the beginning of the project, we defined a target User Experience KPI for each release and measured achievement at the end of the release. We used benchmark usability tests to measure user efficiency, effectiveness, and satisfaction. It was obvious for us that we could not achieve our final goal with the first release. For the first release, we defined a target usability KPI of 6 out of 10. The result of the first benchmark usability test for selected key use cases was only 4.8. We did not achieve our target goal for the first release! After we reported the result to the management team, the need for further investment was obvious, and we defined activities to improve the next release significantly. User Experience became a top priority topic for the next release and a major part of the development capacity was focused on UX improvements.

Phase 2: Get Closer to the Target Design

In Phase 1, as we intended, the design of the target solution and the development of the technology platform were done in parallel. Solution managers and the UX designers did a great job in iteratively designing the solution with continuous involvement of end users. Technology and application developers also did a great job in implementing the new software architecture and building the first version of SAP Business ByDesign. However, it was obvious that there would be a gap at the end of the first release.

The goal of Phase 2 was to get the implemented solution closer to the target design.

"The UI Polishing Story"

We launched a UI Polishing project to improve the User Experience of the implemented solution within and across applications based on end-user and internal feedback. Although we already used UI patterns in the development tool, a developer could still create inconsistent screens because the UI patterns were more flexible in the beginning. One experienced colleague from the development team and I were asked to take over the lead for the project. It was good to co-lead the project and to combine development and User Experience skills.

We formed a core team with people from application development, User Experience, UI architecture, and technology. All necessary parties had to come together at one table and agree on a joint plan. After two days locked in a room, we came out with the plan:

- **Identify** The UX team was responsible for identifying and monitoring all UI issues for the implemented solution.

- **Prioritize** The Core team would jointly prioritize the UI issues based on customer and user feedback.

- **Solve** The Technology team was responsible for solving technical issues, the UX team for UI Styleguide issues, and the Application Development team for application-specific issues. All had to work as one team to ensure feasibility.

- **Document** The UI Architecture and the UX team were responsible for extending and rolling out the UI polishing guidelines to developers.

- **Execute** The Application Development team had to drive the consistent implementation of the UI polishing guidelines in all applications.

UI issues could be separated into three categories: technology, application, and UI Styleguide issues. For each category, we assigned one person on our core team to drive these issues.

After the project setup was done and the plan agreed upon, we started with the painful execution process. After we collected all UI issues, we prioritized them and identified the high-priority issues.

We decided to make these high-priority issues very visible to the organization and the board. Every month, we created a UI polishing report detailing the status of the issues. The most important slide was a timeline showing when our customers would receive the fixes. Each issue was described on one slide with pictures and only one or two sentences. It was important that an executive understand the issue quickly and easily.

The most challenging issues were the ones in which the technology team had to develop a new feature and all our application developers had to implement this feature into their UIs. At that time, we already had thousands of screens. Even if you assumed that this new feature had to be implemented in only a subset of the screens and the required development effort per screen was just a few hours, the development organization had to plan a high number of person days for implementing the new feature in all affected user interfaces. Fixes that could be done only by the technology team were much easier to accept. They just made it into the release and no application developer had to react to the fix.

It took us some time to get most of the critical issues solved. This was a painful process for technology developers, application developers, and UX designers. As soon as the technology platform implemented a new feature, the UI Architecture and the UX team created very precise UI polishing guidelines. The guidelines had two parts: the UI Styleguide description and a detailed technical description on how to implement the feature.

We also had to estimate the effort for application developers to implement the new feature and get the commitment from each development team to do so. It was always a fight for resources and time, but the ByDesign Management team made it a priority. In most cases, we were successful. Day to day, we fought hard for every single UI issue.

The UX team together with the Development team set up a joint execution plan. Each application area had to nominate one developer as primary contact for UI polishing. On the other hand, we nominated one UX designer per application area. The developer was responsible for implementing the guideline as defined, and the UX designer was responsible for testing to see if the guidelines were implemented correctly and to support the developer in case of questions. This task is not one UX designers are necessarily enthusiastic about, but it was necessary to meet our product quality goals. We used a huge Excel spreadsheet to monitor and track all UI polishing issues for all screens. After a developer implemented a UI polishing guideline, he or she set the status to "implemented" in Excel. Afterward, the UX designer performed testing and set the status to "ok" or "not ok." In the beginning, participants found it hard to follow this approach, but after some weeks, the process worked better and better.

We published a weekly status report of successfully tested UI polishing implementations per application area. This weekly report made it very obvious that some areas were progressing as planned and some areas were not. It was a good instrument for neutrally showing the status of each application area and it lead to a small competition among the different areas. Finally, we implemented and tested thousands of UI polishing issues and achieved 100 percent test coverage for all polishing issues. This was a great success for the whole organization.

The UX team invested about 50 percent of their time in an activity that UX designers typically do not do. But it was worth the effort! This activity helped us to establish a closer relationship with the developers. It also helped to increase the trust in the UX team because we got it done and got our fingers dirty. Sometimes you have to decide to do something different to achieve your goals!

Are you in a situation in which UI issues don't get treated with the right priority in your company? If so, here are some recommendations:

- Make the issues visible to the management team and the organization.

- Get a sufficient budget and development time for getting the issues solved.

- Penetrate—promote the status of the project and make progress visible again and again.

- Get commitments from the right people.

- Set up a good execution plan.

- Execute until the end!

"The Share-the-Pain Story"

At the beginning of Phase 2, the first SAP Business ByDesign release was shipped to customers. We held a big launch event in New York and had customers on stage speaking about how this innovative solution was helping them to grow their business. Real users started to utilize our system day-by-day. We conducted many site visits and observed how users worked with our new solution. Most of the customers were very open and helpful. They allowed us to record the end-user sessions on video. The observation of real users working with the system helped solution managers, UX designers, knowledge managers, and developers to better understand where the solution needed to be improved.

After we conducted many of the end-user sessions with our live system, we presented the results to the complete ByDesign Management Team. One executive board member and all his senior vice presidents were in the room. All were looking forward to the presentation and the feedback from customers. We decided to show fewer PowerPoint slides and instead show a video of a real user working with the system. The video showed the following:

> A woman working in the HR department of her company was responsible for new hires. She was a very experienced professional in her fifties. Her task was to enter a newly hired person with an unlimited contract efficiently into the system. But the system did not let her do her work in the way she was used to doing it.
>
> After entering the employee details, she came to a screen to enter the duration of the contract. On the screen, she saw the fields "valid from" and "valid to." Both fields were mandatory. The "valid from" field showed, by default, the current date. The "valid to" field showed, by default, "31.12.9999." This means the contract

is valid forever. She was wondering about the "valid to" date, and so deleted the value "31.12.9999," and received an error message saying she needed to enter a date. The field was mandatory. She was totally confused by the reaction of the system. She again started entering the correct dates and successfully came to the next screen. It took some time and the people in the room were laughing. Finally, on the next screen, she finished the tasks and thought that she could just save the data. But the system responded with a simple message "error" without any further explanation. She was totally confused and closed the UI.

The people watching the video grew quiet. Somebody said that he did not expect this would be such a big issue. This was the day when upper management again realized that user experience is important and that this needs to be a focus of our development teams. Two days later, the issue was fixed in the system, as it was not a big deal to correct this. After the fix was implemented, the customer and particularly the woman using this UI were happy with it.

A picture or video tells more than 1000 words! People have to understand how users work with the system and what issues they have with it. Preparing such a video to make a point is a lot of work. You can only do this for selected and important cases. But videos are good vehicles for showing the user's feelings and demonstrating the value of UX design. You do not get the emotions if you just list the issues in a slide.

"The UI Process Improvement Story"

We made user-centered design mandatory for the whole organization from the beginning. Many things went very well, but we identified areas where the process could be more efficient.

At the beginning of Phase 2, I set up a small team of UX designers and solution managers, asked them to analyze the issues of the current process, and make some proposals for improvements. This was a very valuable exercise. They found issues in the following categories: focus on quality, user involvement, use case definition, one team approach, role definition in teams, UI validations, prototyping, and UI tools. For every issue, the team prepared proposals for improvement and described the benefits of implementing the change.

The team presented the outcome to the senior vice president (SVP) of the Solution Management organization. He liked the proposals a lot and helped us to drive the process improvements. Then the team presented the proposals to some development SVPs and got their help to improve the process. We decided to set up pilot projects to prove our process improvements. The pilot projects worked very well and people outside the UX organization spoke positively about user-centered design and the recommended process improvements. Here are some quotes from solution managers and developers:

> *After rolling over to a field research & use case–oriented solution definition approach, the return on our investment has been unbelievable.*

> *The One Team approach helped very much to achieve a technical feasible solution faster and more efficiently.*

> *The Solution Blueprint as well as Use Cases helped to achieve early alignment on requirements and to design wireframes fast and efficiently.*

The responsible executive board member at this time also liked our ideas and the approach we took. He gave me and a development Vice President the task of defining the future development process. The development process improvements became a major topic for the ByDesign management team, and we got a lot of attention and support.

Having one person from development and one with a UX background drive the development process jointly was a good decision. It took us some time to involve all the required stakeholders in our project. People from Solution Management, UX, Knowledge Management, Translation, Development, Operations, and the service organization had to support defining the process.

One of the main things we learned is that the UCD process is not separate from the development process!

We needed to have only one overall product development process description in which user-centered design activities were smoothly integrated. This small change helped us to better position user-centered design in our organization. Before this change, many people saw user-centered design as something that only UX people do. We all knew that this was wrong, but many people in our organization had this perception. We combined two process descriptions into one. All people in the organization use the same process documentation, templates, and examples. Elements of the user-centered design process like use cases and wireframes are mandatory deliverables during a project. Use cases, for example, are now an integral part of the solution blueprint document that describes the high-level business solution. It became obvious that use cases were not just important for the UX team, but they needed to help everybody to understand what needed to be achieved with the solution.

All requirements (including UI requirements) have to be documented and prioritized. UI-related requirements are described using wireframes and UI specifications. They are the basis for the development team for the implementation. The detailed interaction of a UI pattern does not need to be described by the application's UX designer because the pattern is described once centrally within the UI Styleguide, and the UI pattern is implemented in the development tool. The application's UX designer only has to describe the application-specific part of a UI pattern, for example, which columns to use in a table and which configuration options to use from a UI pattern. An example of such a configuration option is the number of lines that are visible in a table by default.

It took us some time to finalize the process description and get it reviewed and approved by all stakeholders. After this was done successfully, the process was officially accepted by the management team as the process for the next release. This was a big milestone for me and the UX team. We were again able to influence the organization and help to get to the next level of process execution. The amount of effort I had to invest to define such an end-to-end process was much higher than I ever expected. User-centered design was only a small part of the overall project, however. I had to deal with knowledge management, translation, development tools, and operational process execution to get the project done. However, even though the effort went much further than the normal responsibility of a UX team, it was worth it.

In Phase 2, we institutionalized the next level of User Experience. Awareness for UX improved throughout the overall organization, and we achieved a smooth integration of user centered-design activities into the overall development process. The relationship between the UX team and the development team grew much closer because of the UI polishing project and the strong collaboration required. Developers proactively approached UX designers when confronted with UI design-related questions. At the end of Phase 2, the usability KPI value was 6.8 out of 10. Compared to the usability KPI value of 4.8 at the end of Phase 1, we significantly improved the user experience during Phase 2.

Phase 3: Move to Lean Software Development

The changes we implemented in Phase 2 helped to improve the process and the user experience of our solution a lot. The goal of Phase 3 was to continue to improve the process and become more efficient as an organization. We decided to move the whole organization to *Lean software development.* We implemented the first stages of the core Lean elements and introduced Scrum to the development organization. We had to find a pragmatic approach to reconcile Lean software development with user-centered design and to combine the advantages of Lean software development with a more structured approach to user involvement. This new approach required UX practitioners to rethink old practices. User Experience methodologies needed to be adapted and smoothly integrated into the overall software development process.

The most important changes in Phase 3 were the "one-team approach" and "co-location." Cross-disciplinary teams work most efficiently if they work in the same location or in the same room. Members of these teams are taken from all organizations relevant to the work package in question: solution managers, UX designers, information developers, development architects, developers, and so on. All required skills are present in the project at all times. This not only gives the team a greater flexibility but also speeds up decision-making processes. The team has a common understanding of the problem space and user research is done as a team. This makes communication among people of different backgrounds much easier because they have a common language.

We introduced one backlog describing the high-level scope for the next software release. All backlog items were ranked in descending order. The availability of a prioritized backlog in each stage of a release makes resource decisions transparent. When resources—especially user researchers and UX designers—become scarce it is easy to decide which projects to support. The ranking of the backlog also helped to decide which topics to validate extensively with customers and users.

The major challenge for the UX team after introducing Scrum was the short development cycles. We had development sprints of two weeks, and the time for working on new designs was very short. Also the time we could use for end-user validations was shorter than before. If we wanted to get the user feedback from a usability test into the backlog of the next sprint, we had to be fast in analyzing the results and fast in making recommendations for improvements.

One approach to compensate for the short sprint cycles is to introduce a sprint zero that focuses on requirements and design. The duration of sprint zero is typically two to four weeks. This can help give team members some time to outline the high-level design before coding starts, but it is not sufficient for conducting solid field, market, and user research. You need to have a long-enough product definition phase that includes user research and a high-level design for those tasks. The high-level information architecture needs to be available before development starts coding to avoid costly late changes. The detail design can precede one or more sprints ahead of development, but flexibility needs to be ensured so the design can be adapted during the sprints based on user validations that are conducted in parallel with the development sprints.

In Phase 3, we not only improved the development process, but also improved the UI development tool to better integrate the UI guidelines.

"The UX Rules Story"

Much effort was invested in testing and quality checks of implemented user interfaces during the UI polishing project during Phase 2, which improved the quality of the user interface and compliance with the UI guidelines significantly. However, the effort invested was high, and we wanted to do something different.

We thought about how to become more efficient in this aspect as an organization and, therefore, invented the "UX rules."

We already implemented the UI pattern into the development tool to ensure consistency, but the UI patterns still need to give developers some flexibility. Many UI guidelines are just recommendations, and you cannot hard code these guidelines into the development tool. We provided the UI Styleguide to explain when to use which UI patterns and also to describe the UI guidelines that could not be hard coded in the UI patterns.

It was obvious to us that most developers did not read the UI Styleguide in detail; some probably never even looked at it. We concluded that we had to find a way to implement more UI guidelines in the development tools. If you look at a UI Styleguide, you'll see two kinds of UX rules: hard and soft rules. *Hard rules* are rules that no application developer can break. An example of a hard rule in our case is that a "close" button has to be on every screen, and a developer cannot get rid of the button. More difficult are the soft rules. An example of a *soft rule* is that a table should not have more than seven columns. Yes, there are exceptions where more columns make sense, but you have to treat them as exceptions.

To better understand how the UX rules are handled in the tool, I need to explain how the UI development tool works. The UI development tool is pattern-based and model-driven. When a developer starts building a UI, he or she first decides which UI pattern to use. He has to implement the business logic, queries, and the backend services. In the UI development tool, for example, the developer has to configure which queries are available for the user, which fields are displayed in the table, and which fields are displayed in the preview area. This is done via configuration. You can also call this UI modeling. UI and backend data logic are clearly separated. All a developer has to do is to fill the pattern with content and to bind the UI with the backend. The UI configuration is done during design time. During runtime, that UI model is interpreted and the UI is rendered. With the separation of the UI model and the runtime, we gained a lot of flexibility and could easily switch to another runtime environment using another UI technology. The UI models are stored as XML files. This enabled us to develop a tool to interpret the XML and to run some rules against this XML. This approach was used for the soft rules.

One of the developers built an engine that was able to check if a UI model (XML) created by our application developers violates a UX rule. In case a violation is detected, the developer receives a warning message in the development tool. He or she can correct the model and get rid of the warning or, by pressing a button, declare it an exception. All exceptions are centrally tracked and so we can see which rules have the most exceptions set. This could be a sign that the rule in the UI Styleguide needs to be revisited. The warning message for the developer consists of a link to a wiki page that describes the reason for the rule. From there, the developer can jump to the detailed chapter in our UI Styleguide to get more information. Getting the rules implemented into the development tool and linking the UI Styleguide to the tool helped us get developers to pay more attention to UI guidelines.

We turned the UI Styleguide into about 300 rules and classified them as "hard" or "soft." Obviously, the quality of the rules had to be perfect. If the developers received warnings that did not make any sense, they would blame the tool and discredit this automated approach. We had to be careful in introducing the rules and extensively tested the UX rules with real UI models.

After we implemented some of the UX rules, we showed the ByDesign management team how a developer works with UX rules in the development environment. They liked the approach and asked us to continue. We started a pilot project with one application area to see how the UX rules were accepted by the developers, and it worked very well. We then implemented more and more rules, tested them intensively, and released them for developers. The UX rules helped to improve the quality of the solution and finally saved the UX team and the developers a lot of manual testing effort.

We finally got the management commitment to define UX rules as a formal release KPI for our software. Developers now have to solve all mandatory UX rule violations before we ship our software to customers. This was another major highlight for the UX team and a further big step toward institutionalizing User Experience. At the end of Phase 3, the usability KPI value was 7,3 out of 10. Compared to 6,8 at the end of Phase 2, we again improved the User Experience.

Key Lessons and Recommendations

In every phase of the project, we learned a lot about what worked well and what had to be improved. It was and is a continuous learning process.

Many of the recommended UX practices used in this project might work for you and your company. Some are more specific for large companies with more complex processes and globally distributed organizations. Take some of the recommendations and try them out in your company. You will see what works and what has to be adapted to your circumstances.

Recommendations for Impacting the Technology

- **Define clear priorities for UI requirements** Prioritize UI requirements from a customer and user point of view. Use research data and results of UI validations with end users to justify priorities.

- **Make UI requirements easy to understand** People making investment decisions need to understand UI requirements. Use screenshots for a visual impactand use easy to understand terminology. If you have requirements dervived from a usability test, show a short highlight video of an end user struggling with the user interface.

- **Own the UI requirements for the UI framework** The UX team should take the lead in the UI requirements process for the UI framework and should have a strong voice in defining priorities. The UI Framework team is part of the technology team and develops the technological foundation for the Application Development team to develop user interfaces. UI patterns are, for example, implemented by the UI framework team.

- **Report on the implementation progress of UI requirements** Regularly report to the management team about the implementation status of UI requirements. Show them when the improvements will be available for customers.

- **Establish a good personal relationship with the UI Framework team** Set up a strong collaboration model between the User Experience team and the UI Framework team. If you establish a good personal relationship, you will get support from the UI Framework team to implement UI requirements that are important to achieving a superior User Experience.

- **Fight for every real user requirement** You have to fight for each and every requirement that improves the User Experience. Just putting the requirement on a list and hoping that it gets implemented in the way you would like will not work. You have to fight for every requirement and come up with alternative design proposals if your target design cannot be implemented.

- **Define a reasonable pattern library** The pattern library should be large enough to enable application designers and developers to create user interfaces that fit the task the user needs to perform.

- **Integrate a UI styleguide with the development tools**   Integrating the UI Styleguide with the development tools helps you to significantly improve the quality and efficiency of the development process. Make the UI pattern part of the UI framework. A pattern-based tool allows consistent and comprehensive design and development. Your styleguide will have "hard" and "soft" rules. "Hard" rules can be hard-coded into the development tool. "Soft" rules are sometimes recommendations or best practices. They apply to 90 percent of cases, but there are instances where exceptions are needed. Implement these "soft" rules into the development tool and inform the developer during development in case he or she violates a rule. If the violation is intentional, the developer can easily set the "exception" flag and continue working. If it is not an exception, he or she can immediately solve the problem. UX rules bring the UI styleguide closer to the developer.

- **Plan for iterations in UI framework development**   The consolidation of requirements to optimize the UI pattern is challenging. You have to plan sufficient time for iterations during development. Test the implemented UI pattern with end users and iteratively improve the pattern.

- **Invite developers to usability tests**   Developers need to see real users and feel how they struggle with the software. They need to experience if users are excited or struggling.

- **Introduce automated UI tests**   Automated UI tests free up people to do productive work. Automated tests should be used to do regression tests. They help to increase the quality of your product.

Recommendations for Impacting the Organization and People

- **Get top management buy-in**   Top management has to be convinced of the value of user-centered design to approve sufficient resources and budget. If you do not have the buy-in from top management, you should probably look for a new job.

- **Train and coach user-centered design (UCD)**   Enable solution managers, UX designers, and developers to execute the process successfully by providing training and coaching (for example, site visits and "how to write good use cases" training). Many people in your organization may not be familiar with UCD methodologies, and even if they have had previous exposure to it, new people have probably joined the organization over the course of the project, so the educational refresh process must be an ongoing one. The training should be practically oriented using many examples and practices. The goal is to learn by doing.

- **Understand the needs of solution managers and developers** Understand the needs of solution managers as well as those of developers and help them to become successful. Let them experience the value of user-centered design by taking them on site visits to customers and end users. We invited developers and solution managers to participate in site visits and usability activities with end users. People learn much better by experience—just "preaching" UCD does not help. Often, solution managers have a market research background but are not familiar with user research. User research helps solution managers obtain accurate data and enables them to better communicate with developers.

- **Share the same goals** Solution managers and UX designers and developers have to work as one team and share the same goals. Make the goals part of the individual objectives of UX designers, developers, and solution managers.

- **Be visible and sell user-centered design** Report end-user test results regularly. Use highlight videos to transport end-user impressions to the teams and the management. Offer remote observation for usability tests for people who cannot participate in person.

- **One-team approach** Build cross-disciplinary teams and ensure that all required skills are being used in the project at all times. The team should consist of a solution manager, a UX designer, a developer, and a knowledge manager to make the team most efficient and productive.

- **Co-locate teams** Teams should be located in one geographical location if possible. It is not a problem to have teams in multiple locations, but each team should have all skills in one location and ideally in one room. Our clear goal was co-location, but this was not possible over night. We became more co-located with each release, and we only allowed two locations maximum per team. This was not ideal but a good step in the right direction.

- **Take your time** The mind-shift required in a large organization to live a user-centered design approach takes time. It takes years to make it happen naturally, and it will never be perfect.

Recommendations for Impacting on the Process

- **Define *one* product development process** Define one overall product development process where user-centered design activities are smoothly integrated. There is no separate UI process!

- **Document the process clearly**   Provide a clear process description with defined deliverables. Each person needs to know what is expected from him or her. Make the process easy to understand. Start with a high-level description per process phase with the possibility to go into more detail if required.

- **Define clear roles**   Define clear roles and responsibilities across teams to avoid the "who owns the User Experience" discussion.

- **Define use cases as a mandatory deliverable**   You should not start designing the UI without knowing the user's main goals and tasks. To ensure high-quality use cases, talk to customers and end users, review existing applications, review results of prior usability tests, and interview the support organization representatives responsible for maintaining existing products about problem areas in the UIs.

- **Prioritize use cases**   Focus on high quality for the most important and most frequent use cases. Not every use case has the same priority.

- **Provide easy-to-use templates and best practices**   Templates for deliverables and best practices for how to use them will increase their acceptance by the people who need to follow them. It is easier to learn through good examples.

- **Define one product and release backlog**   Define one overall product and release backlog with a clear ranking of the high-level requirements. The prioritized backlogs help you to define the right priorities for User Experience activities. The product backlog covers the high-level requirements for the next two to three years. The release backlog covers only the requirements for one release.

- **Align requirements early**   You have to align the requirements early within the team. Developers should participate in the early phase of the project. They need to be involved from the beginning to avoid the "throwing of concepts over the wall" from solution management to development.

- **Plan sufficient time for concept work**   You have to plan sufficient time for user research and conceptual work. This is especially important if you go for an agile development approach. We decided to go for a six-month release cycle and planned for more complex conceptual projects with three to five months lead time. The conceptual work had to be done in parallel with the development phase of the previous release.

- **Plan for iterations**   User-centered design is an iterative development approach. You have to plan time in development for iterations.

- **Run pilot projects**   Set up pilot projects for improvements you want to make mandatory in the process. Invest time in coaching the pilot projects to ensure good results. Successful projects help convince management as well as the people participating in the project of the project's value. Use these people as multipliers to convince others in the organization to follow the approach.

- **Provide an end-user involvement infrastructure**   Provide an infrastructure for the teams to get in contact with end users and customers easily and quickly.

- **Involve developers in user research activities**   Developers get a better understanding of user requirements and a respect for real data collected in the field by participating in user research. A developer does not need to participate at each site visit, but should at least attend the synthesis workshop when the site visit results are consolidated.

- **Make UX rule violations a mandatory quality gate**   Regularly monitor UX rule violations in the development tool and report the status of violations. Make the solution of high-priority violations mandatory to release the product for customer shipment.

- **Measure the achievement of UX goals**   Define UX goals using key performance indicators (KPIs) and measure the KPIs using benchmark usability tests. Report the benchmark results to the management team.

- **Continuously improve the process**   The process will never be perfect. You have to continuously evaluate the process and work on iterative improvements.

Conclusion

Customers' quotes like *"The Silverlight UI rocks! It is fast and slick. It is a major improvement"*; *"The way it is structured is good, we don't have to send the employees to training. That saves costs. Every employee can virtually qualify himself"*; or *"ByDesign looked like it was designed for us"* prove that the effort we invested in User Experience design paid off. But we are still not finished and continuously have to improve our solution to meet market and customer expectations.

During the growth of SAP Business ByDesign, we learned that especially in a global environment, working together as one project team was essential when defining, designing, and developing new features. All team members—solution managers, UX designers, knowledge managers, and developers—need to be involved from the very first step in a project to align objectives and gain a common understanding of users' needs and the business processes. Besides the one-team approach, it is important to negotiate contracts between all involved persons. Working this way is much more efficient and reduces iterations in later process phases.

The UX team has to lead the process of institutionalizing user-centered design within a company. As the UX leader, you need to be visible and sell UCD within your organization. However, the context for this process needs to be set up as a win-win situation for all parties, not a competition.

It is essential to have top management support. But institutionalizing User Experience requires much more than just management buy-in. You have to influence processes, people, and tools to be successful.

Once the process is in place, it requires continued nurturing and support. You have to fight for User Experience until it is in the genes of every employee. Prepare yourself and the UX team for a long, but interesting journey.

Year-by-year we achieve the next level of institutionalizing User Experience. Developers and solution managers proactively involve UX designers in their projects and ask for resources and support. They clearly see the benefit of User Experience work.

How long does it take to fully institutionalize User Experience in a large organization? The answer is simple: It takes years to change the way a large organization works. You constantly have to learn and adapt the process to the individual needs of the organization. You always have to think about and articulate how UCD makes solution managers and developers more successful. If they see a benefit, they will follow the UCD process, provided you cast the whole process as a win-win situation and not a confrontational one over who owns the User Experience.

However, in the end, like all management challenges, it is not a question of having the best process in place. It is more a question of mindset and building successful relationships among solution managers, UX designers, and developers. They have to share the same goals in a meaningful way in order to work as one team.

Summary

- **What is the business context (e.g., product, customers)?**
  Some years ago SAP decided to build a game-changing business solution. The goal was to extend market penetration significantly into the small and medium enterprises (SME) market.

  The solution is called SAP Business ByDesign, and it is the world's most complete and adaptable on-demand business solution. Unlike any other on-demand business software, SAP Business ByDesign delivers transparency and control of the entire business end-to-end from Customer Relationship Management (CRM) to Supplier Relationship Management (SRM), to Supply Chain Management (SCM), to Financial Management (FIN), to Human Resources (HR). It provides companies an immediate 360-degree view of their business, is easy to use, and adapts quickly to changing business needs.

- **Which (business) problems did you address with your UX practice?**
  SAP Business ByDesign places user's needs right at the center of its design by addressing the "human" side of business software. This was important, because buying decisions for business software are no longer made by the CIO, but by the departments that use the software. The goal was to design a solution that meets the expectations of users, ensuring that users could work efficiently and effectively with the system. To achieve this goal, we defined a user-centered design process that was mandatory for the entire organization.

- **What were constraints and prerequisites?**
  To develop a new breakthrough on-demand business solution, we had to create a *new technology platform* that enabled us to develop open and flexible business applications. We developed a pure service-oriented architecture (SOA) and implemented UI patterns into the development tools. We also radically changed the *development process*. Superior User Experience was a key goal, and to achieve this, we defined an outside-in driven, iterative development process. In addition to the new technology and the new development process, we set up a completely *new organization* that grew very fast into a very large and global organization. The biggest challenge for us was that the *technology was not available at the time we started designing the solution*. We had to start with understanding the new market and the user requirements when the technology architecture was just paper work. We could not wait for one or two years until the technology was available. The time to get the product to the market would have been too long.

- **In which development context did you apply your UX practices?**
  The UX practices covered the complete development lifecycle of a new business software solution. The practices provide recommendations on how to impact the technology, the organization, and the people as well as the development process.

- **What compelling events supported you in applying your UX practice successfully?**
  At the beginning of the project, we convinced top management about the value of user-centered design, and, as a result, they provided

sufficient resources and budget. The decision to implement UI patterns into the development tools helped us to achieve consistency, which has led to higher developer productivity and reduced learning time for end users. Another compelling event was that user-centered design was mandatory for the complete organization.

- **What was the achieved product impact?**
  Our solution's User Experience improved significantly from release to release. We defined a User Experience key performance indicator (KPI) and measure user efficiency, effectiveness, and satisfaction after each release. The results proved that the investment in User Experience paid off. Finally, the excellent feedback from customers and users proves that the UX practices helped to achieve this success.

- **How did you do apply the UX practice?**
  We applied several UX practices. In general, we highlighted the value of user-centered design in the organization and came up with realistic and pragmatic proposals on how to develop a highly usable solution. It was a question of mindset and building trustful and successful relationships among solution managers, user experience designers, and developers. They have to share the same goals in a meaningful way in order to work as one team.

- **Which recommendations do you have for our readers?**
  The UX team has to lead the process of institutionalizing user-centered design within a company. As the UX leader, you need to be visible and sell UCD within your organization. However, the context for this process needs to be set up as a win-win situation for all parties, not a competition between parties. It is essential to have top management support. But institutionalizing User Experience requires much more than just management buy-in; you have to influence processes, people, and tools to be successful.

  Once the process is in place, it requires continued nurturing and support. You have to fight for User Experience day by day. Prepare yourself and the UX team for a long, but interesting journey.

Chapter 3

Influencing the Establishment and Sustainable Development of UX:
Strategic Selection in Different Phases

By Li Ming and Shui Shiwei

Ping An®

As a professionally managed and world-class organization, Ping An Insurance (Group) of China Ltd. is the first Chinese insurer to have introduced foreign investors into its shareholding structure. Operating along the principle of "Group Holdings, Segment Operation, Segment Supervision, Group Listing," Ping An has been able to ensure that the Group as a whole moves toward its goal of uniting strategy, branding, and corporate culture. Its financial platform is the most integrated among China's financial services sector. Its national back-office support operation in Zhangjiang, Shanghai, is a leading financial backend support center in Asia. Through this center, Ping An has established a systematic backend operation. By having in place a service infrastructure that includes telephony, the Internet, and customer service staff, Ping An can deliver a full range of financial services to customers in a professional, standardized, and comprehensive manner. Value-added services are also delivered to customers through its development of Customer Service Day and other innovative services such as Wanlitong for long-time customers and One Account. Wanlitong is a long-term customer reward plan that covers discount and other value-added services based on accumulated points. Run by a PingAn subsidiary, it aims to enable customers to enjoy diversified financial services and gain more long-term rewards with varied experience. According to authoritative surveys in 2009, customers ranked customer services at Ping An Life and Ping An Property & Casualty number one in their respective areas.

The Group provides comprehensive products and services in insurance, banking, and investments to more than 51 million retail customers and 2 million corporate clients. Ping An's organizational structure is shown in Figure 3-1.

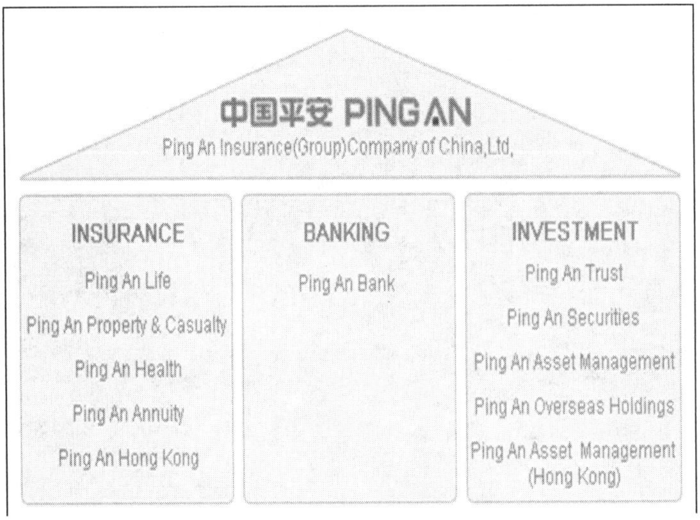

Ping An has about 417,000 life insurance sales agents, over 83,000 full-time employees, and a network of more than 3,800 branch offices. As of December 31, 2009, consolidated total assets and total equity of the Group were valued at 140.3 billion US dollars and 13.7 billion US dollars, respectively. The Group posted total income in 2009 was 22.9 billion US dollars with a net profit of 2.2 billion (using the exchange rate of 6.6693 US dollars on October 13, 2010). Ping An Life is the second largest

FIGURE 3-1 Ping An's organizational structure

life insurer in China by insurance income, whereas Ping An Property & Casualty is the second largest property and casualty insurer in China.

In 2008, Ping An was included in *Fortune Magazine*'s "Global 500" list, ranking first among China's non-state-owned enterprises. In June 2009, Ping An was included in *The Financial Times* Global 500 list of companies, ranking second among insurers globally, eighth among Chinese enterprises, and first among China's non-state-owned firms. In *Forbes Magazine*'s Global 2000 list of companies, Ping An was ranked number 141.

The Role Played by Ping An's E-commerce Website

In addition to promoting the Ping An brand, the Ping An's website also promotes online sales of financial and insurance products for the company.

Ping An Website Customers

Ping An website customers can be classified into four types: new customers, highly skilled customers, potential customers, and investors. The new customers are Ping An customers who log on to the website for the first time or only visit the website occasionally; highly skilled customers are those who visit the website frequently; potential customers are those non-customers who log onto the website for the first time or visit the website occasionally to research Ping An and its products; and investors are customers who invest in Ping An; generally, they visit the website to check on developments within the company.

The website enables these four types of customers to learn about all of Ping An's products and allows them to purchase those products online. Additionally, as far as cost is concerned, online services are preferred as they cost less than telephone and in-person services conducted in branch offices.

Ping An Website, User Experience Goals

In an effort to improve User Experience, or UX, Ping An has come up with four goals to improve its website:

- To design a website that allows all visitors to find the services and products they need quickly.

- To enhance the usability of online services and sales so visitors can complete every operation smoothly and to avoid unnecessary loss.

- To allow website visitors to locate solutions easily when they encounter problems using the website.

- To explore the functional requirements that users expect from the website to improve sales of Ping An's products.

Why UX Is Important

Many Ping An products, such as customer service, product marketing, and information communication, are all promoted using conventional marketing approaches, including branches, agents, and via telephone. As a result, marketing costs far outweigh the cost of online sales. By improving UX, when visitors use online services, purchase products online, or consult the website for information, and do all this easily and quickly, many will begin to utilize online services primarily, therefore reducing costs. Ping An can also focus on promoting its products on the Internet, utilizing the latest communications channels. Therefore, UX is very important for Ping An's profit.

Advantages and Limitations of Developing UX at Ping An

The advantages to developing UX include the UX department's accumulation of various available resources, including long-term cooperation with professional UX vendors, resources including personnel, and funding to conduct UX explorations.

Some of the limitations we've encountered include not all sections and subsidiaries have been willing to accept the new UX before they can see notable profits brought about by improved UX. In addition, existing widespread qualitative-focused conclusions in UX research have had less persuasive impact because other departments have more faith in quantitative data. For this reason, we have tried to ensure them through using quantitative data in daily work that UX can increase profits.

Status and Development

At an industry forum in 2006, we learned about the UX concept. As a result, we began to pay attention to this issue and apply it to our own e-commerce websites. Since then, we have employed UX methods in some of our projects through contact with a company that specializes in user research. After conducting several tests, we discovered that our original opinions of our website's usefulness deviated from those of our website visitors. We realized that in designing our website we should not only take into consideration the usability of filling out forms, but also users' desire to fill out those forms. Only after users visited our website and filled out the forms were we able to acquire our prospective clients' contact information; otherwise, we had no way to contact them about our products sold online. We needed to know why users were not willing to fill out the forms. Only when forms can be filled out easily does the transaction success rate increase.

In 2007, the company formally introduced the concept of UX, which was initially applied to a few project-based works to figure out some difficult or controversial problems. Gradually, we came to understand the importance of UX for e-commerce websites. Whether considered from the perspective of evaluating data from the website, users' emotional experience, or connectivity between users and websites, the concept of UX is of great significance.

We attempted to establish a successful integration of UX and the enterprise's development goals. We worked hard to develop the company's website into a leading e-commerce website, while also trying to increase online sales. We wanted not only to apply the UX concept to decision-making solutions, but also to contribute toward increasing commercial profits. And we hoped the UX concept could be efficiently applied to each product, link, and procedure. The company now requires that all staff along the whole workflow have a deep understanding of UX, which exerts an important influence on improving the UX of the entire website.

Nowadays, in the Internet era, apart from maintaining customer relations through our website, we must be fully aware that the company's development goals and sales performance are inseparable from the usability and efficiency of the User Experience, which coincides with the long-term operating purpose of any e-commerce website. As a result, we continue to expand the influence of UX on the operation of the company's website to further apply UX to tactical decision-making at different stages, such as product planning, development, and launch.

Facilitating Cooperation Among Various Roles in the Whole Process

In the process of designing UX, personnel from multidisciplinary teams such as the marketing department, technical department, experience design department, and product management department are involved. Because each team has different goals and criteria for success, and team members often have little understanding about the work procedures and barriers for other teams, contradictions and conflicts can exist among different teams. In this case, to achieve UX impact, the first thing we do is to unite teams with different professional backgrounds through application of UX.

Before the UX is brought to bear on the work, the different departments set their own goals, thus creating different criteria for teamwork efficiency, the satisfaction of cooperative departments, and so on, as a way to assess their achievements. Using UX as the link, we then try to come to an agreement on common goals and criteria for success among the different teams, specifically focusing on the profits earned via our website. With user behavior and habits at the core, we organize the work of different teams, so every member on every team develops a deep understanding of UX and its resulting profits.

As mentioned previously, a prerequisite of good cooperation is for the company staff at all levels to be aware of the value improved UX brings to the website, and to understand that all staff play a key role in promoting the operation of UX. The staff includes company leaders, business teams, project managers, product managers, user research staff, interactive design and visual design staff, as well as IT developers. Among these personnel, the leaders' approval is most important.

How Do Departments and Colleagues Cooperate with Each Other?

In the organization chart for Ping An's website, shown in Figure 3-2, the owners of Ping An's products in online sales are product managers, and the employees responsible for promoting products through the Internet are sales managers; this group is called the *business team*. The people in charge of user research, interaction design, and visual design are the *UX team*. The personnel providing IT technical support for the website is called the *IT team* and includes front-end development, IT technology research and development, and website operation. In addition to these three teams, we also have a special team comprised of all the subsidiaries of Ping An who are responsible for product prototype research and development; these teams are known as the seeding operation parties.

As a general rule, the seeding operation parties contact the product managers for corresponding products with information about their own products when selling or promoting their products online. After ensuring the feasibility of online sales, they determine whether the products will be purchased by Internet users and that the sales management procedure is feasible by employing user research methods. In the end,

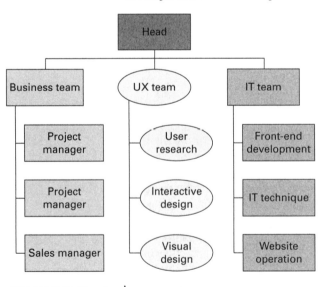

FIGURE 3-2 Ping An organization chart

they submit the optimal Internet sales management procedures to the IT team, who implements these procedures online. To enhance the products' popularity and sales, the seeding operation parties negotiate with sales managers about online promotion approaches, marketing the product among Internet users through marketing and search engine optimization (SEO).

UX Team Members' Responsibility

The UX team consists of the user research department, interaction design department, and visual design department, with members of each department working on different products. For instance, user research is responsible for researching product lines. When a new product is ready to launch, the user research manager is appointed as the project manager and organizes the necessary work, while interaction design and visual design are still ongoing in their corresponding departments. To better describe our work, we will employ several fictional characters in the following sections to refer to different UX-related stakeholders in the whole process.

Leaders Play a Key Role

UX has been part of the Internet industry for some time now. Being a relatively new discipline in China, however, it is still a challenge to enable every team member to use UX methods in their daily work and apply the UX concept to every product line.

In order to establish good UX, every team needs its own executive management who fully understand UX. Team leaders play an important role in promoting the UX operation. They not only communicate UX cases with each other; they are also the pilots guiding the communication and cooperation among different teams. The management team needs to understand the UX concept so as to make the company's benefits coincide with customer requirements. They also need to make UX an important part of the company's strategic planning process and promote user requirements as essential factors in the website's functional design.

First, leaders must understand the values brought by improved UX. Rita is the senior executive of a company. She is responsible for setting up the website for network marketing, which means the website's UX should be of great significance for her. However, because she had a limited understanding of UX, she hadn't paid enough attention to it in her work. Under the stress of fierce competition from similar businesses and sales performance appraisal, the sales team urgently needed various means or methods for analyzing and solving problems. Their top priority was to help Rita understand that UX testing could be a useful way to discover problems in a timely fashion. And she also needed to find the problems before the launch of the online sales process instead of remedying or solving the problem after the launch.

The sales team invited Rita to watch a usability test. Rita realized that the website's usability was a key factor in network marketing when she saw the failure of a purchase caused by an inconvenient online sales procedure. And she also realized that applying UX did help in discovering problems and proper solutions quickly.

Since then, Rita has required video clips be included in briefing reports so more colleagues can solve problems quickly by applying UX research methods. She also requires that all sales procedures go through usability testing and any major problems found in the testing be solved properly before they are launched.

Second, leaders need to understand to which problems UX can be applied. In network marketing, in order to buy product A, clients are required to register on the website first and then fill in all personal data, including name, gender, cell phone number, telephone number, e-mail, mailing address, zip code, and so on. During usability testing, we found that website users tended to hesitate to fill in these data or even enquired if they could leave these questions blank. Obviously, website users were not willing to fill in their personal data. However, users were forced to fill in all the data because they were required to do so under pressure from product owners who felt that product sales could only be promoted after the blanks were filled in. So although we launched this sales procedure, we found that the rate of successful registrations was not satisfying.

According to the analysis of website monitoring data, the website lost a certain number of registered users with every input that visitors were required to fill in with their personal data: 8 percent of visitors closed the page immediately and left the website when they were required to enter their cell phone number; 25percent of visitors stopped registration when they had to enter their mailing address; 6 percent of visitors didn't click the Submit button after being asked to enter their zip code.

Based on the testing results and analysis of website monitoring data, we not only recognized but also acquired quantitative evidence that website visitors were cautious about revealing their private information and our sales procedures needed to be adjusted as a result. Specifically, visitors should be required to enter only their name, cell phone number, and e-mail address, which are the basic requirements for online shopping.

As shown in Figure 3-3, since the new sales procedure was launched online one month ago, the rate of successful registration has increased by 75 percent because users are no longer required to enter so much personal information. When the test data was reported to leaders, the increase in number of registrations led to their paying more attention to UX before the launch of product sales procedures as well as during the early stages of product development.

Chart 1

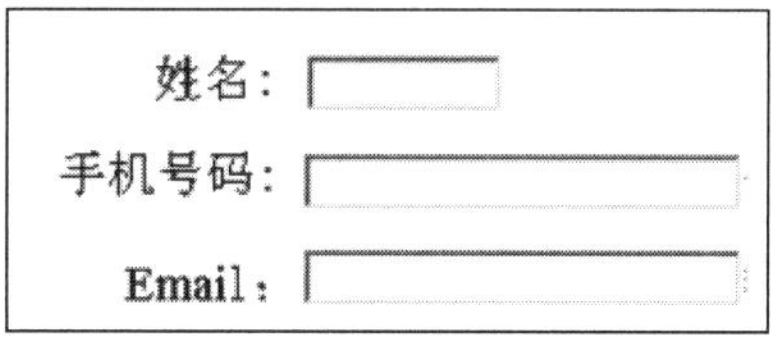

Chart 2

FIGURE 3-3 Chart 1 requires users to enter their name, gender, cell phone number, telephone number, e-mail, mailing address, and zip code so they can register on the website. Chart 2 requires users to enter only their name, cell phone number, and e-mail. The rate of successful registration increased by 75 percent when the required registration information was reduced to three items, namely, name, cell phone number, and e-mail.

For the customer information we didn't get from the initial registration, we obtained during subsequent activities, service, or communication with the customers, which not only meets the needs of current sales but also fulfills the company's demand for more detailed customer information. As a general rule, it is much easier for a current customer to reveal his or her private information than for a potential customer to do so.

Besides encouraging leaders to participate in the usability test themselves, we also shared successful industry stories and user research conclusions with other departments frequently, with cases and conclusions usually containing convincing data. By doing so, we enabled leaders to understand the effect of UX. These stories and conclusions also facilitated sharing and communication among leaders. Gradually, they began to ask their team to seek help from the UX department for UX-related problems.

How UX Data and Conclusions Helped Sales Managers Understand the UX Profits

Sales personnel were ranked as the new "driving force" of the UX project in the company. They used a series of instruments to improve sales performance, including various UX methods. The influence of UX on the company's sales performance was demonstrated when a good UX enhanced sales performance by 5 percent. We shared these successful experiences with the whole work team so the results of UX could be better applied to increase profits. Therefore, the company required that sales managers understand the importance of UX and carry it forward to team members. The comparison between pages conversion rates before UX testing and after UX testing implemented improvements was assertive evidence for sales managers to persuade team members to pay attention to the sales performance increases brought about by improved UX.

During the early stage of product sales procedure design, the design team strove to understand consumers' needs for a product based only on past experiences accumulated by the sales team. Because the sales team had direct contact with consumers, they knew the opinions and needs of consumers best. As a result, the sales team became the new "driving force" of the UX project in the company. However, as far as network marketing was concerned, sellers could not be fully representative of consumers. No matter how the design and IT technology developed, the ultimate product users are only a portion of the people who need networking products. And these people will not visit the website to purchase products only because of its elegant design or advanced IT technology. As a result, when determining user needs, we still need to listen to the voices of users, which simply refers to a group of people with common characteristics instead of all people in the world.

Consequently, sales managers should not consider themselves as representatives of target users. The target users of products are not sales managers, who may seldom use or buy the products they sell in their daily life. On the one hand, sales managers need to understand that, although their suggestions are inspiring for products sales, in the decision-making process, they should analyze cases in combination with feedback from target users. Real cases were utilized, for example, by having sales managers directly experience operational procedures for high-fidelity prototypes of the products so they could consider the products from the perspective of a beginner. Playing video clips of testing operations was another efficient way to give the sales team direct access to users' opinions.

Jackie is in charge of sales of a consumer card, which contains cash value and can be used in appointed shops. To expand the sales channels, Jackie wants to sell the consumer card online. After communicating with the UX team, the product manager in charge of sales utilized UX methods to research users' needs for online purchases. When conducting user group segmentation, the product manager discovered that the user groups willing to buy products online were limited. Hence, they were concerned that no one would show an interest in the card after its launch online. In this case, the IT development and publicity cost incurred during the earlier stages in addition to operation costs in the later stages would be wasted. The UX department carried on network research aimed at immediate test results. The analysis showed that the user group willing to buy consumer cards online was limited. The reasons for users' unwillingness to buy were varied, such as low discounts for online shopping, knowing little about network operations, the unavailability of invoices when paying by card. With this knowledge, Jackie changed his marketing strategy, which was not to sell the consumer card through an online approach. From this UX test, Jackie began to understand the consumer card's weakness, and he is trying to improve the card's function so as to achieve better sales performance.

Ensuring Project Manager Involvement by Solving Problems with UX Work

Product development requires that staff at all levels coordinate with each other. As the coordinator, the project manager generally doesn't have a UX background and thus has little understanding about the relationship between UX and other work and, as a result, sometimes will delay or ignore UX work. Therefore, a key point in promoting UX applications is to help project managers gain a deeper understanding of UX. To accomplish this, our company has carried out various communications to increase project managers' interests in UX via real cases as well as tactical exercises. Meanwhile, we helped project managers understand that using UX methods could solve some difficult problems.

Jason, and Thomson, both product managers, had different ideas about how to classify items on electronic banking menus so website visitors could complete their expected task quickly. Jason believed users visit the bank websites for two reasons: to inquire about their balance and to transfer funds between accounts. But Thomson thought that more users visit the bank websites to check details about their accounts or to buy bank products. Jason sought a communication meeting with the UX team one week ago, in which they analyzed how to classify site navigation. From the meeting, Jason learned that card sorting could be helpful in understanding users' needs for classifying items on the e-bank menu. He then contacted DK, a member of the UX team, and gained DK's support after expressing his opinion.

After the test, however, Jason was enlightened by the test's conclusion. He realized that the main purpose for bank customers visiting the bank's website was not to check their balance, as customers received SMSs informing them of their account balance if there was any change; instead, their main purpose was to transfer funds between accounts, to purchase funds online, or to inquire about fund payoff. Through cooperation with the UX team, not only did Jason understand how to design the items on the e-bank menu, but also he realized he could use UX methods to find solutions when he came up with difficult problems in his work.

Letting Product Managers Listen to Clients' Voices in the Field

In teamwork with the product line, a lot of UX work needs to be done. If team members with different professional backgrounds think that the newly added UX work cannot make a product more profitable, then UX cannot be applied to daily work.

During usability testing for a product, the UX team chose eight candidates who met the characteristics of a target user group to experience the product operation procedure. During testing, a candidate clicked the Next Step button and prepared to go to the next page. But the progress bar disappeared one second after it indicated it was "submitting data" and the website stopped on the page with no feedback. The website user stared at the page confusedly and then tried to find out the reason the page froze by checking the Help Section of the website. However, the user could not find the solution, so he gave up on the purchase. At this point, the product manager shouted, "Look at the prompt message on the page!" It was later discovered that users forgot to fill in the E-mail field. The red font behind the E-mail text box was supposed to remind users to fill in this field. However, as other prompt messages appeared next to this prompt message, users didn't see the e-mail prompt message at that moment.

When observing the whole testing process, product managers constantly complained about the poor quality of the candidates who casually filled in the blanks without reading the rules carefully and who didn't know how to correct mistakes after receiving the prompt message. The test results indicated that six candidates out of eight had this problem during the test.

Facing complaints from product managers, the leaders replied, "We cannot expect too much from website visitors when selling our products online. There are over a hundred million Netizens willing to buy products online in China. We should provide convenient purchase procedures for website users so that they can complete purchases easily. It also means that the personal behaviors of network consumers are uncontrollable. What the product managers need to do is to lead website users toward smoothly completely the purchase procedure step by step."

At this stage of product design or requirements analysis, product managers may have many ideas and users' requirements may change accordingly. During this process, product managers usually believe that website users are able to operate the sales procedure smoothly and complete the expected task easily. However, some problems concerning usability will appear during Expert Evaluation (this refers to Heuristic Evaluation, a UX method). For this reason, allowing product managers to listen to users' opinions about sales procedures is of great significance.

After the test, when planning new web pages, product managers considered usability issues for website users viewing web pages from different perspectives, and they also paid more attention to the influence of UX on web conversion rates for product sales.

Making Use of Bench Marketing and Sales Data to Help IT Technicians

IT technicians are not responsible for sales targets. They tend to work on web page development strictly according to requirements in the instruction book. In their opinion, the purpose of website development is to satisfy all the functions required by the specifications. They seldom take the website's usability into consideration. Therefore, when users' requirements change, the two parties often cannot come to an agreement easily.

At this moment, our aim is to convince IT technicians that their work on UX will benefit network marketing. Improved UX can lead to faster web page response and make interactions friendlier. And, as a result, users are more willing to buy products on the company's website. Meanwhile, the sales team, project managers, and product managers should understand the pressures, difficulties, and complex working procedures that IT technicians endure. Website UX cannot be improved without IT technicians' doing the work, which requires close coordination to solve problems.

First, we shared examples of websites with good UX among all members of the team, and IT technicians were also invited to analyze these websites and compare them with the company's own website. When we tried to discover our own merits and demerits and make comparison to work out how to surpass other websites in the same business, suggestions from IT technicians were taken into consideration.

Kyle, an IT technician in the company, had different opinions from the product manager's during the product development stage. The webpage he developed had shortcomings, namely, users had to spend a lot of time logging onto the website. In UX testing, we discovered that it took nearly one minute for website users to choose an option. Seeing that, Ann, the product manager, shared the websites from similar businesses with Kyle. On these websites, controls were widely used and the application of these controls in the sales procedure of different products was very flexible. By operating the controls on these websites and on the pages he developed, he realized his controls were not as convenient as the ones on other websites. Seeing the video that recorded users becoming entangled in operating his controls, Kyle felt obliged to improve the performance of controls on his web pages.

Due to the limits of technology, developers can't always fulfill the ideal UI concept, but they can improve it to the largest extent possible by fully understanding the UX. After comparing the results, we provided them with the version that could practically promote sales.

Second, we showed IT technicians how sales performance increased due to their work, which motivated the team's passion and made them understand how their work played an important role in increasing the website's sales performance. After the launch of new controls, online shopping became more efficient and the number of users who left before completing a purchase was reduced. Seeing the decrease in users' wastage rate and the increase in sales performance, Kyle rejoiced at the benefits brought about by his work. He understood that his work influenced the company's sales performance, which was also a great motivation for him. In order to enhance team members' understanding about UX and further improve UX work, a culture of continuous learning must be established that encourages different teams to regularly exchange ideas about UX work.

By cooperating with each team, we often invite colleagues to participate in tests, share cases, and communicate with each other, so they can gain further insight into UX, which is also an important approach in promoting UX.

Implementing UX

We first implemented UX in one product and then gradually applied it to other products and then the whole production line. During the UX process, efficient communication guarantees the smooth completion of UX testing. And the understanding of each role in the whole process of product development comes from the Requirements Document provided during a UX test.

In this document, we first try to clarify the purpose and contents of the test. Knowing the test's purpose enables testing staff to have a clear understanding about the test and its objectives. If the test purpose isn't clear, we may gradually wander off onto other topics or even choose wrong methods in the process of executing the test.

Second, we try to clarify the screening criteria for users in the test. As far as the network sales channel is concerned, all users must have some experience on the Internet. We don't choose people who cannot use a computer to participate in the test. And there are other required conditions. For example, when conducting a test of network sales procedures for tourist products, we selected a user group who traveled frequently and had experience in online shopping. In the screening process, we listed some questions to access certain conditions in choosing test candidates. For example, two conditions we assessed are listed here:

- Traveling frequency during the past one year. (If traveling frequency is less than two times a year, the user belongs to the group who don't travel a lot and have less purchasing experience and, therefore, should not be included in the testing.)

- When did your last online transaction happen? (If the time interval is more than one year, it indicates that the user isn't in the habit of buying products online and should not be included.)

Third, we try to clarify the focus of the test. A complete online purchase procedure generally does not use only one web page; it's usually made up of several web pages. Hence the test operational staff needed to focus attention on the descriptions in the Requirements Document for each time users operated a new web page. For example, when conducting a test of network sales procedures for tourist products, we needed to know whether the candidates of non-member groups would compare the non-member price with the member price. By focusing attention on each web page specifically, the test operational staff paid special attention to the individual pages and noted the results. Thus, complete data for every test were recorded, which contributed to improved data analysis after the test.

Last, but not least, the Requirements Document should be enclosed with other items used in the test and ID numbers, which helps guarantee a smooth and efficient testing process.

Using Persona and Focus Groups to Understand Target User Group Requirements

In the earlier stages of product planning, we didn't know users' requirements, so we initially learned from other similar products sold in the market. Later, when we found our users hesitated to click certain buttons on our website, we began to realize that the user group for our product wasn't in full accord with other user groups of similar products on the market. As a result, it would be a mistake to keep using market demands as a guide to our users' demands; it was time to utilize real target users of our own products.

This is when management needs to know who their users are and their character. Since management already understood, as mentioned previously, that the UX team could help them to answer these questions, they asked their own teams to communicate directly with the UX team and submit the answer.

Understanding the Target User Group's Characteristics

Business Problem   E-mail Direct Marketing (EMD) is one approach to business promotion. Every time we send an e-mail to our clients, we hope they are willing to go to our website and take part in our business activities, which will increase our profits. Therefore, determining the unique open rate and click rate for the e-mail is very important. In our experience, however, even when the open and click rate of two e-mails looked the same, the success rate differed greatly, and it became a problem we needed to solve.

Nikko is the sales manager for a product on a website. He is responsible for product promotion and for encouraging web users to buy products in the website's partner shop. When conducting a sales procedure test, Nikko was asked about the features of the target user group. Until then, Nikko hadn't considered the target user group for his products, such as the age group of users, their Internet habits, educational background, and under what condition these users utilize his products.

Having recognized this problem, Nikko realized he needed to understand the users of his product. He discovered the click-through rate (CTR) of the e-mail he sent was 0.1 percent, which was lower than other e-mails sent by similar businesses. Nikko then consulted investigative materials provided by the marketing department, including the market occupancy rate, market prospects, and analysis of other products from the same business. There was no research available about the fractionalizing, or dividing of, the user group based on individual characteristics.

This was not just Nikko's problem. This problem existed throughout many product lines. Some sales mangers even believed that all people who could use the Internet were their target clients. At this time, we realized that efficient measures were needed to help sales managers be more profitable with fewer resources and to optimize sales procedures. For instance, let's say the age range of product A's user group is from 20 to 45. And the age range of users willing to buy products or to make frequent online purchases is from 29 to 36. As a result, when we promoted our products to optimize the UX, we paid more attention to the feelings of user group members who were 29 to 36 years old, maintaining and increasing the benefits brought to the company by this portion of the user group. On the other hand, we also tried to understand the deeper reasons for the low operation frequency of the 20 to 28 year olds and 37 to 45 year olds in an effort to optimize product and sales procedures and promotions and to increase sales performance by encouraging these users' consumption of the product.

We adopted persona methodology for researching the product's target user group, so the research conclusion would better serve the product and maximize the input-output ratio. In the example discussed here, after receiving the research results, Nikko geared his promotion plan according to his specific user group's characteristics. By sending more accurately geared e-mails, in a short time the CTR of e-mail increased to 4 percent.

In attempting to design a web page that will possess all the desired functions and satisfy all visitors, you may end up creating a web page that no one will like in the end. Trying to satisfy all users only decreases users' degree of satisfaction. That's why we researched specific user group personality traits to help product managers create different sales procedures geared toward specific user groups, and, as a result, we found that market needs were better satisfied in the end.

Exploring Users' New Requirements and Understanding Users' Attitudes Toward Online Sales Through Focus Groups

Business Problem   Enhancing a website's business volume to increase profits is a problem. Projects that have already been launched tend to have a hard time further increasing their volume of business after a period of operation.

As the Internet is a main market channel, all areas of our company need to explore online sales and services for their products. However, not all users want to purchase products online, and users generally have higher standards for products sold online.

Online sales procedures exist for products being sold online. In order to meet users' needs, besides fully understanding users' requirements regarding a product's function and service, we also need to understand users' attitudes toward online sales procedures through UX methods, taking into consideration that if our products attract buyers, we can anticipate achieving our sales target. Thus, research on users during the earlier stages of a sales procedure is of great importance. We combine qualitative studies, which are based on personality characteristics and serve to identify potential problems, and quantitative studies, which provide more references for product planning.

Eva is the project manager for an upgrade project for an individual e-bank website. After fractionalizing the user group for e-bank operation, she already knew users' motivation for using e-banking and users' operational habits when using e-banking. What Eva also needed to know was other requirements e-bank users had regarding the website, so she could propose more detailed requirements for e-banking when discussing the project with bank leaders and IT technicians. As a result, she needed professional help before undertaking product planning.

Linda is the user researcher responsible for e-banking UX. She coordinated with Eva by organizing three focus groups based on the user group's characteristics. In addition to demands for purchasing financial products and services online, e-bank users also wanted reminder functions included in their e-bank experience. For example, users wanted to be reminded of the time of online transactions, payments, or finance product redemptions before closing time. The whole process of user requirement research indicated a conclusion close to users' ideas. Eva added such functions after discussion with bank leaders in charge of the section, thus strengthening users' feelings of reliance on e-banking. The transaction volume increased after the new functions were launched.

Because focus groups can help uncover user requirements in a short time without too much pretask preparation, they are a good approach to solving problems quickly for burgeoning e-commerce websites.

Setting Priorities in the Execution Process of Product Development

During product development and execution stages, many colleagues aspiring for perfection hope the visual design is as perfect as artwork. As for e-commerce that meets the need for quick online sales, we have to consider whether a design can benefit the company and decide which elements can be postponed and which should be executed immediately.

Paying Attention to Input-Output Ratio of Product Development at the Very Beginning of Product Planning

Business Problem   During the launching of a new project, the deadline is an influential factor. Being perfect is almost impossible and some work has to be left incomplete. When the time for launch and promotion is fast approaching, as far as the uncompleted work is concerned, how do you decide which work should be given priority?

In the beginning of product planning, we had already begun to pay attention to the product's usability. Prototypes of various types including freehand drawings, wire frames, screenshots, HTML files, and even partly functioning web-page prototypes were used as testing objects.

At this stage, problems were discovered that only had a little influence on usage, such as a visual pattern or style that could be improved at a later stage, but some bigger issues resulting in decreased user experience or even a possible negative impact on sales performance were corrected immediately, and sometimes project teams suspended other work just to solve such kinds of problems.

MK, the product manager, thought that visual design in the product sales procedure was not "good enough." He asked other colleagues how to improve the visual design. In this case, UX team members gave some suggestions: under the circumstances, the sales procedure needed to be launched online in order to ensure the complete functioning and usability of the sales procedure; it was determined, therefore, that the current visual pattern did not need to be adjusted because it already met users' needs. According to the tests, users didn't pay too much attention to the visual style and elements on the web page; completing the expected task was much more important. However, MK didn't agree with the UX team's suggestion. He thought that "not good enough" visual design would have bad influence on users' purchases regardless of how perfect the sales procedure was. On the other hand, the project manager worried that the time to optimize visual design would delay the launch of the product sales procedure and not only project costs would increase but also market opportunities would be lost.

To resolve the argument between the project manager and the product manager, leaders demanded a feasible scheme be proposed from the users' point of view. After the user acceptance test, we found that users paid more attention to the product's usability, and the now available visual design didn't influence users' purchases. The conclusion was that the now-available web page could be put online. Although later, based on MK's strong request, the visual design of the website was updated to a more satisfying version after the product was launched online, the website's monitoring data saw no significant increase in the product's transition rate after the adjustment of the visual design. At this moment, MK realized that the optimization of visual design had proven to be a waste of efforts. The cost did not have an influence on transition rate or sales performance.

In addition, solving some usability problems can also be postponed. Usability changes as time passes. The UX upon the product's launch may not necessarily be 100 percent perfect. The main purpose is to help users understand the product and purchase it online smoothly. The optimization and correction of details can be done in later stages. Usually after the launch of a new product, web analysts analyze users' behaviors via other software, such as Webtrends, to determine page views and users' online operations, operational duration, and browser habits. After several weeks' analysis of this quantitative data, we then fully understand that users may come up with problems concerning availability. And that's when we further improve the website's usability according to the analysis.

Through tests, colleagues aspiring for perfection soon realize that in optimizing a website, they need to pay more attention to the process of completing the expected task as well as the return on investment (ROI). If the perfect art form or creative effect cannot provide a benefit, it will cause increased input cost; the priority of such work should be decreased because ROI is the most important factor for a company.

Determining Which Is Better: Web Page Transition Rates and Their Direct Influence on Sales Performance

Business Problem   The transition rate of a web page is a key element in the profitability of a website. Hence, during product marketing, popularizing the web page that can bring about the greatest profits among clients is key. Frequently at this moment, however, as you are confronted with various overall arrangements and designs, how do you choose the best one?

Network promotion is an approach to improving network marketing performance. When there is online promotion, in order to maximize the web-page transition rate, the marketing manager and activity planning manager will propose two choices for leaders to decide between. Sometimes, leaders have a difficult time making the decision regarding which choice will increase the transition rate from one page to another.

Betty is the network marketing manager responsible for mortgage lending. Her work is to gather users' information during promotion activities. Then the bank's customer service specialists contact visitors to discuss details about mortgage lending. John is the plans manager responsible for this activity. The web-page transition rate is one of his criteria for evaluation, which means John has his own opinion on how to increase the web-page transition rate.

When designing visual effects for a promotional web page, Betty and John have different ideas about whether to let clients understand the transaction process first or to fill in their personal information first. Betty thought they should first communicate with visitors about the purpose of the loan, and then inform clients about the requirements for a loan, and finally let users submit their personal information. But John thought that website visitors should intend to get a loan before visiting, so they first should let visitors fully understand what they need to do. Both ideas sounded reasonable, and there was only a small difference between the two options. Because we had no available similar experience to draw on, we decided to conduct an A/B Test between the two web pages to learn the transition rate of the two web pages from the backend data (see Figure 3-4). To make the tests results more reliable, we asked our developers to establish two real websites reflecting two different ideas for tests. After testing for a while, it turned out that the conclusion ran counter to Betty's idea. There was deviation between her conclusion and the actual conclusion, which showed the transition rate of Web Page B was higher than Web Page A by 70 percent. Betty was surprised at the fact that such a tiny change in a web page could result in so big an increase in sales performance.

However, later in the monthly Sales Analysis Report, Betty discovered that Web Page B did not increase sales performance by 70 percent; in fact, Web Page B had even lower sales performance than Web Page A. Finally, after analyzing the data between two versions, we concluded that, although the transition rate of Web Page B was higher than that of Web Page A, the success rate of Web Page B was not as high as that of Web Page A. As a result, in determining the transition rate, a comprehensive analysis of the project fitting the company's goals ought to be adopted before deciding on a suitable online promotion scheme.

Determining Which Design Attracts More Attention and Is More Efficient for Users

Business Problem   When a new credit card is launched on the market, card owners often need to activate it on the website. The goal of the company is to help users find the right entrance on the home page and to activate the card easily. There were three opinions about the visual design of the activation entrance. Version 1 adopted the form with clear plaintext and a button to

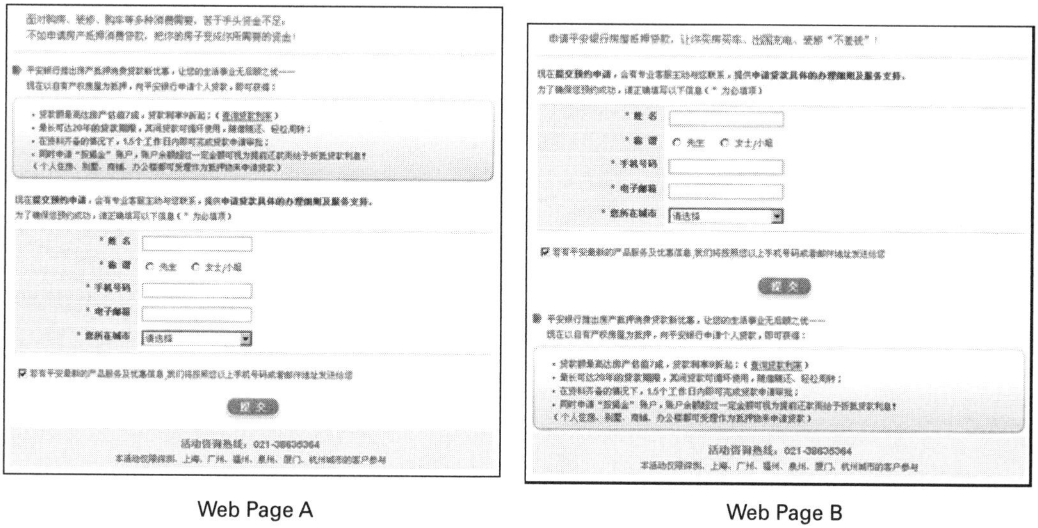

Web Page A

Web Page B

press; version 2 adopted a press-button form; and version 3 used the form with the advertising copy. The three forms are shown in Figure 3-5.

But it was hard to decide which version would increase the success rate for online activation. By using eye-tracking testing, we came up with an answer. We put the three versions in the same position on the home page, conducted eye-tracking testing on different user groups, and compared the test results for each group. The "Card Activation" button used in version 1 attracted users' attention in the shortest time, with a 95 percent CTR, from which we concluded that the form with characters, a button, and a gray background received more attention from website users. On the contrary, the white characters and warm color background in version 2 did not attract website visitors' attention. And version 3 was regarded as an advertisement instead of an activation entrance.

FIGURE 3-4 Web Page A asks the purpose of the loan first and then informs clients of the requirements for a loan and finally let users submit their personal information. Web Page B shows users what they need to do on the web page first and then lists the necessary conditions for a loan after users enter the data.

Version 1   Version 2   Version 3

As a result, in the product online promotion, test conclusions were used to help us decide which version would bring more value to the product.

FIGURE 3-5 The visual designs for a form to activate a credit card: version 1 is a form with clear plaintext and a button to press; version 2 is a press-button form; and version 3 is the form using advertising copy.

Using Other Methods and UX Office
After Product Launch

Applying the UX method helps us find 80 percent of problems for a relatively low cost. But for the remaining 20 percent of problems, long-term optimization is needed. Although we could not find all problems and solve them, our aim is to find and solve 90 percent of them.

Web pages need to be constantly optimized during a period of time after the product launches. The whole optimization process tests and verifies the usability of the online sales procedure and users' feelings according to different user groups. During this period of time, we often discover some problems that lead to users not being able to complete their expected task. UX testing is a good way to discover problems.

We invited some users to complete their expected tasks on their own in the laboratory while the product manager observed them operating the website from the observation room. By using this method, we had clear view of the whole operational process when users completed their tasks, users' own solutions to problems, and under what conditions users quit the operation. Knowing these situations, we discussed them with users to find out the reason for the problem and to create the solution.

Apart from the above methods, we probed users' behaviors by using such backend monitoring device as Webtrends; through monitoring SEO data and by using qualitative-quantitative methods, we understood their purpose for visiting and their behaviors.

Some testing devices make our communication and testing more efficient. UX Office software, shown in Figure 3-6, provides us with a complete UX management platform, which not only enhances the management quality of UX projects, but also improves the efficiency of the usability evaluation. The function of UX Office enables all roles in the UX working process to know every aspect of the project process timeline, including project target, tasks, deliverables, resource coordination, and progress situations. Project members can update their working progress in UX Office so other colleagues are updated on their progress simultaneously, which is convenient for follow-up and project management. It also reduces the progress reporting time cost and shortens the test preparatory period.

There is standard guidance for an evaluation process in the UX Office evaluation module, as shown in Figure 3-7. Even first-time test executors can get started easily rather than ignoring items because they are unfamiliar with the work. UX forms offer an orderly system for test preparation, user recruitment, test execution, test subdivision, data analysis, and video clips for reporting output. It has reduced the workload for each procedure and shortened the project cycle.

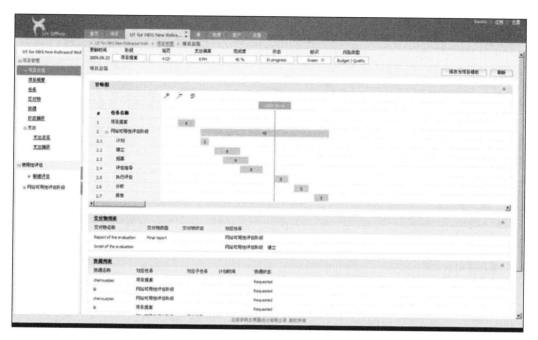

FIGURE 3-6 The project management console in UX office

By using UX Office software, managers can observe test-sites in other locations from the local observation room, as shown in Figure 3-8. And other colleagues can see the test conducted from their offices in other cities. It has greatly enhanced the efficiency of participation among colleagues so that staff find solutions to the problems in their fields in a timely fashion. And test costs have been reduced accordingly.

Using UX Office, we don't have to spend extra time on training or monitoring new staff's execution in usability evaluation, as the system evaluates usability according to standard flows, detailing all the evaluation work.

Sometimes a product has to be tested several times. With UX Office, we only need to call up some data from previous tests and design new scripts based on what we already have, thus completing new tests in half the time.

Before we began using UX Office, we had no specialized labs. If we wanted to have video materials, we had to use a DVR, which cost us much time to look for what we wanted to call up from the video.

When recording data, we now needn't write it down and then transfer it to Excel for analysis. We only need note the problems and then analyze and record the video clip quickly, which enables us to complete a test of five to seven participants within a week, which took double the time before.

FIGURE 3-7 Usability testing employing UX office software

Maintaining Long-Term Communication to Further Improve Sales and Explore Requirements

To establish online relationships between users and the company, besides building users' confidence by using the company's brand, we also need to dispel users' doubts about online purchasing and persuade more people to purchase online, which not only reduces aggregate costs but also provides more convenience for users.

The company's insurance product is periodical and bought by users annually. We expect that users who have bought the product will go on to buy the product in the next year. But from the online transaction data, we found that users had been lost who didn't buy the product online again. Besides maintaining normal transactions for new users, we also tried to discover the reason for the loss of old users and how to make up the lost value. As more users gave up on online purchases, it became more obvious that user needs had not been satisfied.

The company interviewed the user group who had given up online purchases. In the interview, we found that users had many complaints about the service, such as no customer service support available so that they had to spend a lot of time dealing with problems. The product manager then went deep into optimization of user experience and gradually solved issues of common concern so as to encourage users to buy products online again.

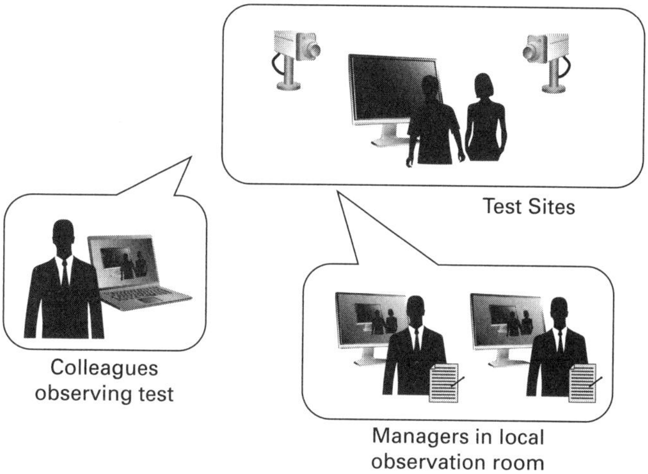

Test Sites

Colleagues observing test

Managers in local observation room

FIGURE 3-8
Synchronous observation of testing from different locations

If the users who used to purchase insurance by phone could be convinced to purchase online, it would also increase online sales performance and reduce corresponding marketing costs. For example, comparing the cost of telemarketing with the cost of online sales, the cost of telemarketing for insurance is 10 yuan (1.5 US dollars) whereas the cost of online sales is only 1 yuan (0.15 US dollars). If we persuade 25 percent of users who used to purchase by phone to purchase insurance online, we can save a lot in marketing costs. So besides finding out reasons that users purchasing by phone don't buy insurance online, we also tried to find a solution to encourage them to buy products online, which is to provide a positive UX. On the contrary, if the online UX is not good enough, users who came across difficulties in online purchasing will return to phone purchases, which will increase marketing costs by ninefold.

We used similar methods to find the problem. We interviewed users who purchased insurance by phone, knowing that some of them could not use a computer, some of them worried about the safety of online purchasing, and some didn't know they could buy insurance online. Based on our conclusions, the product promotion department formulated a detailed promotion program, attracting this part of the user group to purchase online.

Figures 3-9 and 3-10 compare the influence of UX on company costs.

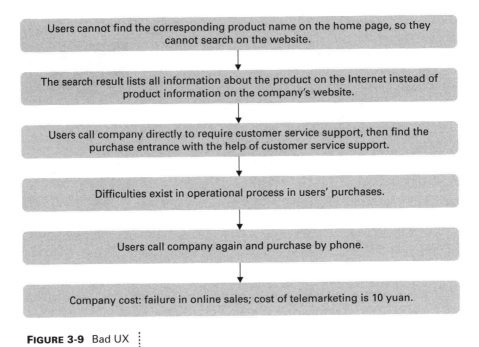

FIGURE 3-9 Bad UX

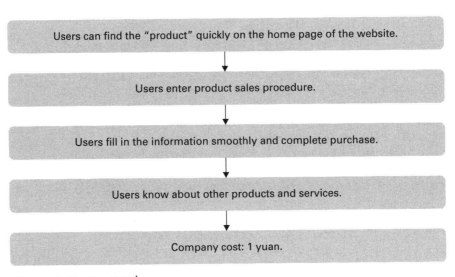

FIGURE 3-10 Good UX

Suggestions

UX refers to all contents involved in the interaction of users with products, devices, or systems, and user perception during the interaction with the product. When applying UX to a company's website, the company should take the commercial value brought by UX into consideration. As a result, sharing data of users' feedback and sale performance with all colleagues along the production line is important.

These data will help other work teams discover problems directly; for example, the design team can adjust the visual design to attract more attention from users; the IT team can consider how to improve web-page response time to satisfy users; interaction designers can improve interactions details to help users operate the site more smoothly; product managers can adjust UX to enable users to understand how to operate the site better. All-round cooperation will gradually improve the quality of a product's UX so as to change the transition rate, trading the volume of user complaints for increased income and reduced cost.

In recent years, the promotion and execution of UX has provided us with many benefits. However, considering the ROI, a company should consider the measurement of UX quality more thoroughly and conduct further quantification of the value brought by UX work. We ought to have more colleagues concerned about the benefits to the company as well as user interest and then reconcile those benefits and interests.

The Internet is a people-oriented network. In such a highly competitive Internet era, the economy of the future is the experience economy. Especially for Chinese e-commerce websites, we can neither copy the experience of others nor ignore the real needs of nowadays Netizens. As long as we fully apply UX to the construction of e-commerce websites, we can be more competitive in the market.

As readers attempt to apply our experience to their companies, we have some suggestions to follow:

- To enable top managers to understand that UX is the core competitive strength for an e-commerce website, make sure there is an abundant budget and resources provided for UX development.

- To establish a multidisciplinary UX team, employ people with professional knowledge to do the work so as to ensure all methodology is understood and carried out properly.

- To communicate, use as interesting an approach as possible, always cooperating with colleagues about problems that can be solved by UX work. After making a deep impression on those colleagues, you can then further explain various UX methods.

- To encourage UX team members to participate in trainings and to communication actively, ensure they have access to the latest knowledge and developments in the industry and that they can apply them in their daily work. Just remember, don't act blindly.

- To motivate team members' positive working spirit, carry out comprehensive performance appraisals for the UX team.

- To support daily work, have a powerful cooperative subcontractor.

- To enhance the cohesive force of the team and make use of relevant resources, share project achievements frequently.

Summary

- **What is the business context (e.g., product, customers)?**
  In our e-commerce business, we sell financial products like insurance, loan, and credit cards, with potential customers who visit the Ping An website or have experience with online purchases.

- **Which (business) problems did you address with your UX practice?**
  Online sales of financial products were stalled due to low web page transition rate, and the promotion didn't bring notable profit as expected. To raise the transition rate, PingAn applied UX to discover the problems with the online sales procedure.

- **What were the (organizational) constraints and prerequisites?**
  Only when we succeed in winning leader's support can we promote the operation of UX in the company smoothly. UX is something new to the company and conflicts with the interests of other sections for the operation of UX means increased time and costs. Besides, leaders and colleagues of other departments don't understand UX, which is another obstacle to the operation of UX.

- **In which development context did you apply your UX practice?**
  When UX has been fully recognized among related departments, UX methods have been well applied when needed in projects.

- **What were compelling events that supported you in applying your UX practice successfully?**
  Large sales promotions and helping leaders or other departments make decisions contributed to the recognition of the importance of UX in Ping An.

- **What was the achieved product impact?**
  By employing UX, we discovered the reasons for the low page-transition rate and improved the sales procedure, improving sales performance and increasing profit at a lower cost.

- **How did you do apply the UX practice?**
  We adopted top-down promotion strategy, namely, we first helped leaders understand the effects of UX and then communicated with colleagues in other departments, helping them learn about the benefits that UX can bring to sales.

- **Which recommendations do you have for our readers?**
  The support of leaders in the company is the essential factor in promoting UX practice.

Chapter 4

From Feature Centric to People Centric

By Sigrid Vandenweghe
and Kris Vanstappen
Human Interface Group

Marc Charlier
BCT

BCT (est. 1985) is one of Europe's major players in the Enterprise Content Management (ECM) market with 180 employees on the payroll. In 2009, BCT had a gross turnover of almost 19 billion Euro, a fine result in a crisis economy. BCT develops, implements, and services its portfolio for the Dutch government market in a direct sales model. All other branches in the Netherlands and the clients in other European countries are serviced through a partner model. In addition to the Dutch partners, BCT has partners in the UK, Belgium, Luxemburg, Germany, Switzerland, Austria, and Sweden.

BCT basically has three product lines:

- CORSA, a very complete and flexible Enterprise Content Management system

- Sha-Peau Enterprise Content Management, which is based on the SharePoint platform

- IDT Capture, an innovative scanning solution for processing and extracting key data from documents

Through its ECM and Capture products, BCT supplies more than 700 international organizations with software for controlling and guiding documents. BCT's core software, CORSA ECM, the subject of this chapter, helps organizations optimize four major business/economic performance factors:

- Cost reduction

- Compliance (with internal and external regulations)

- Continuity (information anytime, anywhere)

- Collaboration (e.g., collaboration and communication)

Human Interface Group inspired BCT to evolve toward a user-centered design methodology and set the example for designing even more successful applications along the full range of document management products.

Guiding the Document Flow

Originally, the request for better document management came from within the market. Existing mail registration software did not fulfill all the needs of BCT's customers because those systems mainly managed paper documents (literally—what came out of the copier or printer) and did not provide any rights management, which is important when dealing with confidential documents.

Document management is actually a *logistic process:* The user initiates and follows a document or another piece of information through the organization. Information enters an organization in a variety of ways: by post, e-mail, fax, scan, and so on. Organizations are confronted almost daily with the processing of hundreds, sometimes thousands, of documents. These documents have to be guided correctly through the organization within a reasonable time after arrival. But reading, judging, and sorting the growing stream of incoming information has become increasingly time consuming. "At the right time, in the right place" has become the credo here.

From the very beginning, BCT chose to work with *Progress,* a US business application infrastructure software (now called *OpenEdge*) because of its transparency and extensive database connectivity, a choice the company still favors today. Progress technology provides the infrastructure for applications as diverse as ERP and financial trading, across industries as diverse as retail, manufacturing, telecommunications, financial services, and government. For BCT's clients, seamless integration with primary systems such as Oracle and SQL databases is crucial: document management always *supports* the primary process and integration with primary systems helps avoid unnecessary and redundant information storage.

Developing CORSA

CORSA was born in response to the market's demand for efficient document management.

An energy company in the Netherlands was the first organization to look for a specific document management system. The most important functionality the company needed was a way to follow documents through the organization that included a routing process to address problems as they occurred (such as documents remaining too long at a certain location) and a way to get management information about the number and type of documents. For example, management needed information about the number of complaints about deliveries or concerning employees.

A BCT consultant searched the market for such a system and could not find it. Because of BCT's experience with ERP consultancy, BCT decided that the functionality the energy company asked for was not very different from the usual ERP requests except it concerned documents and information that had to be in the right place at the right time. This was the beginning of the development of a company-grown document management system. Due to geographic considerations (BCT is located in the deep south of the Netherlands), the system had to be easy to service from a distance (the Internet was not yet a possibility in 1985…). The system also had to have a unique name; one of BCT's first document management customer's suggested CORSA. In ancient Italy, *la corsa* was the route that messengers had to follow, a route that often had to be protected in dangerous places when important messages had to be delivered.

CORSA's functionality grew very fast. Started in 1985 as a document registration system (Record Management System), CORSA added new modules during those first years, such as archiving and relation management in the early 1990s, digitizing in 1995, and a workflow system in 1996. Basically, every minute was invested in extending CORSA's features. What began as a program with approximately 150 little programs related to each other had, by 1996, grown to include over 1700-related programs.

In 1991, BCT founded a CORSA user-group, the so-called SpecTeams (specification teams). For these SpecTeams, CORSA users and developers were brought together to develop new modules or functionality. CORSA users brought knowledge about the work they wanted to do, and developers heard directly from end-users about their new ideas for the CORSA system. Due to the content of the teams, they gave more priority to functionality than to usability. *Featuritis,* the practice of constantly adding features without taking into account the user experience, is, indeed, a disease that makes people blind to the human side of technology.

Here Comes Windows

In 1996, right after the introduction of Windows 95, the market demanded a "Windows way of working." BCT developed a version of CORSA with a Windows flavor, but it still had an undeniably character-based user interface. By integrating C++ and .NET components, BCT was eventually able to deliver a more authentic "Windows look and feel."

More clients, more users, more requests in the new millennium led to organic growth and an explosion of CORSA's functionality, resulting not only in a very complete system but also in a poor user experience and complex, hard-to-use software "meant for specialists in document management."

The Turning Point

In 2004, BCT won a contract to provide document and workflow services to the town of Nijmegen. Nijmegen was charmed by CORSA's features and flexibility, but was not so enthusiastic about its usability and the fact that CORSA required two full days of training. Because the town of Nijmegen employed 2,500 people who had to work with CORSA, this two-day education requirement for each employee would add up 5,000 training days.

The required training would increase the city's investment in CORSA to an unacceptable level.

Empowered users who demanded easy-to-use software along with an awareness that every workplace in an organization should be connected to the document management system—thus multiplying the number of users and training days—changed the way BCT thought about software. BCT realized that CORSA had to be more usable and more intuitive. Using CORSA should be a pleasant experience, enabling users to learn on their own as they explored the software to find ways to maximize its functionalities. BCT also realized that only the department responsible for document flow and archiving needed the type of specialization requiring the two-day course. One of the BCT's most important goals was to build a new user interface for the end-user. The "specialists" would, however, use the old user interface. As the project developed, user tests clearly showed that specialized users also wanted a more user-friendly interface. This resulted in a broader project to improve CORSA's usability.

An Expert's Look

BCT hired Human Interface Group for one important reason: the company *did not want to lose sales because of CORSA's user-experience issues.* In BCT's own view, the competition offered a far better user experience and a more intuitive way of working—and their software did not require a two-day training course to learn the very basics. BCT would gain a great advantage by lessening the days needed for training because a customers' total investment could be reduced.

The goal was very clear from the beginning: deliver a state-of-the-art user experience for the new software. Since functionality had always been "king" at BCT (see Figure 4-1 for the old CORSA search results screen), the company hired usability experts to see what could be done to reach this ambitious goal. Human Interface Group started with a short user and task analysis and an expert review of the document management software, assessing the user interface in accordance with recognized usability principles and the Windows XP Style Guide.

The user and task analysis, based on Mayhews' list (1992), revealed the *heterogeneous nature* of the user group: some users were very IT literate; others only used Office products at a novice level. Some people used CORSA all day long, whereas other users logged in now and then to perform a few tasks. Speed and efficiency was important for a large group of users, but intuitiveness and ease of use was equally important for another group of users. The challenge was to harmonize these different requirements

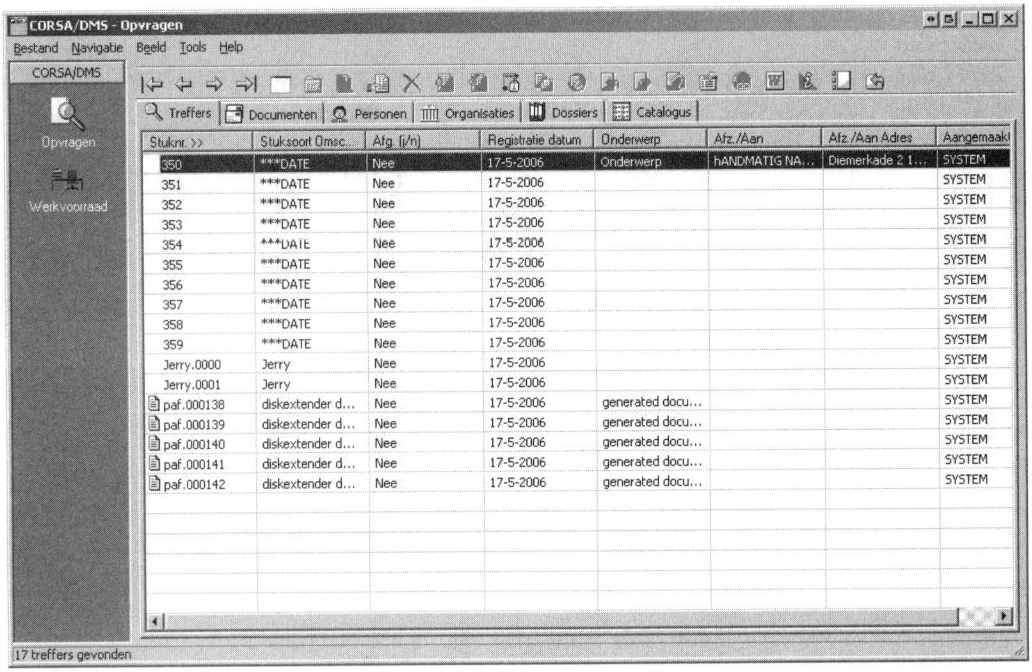

FIGURE 4-1 The old CORSA search results screen

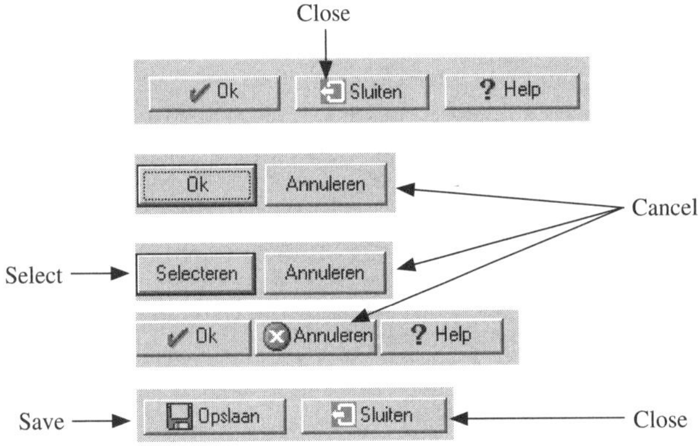

FIGURE 4-2 The various ways to close a window

in the new user interface. The goal was to design a user interface that met the needs of *all users,* not just the document management specialists.

Many usability issues had to be solved, but one of the main problems in the software was the inconsistency of user interaction. For instance, there seemed to be 18 ways to close a window or cancel an action (Figure 4-2). Buttons and accelerators were labeled in more than 10 different ways, and shortcuts were as diverse as the Amazon fauna.

Besides the lack of standardization in the user interface, Human Interface Group also recommended changing the conceptual model, updating the graphical look and feel, and creating an alternative for scrolling in tabbed pages (Figure 4-3).

Detail | Versie | Catalogus | Kenmerken | Memo | Dossiers | Vertrouw. | Route | Relaties

Error messages, such as those shown in Figure 4-4, needed a thorough review as well.

In short, the report pointed out some acute usability issues, and although some problems could be fixed immediately, Human Interface Group recommended a complete redesign of the application.

FIGURE 4-3 Scrolling in tabbed pages

FIGURE 4-4 Cryptic error messages

Moving Forward

Human Interface Group and BCT set up a morning session with all the CORSA company stakeholders. During this three-hour session, which started with a good breakfast just to break the ice, the partners had the following goals in mind:

- Describe the "as is" situation as clearly as possible.

- Create awareness of the change needed.

- Create a common goal for product improvements.

The workshop was attended by the president of the company, the marketing director, two developers, the technical writer. and the CORSA project manager. Human Interface Group guided the session, but BCT's marketing director frequently intervened to make a strong link between BCT's situation and company strategy, which created a natural synergy.

The workshop started with a few starters to catch everybody's attention, such as the following classic usability ROI statistics:

- Every $1 invested in UCD returns between $2 and $100 (Pressman 1992).

- Nearly 80 percent of software lifecycle costs occur during the maintenance phase (Pressman 1992).

- According to the Standish Group, 60 percent of that maintenance phase is due to rework because the user requirements were not clear in the beginning. Approximately 63 percent of software projects exceed their estimates (Lederer and Prassad 1992).

- "The rule of thumb in many usability-aware organizations is that the cost-benefit ratio for usability is $1:$10–$100. Once a system is in development, correcting a problem costs 10 times as much as fixing the same problem in design. If the system has been released, it costs 100 times as much relative to fixing in design" (Gilb 1988, 66).

● "The average user interface has some 40 flaws. Correcting the easiest 20 of these yields an average improvement in usability of 50%. The big win, however, occurs when usability is factored in from the beginning. This can yield efficiency improvements of over 700%" (Landauer 1995).

The roundtable discussion between Human Interface Group and BCT was enlightening for product managers and developers and resulted in the decision to work on a new user interface for CORSA. Human Interface Group then shared the conclusions from the expert review in a meeting with all stakeholders, which was set up as a presentation of the results and an interactive workshop on usability principles (loosely based on Nielsen's ten heuristics, which are ten general principles for usability design). Using visual arguments and real-world scenarios employing the old software helped to move things forward.

Human Interface Group also explained the user-centered design process to BCT, using Apple products as an example (the new iPod mini with its click wheel had just been released and was a huge commercial success). The focus was to reveal the so-called Apple secret as a methodology in which user goals and in-depth user knowledge were crucial and where frequent iterations automatically paved the way to success. Apple also had to ruthlessly remove any feature not core to the iPod's function. For example, a display is nice, but it adds cost and weight, and it doesn't add much to the "play random songs" experience. So out it went. Some customers would be upset, but for the majority, the overall experience would be better. A marketing department focused on feature checklists would never make this decision.

Human Interface Group wanted not only to inform BCT about what was wrong with the software but also to show how it could be improved. For example, using data (evidence) from similar projects with other clients, they demonstrated that user-centered design can be perfectly integrated into a "classic" software development process. The usability expert also brought in some real-life ROI examples to show explicitly the added value of user-centered design. In addition, Human Interface Group presented a realistic user interface redesign roadmap, so stakeholders could actually visualize the next steps.

This awareness session was a very important milestone for BCT and Human Interface Group, because it motivated both the commercial and technical teams to work on the software's "outside" (the user experience) instead of focusing on the "inside" (the technology), which resulted in the creation of a common goal:

To create a state-of-the-art user experience in order to stay competitive in the market.

Goals perceived as realistic are far more effective in changing behavior, and studies on the theory of goal-setting suggest it is an effective tool for making progress by ensuring that group participants with a common goal are clearly aware of what is expected from them if they are to achieve their objective. The commercial team would be able to sell better and sell more and developers were inspired to change their product in a positive way. And, last but not least, the company director was there every step of the way.

After that meeting, it became very clear for everybody that cleaning up the cosmetics would not help BCT to reach the goal of delivering a state-of-the-art user experience. Because this was a group decision, there was a maximum buy in, which again resulted in a strong commitment to the goal: everybody believed in the importance of better usability.

A team was put together, consisting of two developers from BCT and a senior user interface designer from Human Interface Group. Because time and money were short, things had to move quickly. Human Interface Group worked at the BCT offices, right next to the developers, so communication could happen quickly and the usability expert would quickly become a part of the team. This was also a great way to share expertise: Human Interface Group could "evangelize" user experience and train on the job and BCT happily shared its technical knowledge in order to design something that could actually be built afterward. A rewarding synergy developed that quickly proved to be very productive.

The user and task analysis had already revealed that 90 percent of end-users used Outlook on a daily basis and that these people were very familiar with the Outlook tripanel navigation model. A new conceptual model was then developed after intensive iterative design, based on the tripanel navigation model (Figure 4-5).

Based on the new conceptual design, Human Interface Group developed a *static mockup* of one module of the user interface (search documents and display document properties), which, after agile design and iterative fine-tuning, resulted in a Windows XP prototype made with Delphi (Figures 4-6 and 4-7). The new user interface was tailored to the specific needs of the end-users. Because Human Interface Group worked so closely with the developers, only three weeks were needed between the delivery of the expert review and the working prototype, which was baptized "DMS2006." The usability project resulted in a change in development tools. Besides the OpenEdge (formerly named Progress) development environment, the new tools included Delphi, .NET, and Java. These new tools brought usability to the higher level that everyone was aiming for.

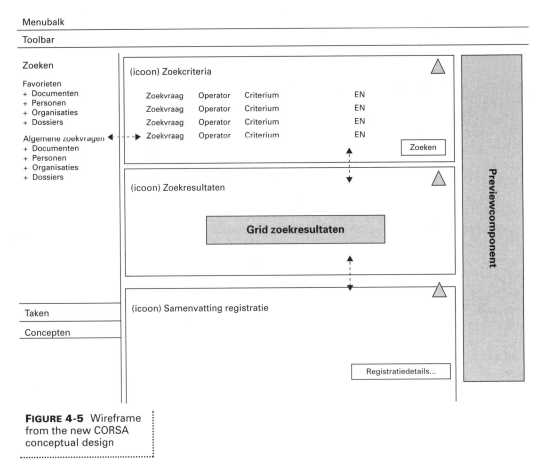

FIGURE 4-5 Wireframe from the new CORSA conceptual design

Test drive

CORSA users then tested the working prototype in a usability lab with Morae software (Figure 4-8).

The first results of the user feedback sessions were very positive:

- "The software is very familiar and recognizable."

- "Clearly a giant leap forward."

- "This looks very good to me; when can we have it?"

Analysis of the test data resulted in some adjustments and adaptations of the user interface and an optimized prototype.

By this time, three BCT employees had become so eager to learn about usability, they enrolled in a postgraduate degree program focused

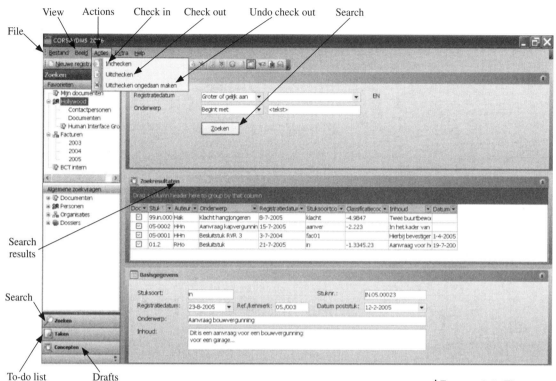

View Actions Check in Check out Undo check out Search

File

Search results

Search

To-do list Drafts

FIGURE 4-6 The new CORSA prototype with three-pane model and multifaceted search

on user-centered design, where Human Interface Group gave most of the trainings. They travelled 200 kilometers for many training days and wrote excellent papers on different user experience subjects. Talk about motivated team members…

Standardize, Standardize, Standardize

After the prototype was tested and fine-tuned, development of the main application began. Because an entire team of developers would do the programming and because consistency was key, BCT needed a *standard* for all future user interface design.

A style guide would make it easier for BCT to develop software in accordance with the prevailing platform standards and conventions and would serve as a means of added value for BCT's product branding and image.

Because BCT already had formal knowledge of usability methodology, BCT drafted the first version of the style guide under the guidance and coaching of Human Interface Group. This way, another period of knowledge

Documents
Memo
Connections
File
Registration   Baseline data   Version management

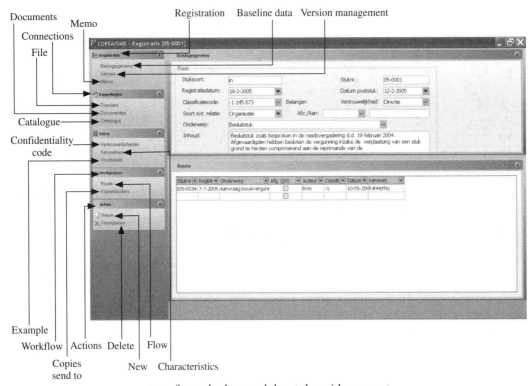

Catalogue
Confidentiality code
Example
Workflow | Actions | Delete | Flow
Copies send to   New   Characteristics

FIGURE 4-7 The new CORSA prototype showing the properties of a document

transfer took place and the style guide was not something "imposed from the outside." The style guide was reviewed and tested by developers, and people working on the user interface could make suggestions and change requests. Information sessions on using the style guide were held and attended by management as well, so internal support was good. The user interface standard really became "a BCT standard," generally accepted as the company's new user interface bible.

FIGURE 4-8 BCT employees monitoring a usability test

Beyond Colors and Buttons: Institutionalization

In general, the team made a big difference in the development process at BCT, as illustrated in Figure 4-9.

BCT management still decides whether to add new features. The usability aspect doesn't change this decision; it only adds a new component to the decision-making process. Building a specific feature and making sure the user experience remains excellent might be more expensive than just building without looking at the feature's usability aspect. And this means a feature might not be added because it is too expensive to deliver with a good user experience.

The big difference in before and after lies in the fact that

- User needs are thoroughly analyzed up front instead of "just adding whatever the customer wants to the software."

- New developers learn about usability during their introduction period and the functionality created by new developers gets extra attention from the usability team.

- Formal evaluations of the software's UX have been established.

- Usability testing is performed during different stages in the product development cycle (from sketches to prototypes).

BCT moved from being a company with a very technical and functional mindset to being a company where the user is king and where new products

FIGURE 4-9
Development process at BCT: Before and after

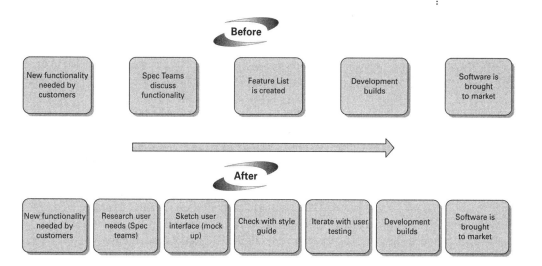

evolve around the people who need to use them. The CORSA SpecTeams user groups still exist, but each SpecTeam has at least one Certified Usability Designer as a member. Usability has become an aspect of development that each developer knows about and considers while developing new functionality. One of the biggest fans of usability is the BCT Research & Development manager. Before 2006, he only thought about new functionality; now he always tells his developers (the "old" ones and especially the new ones) how important usability is in modern software. A good example of this is the new Apple iPad. It inspired the BCT developers to create a new user interface designed for this new device. This version is used in areas where customers benefit from looking up the communications between the customer and the organization using the Apple iPad.

This change was a process in which the product improvement served as the trigger for an organizational transformation. Because of the time needed to build a well-trained usability team within the BCT organization, it took about a year and a half to develop a more or less smooth-running usability assurance operation in the development process. The overall trigger for this change was the common goal of improving one of the BCT's main products, which resulted in an approach to software redesign where several departments were involved in the process.

Creating awareness through clearly showing the difference between the "as is" and "to be" situation was the *first* step in this process and Human Interface Group successfully created new enthusiasm about the possibilities ahead. The *second* step was to bend that awareness into creating the desire to participate in the project.

On BCT's side, management provided maximum support and dedication. Senior managers continually confirmed Human Interface Group as a "change-to-come" symbol and Human Interface Group, in its turn, was open to knowledge sharing and "training on the job."

BCT's management actively supported the vision for the project, ensuring the organization as a whole understood that the changes that needed to be made were ultimately beneficial to the organization. If an organization tries to make changes that are inherently bad or are not received positively by the people, it will be much more difficult or close to impossible to implement these changes without significant resistance.

Human Interface Group's reputation as an international and well-known organization skilled in making software more usable and the fine personal contacts between BCT and Human Interface Group team members gave BCT the trust they needed to assign the work to Human Interface Group.

As an external company, Human Interface Group also maximized its influence by taking the role of an external consultant. As a consultancy contract is usually made for a limited period of time, it improves the chances for a project to be approved and facilitates quick implementation and the overcoming of internal conflicts. The use of external consultants also enhances the legitimacy and prestige of projects, often generates new ideas, and facilitates the discovery of other options. On rare occasions, external consultants also serve as troubleshooters.

For an individual or organization to achieve change effectively, individuals in the organization who need to modify their behavior exhibit buy in, for instance, by learning new tools and methods.

BCT's organizational culture, which has little power distance (this is the degree to which an organization expects differences in the levels of power) and low uncertainty avoidance (the extent to which a culture accepts uncertainty and risk), were real advantages. At BCT, employees were empowered to take initiative and come up with creative solutions to solve problems.

Usability got a place in the software development process because people understood its importance and experienced the benefits of user-centered design themselves. For example, it is now company policy that the development department must have, at any given moment, at least two people trained in user-centered design, so no gap in the expertise needed to work in a user-centered way occurs.

Usability is also given high priority in the review and testing process as well: new functionalities with a less-than-perfect user experience are sent back to the drawing table. The BCT usability team determines usability. They are all university-trained Certified Usability Designers and can decide whether the user experience for a new functionality is good or not.

Perhaps the best example of real change is the quarterly personnel meeting. This meeting used to consist of six or seven managers giving a speech from behind a desk, but it has now been transformed into an interactive talk show with a real host, with usability as a fixed agenda topic. The Corporate Communications Manager, who hosts, talks to an employee about improvements made to the user experience, increasing awareness for more than 200 people at the same time.

Users as Sellers

The new CORSA got a new name: MyCORSA. BCT's marketing department did the "preaching" in the market. After a big presentation during a CORSA user conference in 2006, regional sessions were organized to create awareness for the usability possibilities MyCORSA provided. Press communication increased, too: because of the way BCT started and developed the MyCORSA project with Human Interface Group, journalists were more interested in this "innovative organization." This increased press attention brought a double win. BCT was in the press as an innovative organization and the Unique Selling Proposition (USP) of usability was brought to the attention of prospective customers. This resulted in new business opportunity for

BCT because organizations specifically demanded usable solutions for their document management process—an aspect that had never been considered before the CORSA project.

Success followed almost instantly: a consistent revenue growth of 15 percent and even 22 percent in the recession year 2009, the competition shamelessly copying the user interface, and last, but not least, much more satisfied users. Because the number of document management users is still growing with the growth of digital information, organizations will not buy a document management system that is not user friendly. Users were happy to be ambassadors and advocates for BCT and CORSA. Users became our software "fans," essentially selling our product.

In addition, BCT also saved on hiring new resources. The new user interface required more modern user interfaces, so .NET and Delphi were used to implement the user interface. It's easier and less costly to hire .NET or Delphi developers because these tools are taught in college, whereas OpenEdge programmers are scarce and expensive. BCT still uses OpenEdge, however, because moving to an entirely new platform would be very costly. In short, evolving toward more standard development tools had a positive impact on technical costs.

BCT just launched its *Intelligent Document Technologies* department, which develops input management tools (advanced scanning software). Because of the excellent user experience, BCT is the only European company with a certified extension on the Kodak ScanPartner scanner, a certificate that offers the possibility of delivering software on a platform never thought of previously—an intelligent document scanner. And the only reason that the BCT developers could develop tools for this touch-screen scanner was because of their experience with usability.

Of course, BCT knows that designing a good user experience takes time and money. But these investments pay for themselves quickly: shorter trainings, happy users, and a product that sells itself.

MyCORSA product is now four years old, and BCT wants the company to remain a market leader in their segment. That's why they started another project with Human Interface Group to have a fresh new look at other ways to deliver state-of-the-art user experiences to their customers.

Because they know that attention to people pays off.

And because it is so rewarding to help people do a better job.

Without Human Interface Group we would still be struggling to make our interface user-friendly. Their experienced view and good advice helped us create an interface that is without competition in the document management environment.

Marc Charlier
Manager Corporate Communications
BCT

Summary

- **What is the business context (e.g., product, customers)?**
  BCT is one of Europe's major players in the Enterprise Content Management market. ECM is the generic name for Document, Record & Workflow Management and Digital Filing. BCT's business applications deliver solutions to companies that want to streamline their ECM. One of BCT's core products—CORSA—had to be improved drastically.

- **Which (business) problems did you address with your UX practice?**
  Human Interface Group was hired for one important reason: BCT was anxious about losing sales because of the software's User Experience issues. The competition offered a far better User Experience and a more intuitive way of working—and their software did not require a two-day training course to learn the very basics.

- **What were constraints and prerequisites?**
  Timing was very tight for this project as things needed to move fast and not take months so BCT could beat the competition.
    Human Interface Group had to use the technology chosen by BCT (Delphi) to create a new user interface and had to make sure that UX became a top priority in the organization at the same time. Buy-in from BCT's management was key here.

- **In which development context did you apply your UX practices?**
  CORSA is a desktop software that was built in Delphi. Human Interface Group applied UX practices on the level of analyzing user needs, iterative design, standardization, and usability testing.
    BCT later implemented good UX practices throughout the entire organization.

- **What compelling events supported you in applying your UX practice successfully?**
  In addition to the redesign of CORSA, BCT had to be transformed from an organization that focused on software features and functionality to a user-centered organization. Human Interface Group had to convince all stakeholders in the project about the importance of user-centered design. Changing the mindset of all people involved in product development was the most challenging issue.

- **What was the achieved product or business impact?**
  After the redesign of CORSA, BCT achieved a consistent revenue growth of 15 percent and even 22 percent during 2009, a recession year; the competition shamelessly copied the user interface; and last, but not least, BCT's users were much more satisfied. Because the number

of document management users is growing with the growth of digital information, organizations will not buy a document management system that is not user friendly.

The User Experience of our solution improved significantly from release to release. We defined a User Experience key performance indicator (KPI) and achieved our goals with each release.

- **How did you apply the UX practice?**
Human Interface Group applied several UX practices. First of all, we gave a clear overview of the "as is" situation and drafted a step-by-step approach to reach the "to be" situation. Human Interface Group used industry examples and best practices to create UX awareness in the company.

- **Which recommendations do you have for our readers?**
As an external consultancy, creating buy-in for your vision is key. You need to be honest about the current situation and demonstrate to all stakeholders what a better approach would be. You want to establish a common goal so everybody is heading in the same direction. Not only is management support important, but also you need the support of the people actually developing the software. Have them do some of the work as well (creating a working prototype, observing usability tests, for example), so people feel connected to the solution.

References

Gilb, T. 1988. *Principles of Software Engineering Management.* Reading, MA: Addison Wesley.

Landauer, T. K. 1995. *The Trouble with Computers: Usefulness, Usability, and Productivity.* Boston: MIT Press.

Lederer, A. L., and J. Prasad. 1992. "Nine Management Guidelines for Better Cost Estimating." *Communications of the ACM* 35(2) (February): 51–59.

Pressman, R. 1992. *Software Engineering: A Practitioner's Approach.* New York: McGraw-Hill.

Chapter 5

The Effective User-Centered End-to-End Product Development Process

By Ji Hong
China Telecom®

China Telecom is a giant state-owned telecom operator in China. China Telecom was a Global Partner of World Expo 2010 Shanghai and, for many consecutive years, has been selected as one of the Top 500 Global Corporations. China Telecom mainly provides integrated information services, including fixed-line telephone service, mobile service, Internet connections, and applications services. By the end of 2009, the company's revenue reached 207.8 billion RMB (approximately 30.4 billion USD), which was a 25 percent share of China's total telecommunications market. China Telecom has 194 million fixed-line telephone subscribers, 62.36 million mobile (Code Division Multiple Access, or CDMA) subscribers, and 61.75 million broadband customers. China Telecom's assets total 632.2 billion RMB (approximately 96.2 billion USD). The company has 670,000 employees.

As the telecom industry has developed rapidly, the number of users and the market are approaching saturation. In China, by the close of 2009, the number of telephone subscribers reached 1,061,000,000; the number of mobile communication subscribers reached 720,000,000; and the number of broadband Internet users reached 100,000,000. China has become the largest telecom market in the world in terms of both number of users and market scale. Meanwhile, the competition for telecom carriers in the market is becoming increasingly fierce. Telecom carriers need to develop products targeted to various market segments, yet learning and meeting such requirements is itself becoming increasingly difficult. The year 2009 marked the first year of 3G service in China's telecom industry; three carriers, including China Telecom, China New Unicom, and China Mobile, were authorized by the Ministry of Industry and Information Technology to begin 3G service, which was the prelude to the now wide-ranging competition among China's telecom carriers. To keep up, telecom carriers desperately need to transition from being traditional telecom operators to being comprehensive information suppliers. Product development, which was technology-centered, has gradually become user and market centered, with a greater emphasis on users' perceptions and the business model of products in market operation.

What has China Telecom done to establish and develop its products' user-centered development model? What problems of concern to the company's decision-makers can be solved by User Experience work? How did China Telecom better meet strategic requirements by improving the User Experience? This chapter focuses on how to bring the user-centered design (UCD) product-development model into telecom product development. We explore several workflows and methods for promoting users' perceptions in practice, proposing suggestions that advance an enterprise's strategic values for the User Experience.

Understanding: The Strategic Values of User Experience on Current Telecom Product Development

In the global competitive marketplace, we believe that in-depth research to promote User Experience (UX) is helpful in discovering and satisfying market demand. Instead of price wars alone driving the market, different User Experiences could drive development among competitors. Research on User Experience is of great value and significance to a company's products and its strategies to differentiate those products from those of its competitors. Research can also help solve the following problems:

- *Create new products and market.* At the moment, telecom operators around the world are facing the same problem—how do they develop new business and find new market growth. As the telecom business develops, people's demands for individual services continuously increase. Globally, despite their constant pursuit and explorations, carriers are finding it difficult to discover the next "killer class" product, something like Short Message Service (SMS), or text messaging, which has tens of billions of users worldwide. Apple's success shows us how finding such a product brings great benefits to a company—so much so that we now believe that only by developing a killer class UX can we win customers and the market.

- *Enhance proficient product development.* Fierce market competition requires shorter production cycles and lower costs for product development. Because a product development model based on User Experience pays attention to users' demands, the pertinence and quality of products improve. Complaints after the products are launched to the market are also reduced. Product development becomes, therefore, more efficient.

- *Improve customer satisfaction.* Demonstrating concerns for users and market values is the basis of a company's survival and development. The value of a product is embodied in the value of the market and the product's users. In the past, due to closed-end development, we did not discover problems until the products were already in the market. User Experience best practice requires listening to customers' opinions during the product development process, so we consider the needs and experience not only of the market but also of customers, ensuring that aftermarket feedback will be more positive because customers were involved in the process upfront.

- *Create unique product features that differentiate a company from its competitors.* We hope to create a unique product and User Experience that differentiates us from other companies with whom we compete.

- *Make the product more popular and easier to use.* Sometimes we found that consumers were very interested in the new product, but with poor usability or misunderstanding of the UI, they could not subscribe to the service easily.

Misperception: Limitations on UX Research

As a pioneer, during the introduction of User Experience into telecom product development, I did not spend much time explaining to decision-makers the importance of User Experience. However, I had to spend a great deal of time thinking about how to satisfy our company's business needs through User Experience, instead of just using focus groups or User Experience testing.

We need some time to apply User Experience to product development. The management of a company generally identifies with the concept and significance of User Experience at the beginning, and they are very eager to see how the development of UCD can solve all users' problems. After that, they may be bothered by many of the questions. For example, can the User Experience methodology not only explore the potential needs of users but also lead to the development of a new killer class product? Will the product, having passed dozens of User Experience tests, receive positive feedback from the market? How much will the cost of labor and time increase due to User Experience work? After they discover that much User Experience work leads to advice about improving user interfaces for Internet businesses and user interactions, they may begin to doubt if this work can provide solutions to problems.

Therefore, we found we needed a more comprehensive User Experience methodology due to the complexity, diversity, and variety of telecom products. This methodology should not only consider users' needs and UI design, but also satisfy the two features described next.

Research Should Focus on Multiterminal and Multiservice User Experience

Telecom products are perceived by users as coming through a specific network, resource, device, or service. Products can be classified into various groups:

- **Website pages products**   Website pages, software operating interface, etc.
- **Client products**   Computer users, cell phone users, etc.

- **Hard terminal products**   Gateway, controller, telephone terminal, etc.

- **Voice service products**   Interactive voice response (IVR), manual voice service, etc.

- **Other products**   Yellow pages, mobile Internet service, etc.

Cooperation Among Systems and Departments During Product Development

In addition to the tangible material or service interfaces mentioned in the previous section, many business and technology platforms are needed, such as IT support systems, Business Operation Support systems (BOSS), service provider (SP) service platforms, and so on. Horizontally, the service experience of a telecom service product is the whole process experience from user side to server side, flowing from terminal to interface to network to service system, and so on. Vertically, the User Experience is the whole process that starts from the user side and ends at the user side, moving from the demand analysis stage to the design stage to the development stage to the going-public stage to the User Experience after customers purchase the product, and so on. Therefore, when a product is being developed and improved through User Experience work, this end-to-end development process is necessary. This is when the User Experience contents of every platform and system (every "side") should be taken into account by all the players. Only in this way can an improved product receive good responses at every stage of the process.

Therefore, at China Telecom, we explored and developed a more comprehensive product development model based on User Experience flow: an end-to-end user-centered product development process.

The end-to-end User Experience product development process means applying User Experience to demand analysis, prototype design, product development, and User Experience testing during the entire product development process. Different departments should be part of this process, with the result being presented in multiple user interfaces as well as at all the support service network and platform ends. An end-to-end User Experience process adapts to fields including the Internet, mobile services, Interactive Voice Response (IVR), and other user interface–related products. Applying the concept of end-to-end User Experience requires:

- Commitment to the closed circle of User Experience in product development

- Coordination of User Experience across terminals, platforms, and networks

Implementation: How We Promoted the End-to-End UX Process of Telecom Product Development

From my point of view, the "user-centered end-to-end process of telecom product development" model includes five core aspects. First, we restructured the user-centered development process and carried out User Experience work during important stages; second, we optimized the allocation of resources and established professional User Experience teams and laboratories; third, we tested the whole process to establish an end-to-end User Experience test model and coordinated testing with all concerned parties; fourth, we established an assessment mechanism to ensure a product development practice based on User Experience; and fifth, we promoted user-centered notions among the staff and made UX part of our organizational culture.

Restructuring the User-centered Development Process

We restructured our user-centered development process, as shown in Figure 5-1, to integrate the facts discovered during out research work. Our aim was to solve key problems such as a lack of user-centered practice, inefficient needs-analysis work, and unsatisfactory user perception about our products. Demands analysis and User Experience testing were brought into the product development process. We ascertained demands through a demand-frozen analysis and performed a walk-through test of the whole process to fix, or freeze, the user requirements to avoid the low efficiency caused by changing requirements. During the product development process, we accumulated and perfected a set of methods, instruments, and a flow system for demands analysis and User

FIGURE 5-1 The User Experience process in UCD, with the dark gray boxes representing the product development process before User Experience was introduced, the white boxes representing additional but typical steps after User Experience was introduced, and the two light gray boxes representing steps closely related to our practice, which will be introduced later in more detail.

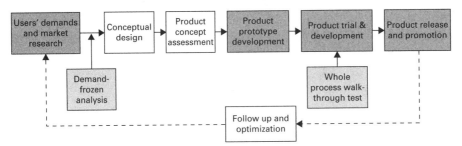

Experience, which instructed the specific work of product development. Our main accomplishments were as follows:

- Demands analysis, comprehensive product design, and User Experience were integrated into a traditional technology-centered product development process, and steps such as product concept design, product concept assessment, product prototype design, product prototype testing, product consistency concern and optimization, and so on, were added to the process.

- During the early stage of product pre-research and market analysis, we focused meticulously on user demands through employing user diaries, deep interviews, field surveys, focus groups, persona models, Kano models, and so on. By analyzing user demands, we provided accurate input for product development.

> **note**   *Persona is a UX methodology whereby user requirements are analyzed by creating a prototype of target users. The Kano model is a theory of product development and customer satisfaction that classifies customer preferences into two dimensions—satisfaction and need—and constructs four quadrants—namely, basic, performance, indifference, and not fulfilled.*

- During product prototype development stage, we added communication and contact with users to the process. The direction of product development was assessed and determined by User Experience to avoid isolating product development from users' needs

- We made the product development process a closed circle. After launch, we followed up on the results of our product in the marketplace and we consistently collected data information about users and the market for product optimizations and upgrades.

Optimizing Resource Allocation and Establishing a Professional UX Team

One of the prerequisites for conducting a user-centered end-to-end product development process is the setting up of professional User Experience departments or teams and laboratories in companies, or consulting with User Experience companies. Professional teams can play the user role within the company. We tried to guarantee that the team had professional competency and a big say in the assessment of product development.

It is important for the team members to convince the development team that they have professional competency and are skilled enough to represent the end users. The UX team's skills include knowledge of a series of disciplines, such as psychology, industrial design, and human factors engineering. Therefore, the professional competency of the teams can be greatly improved if their own quality, process, and practice of the User Experience methodology have been certified by professional certification authorities. What's more, we realized the importance of guaranteeing the UX team's voice was heard. Under the traditional product development system, users' demands were never presented at the initial stage of product development and certainly didn't receive active responses from the product development department. When problems are discovered after the product had gone to the market, a great deal of time and money is lost.

Conducting Whole Process Tests to Establish an End-to-End UX Test Model

A key part of the end-to-end User Experience process is to establish two important steps: a demand-frozen analysis and a whole process walk-through test.

Demand-frozen Analysis

A demand-frozen analysis refers to the process of ascertaining final demands at the demands analysis stage and, therefore, avoiding the disorder and resource waste that occurs during product development due to the constant changing of demands. This work was not just performed by the User Experience department; it was also led by the company's top leaders. All the front and backstage departments (including the user research department, marketing department, product development department, network department, IT department, front-desk marketing personnel, and maintenance department) participated. Together, they assessed the feasibility of the demands and the measures that needed to be taken and then determined the demands. For China Telecom, two issues were confirmed at this stage in the end-to-end process: the needs and classification of needs from target end users, and the usage requirements for selling, charging, and operation proposed by the sales operation staff. After combining these issues, a development direction and schedule were then confirmed. Moreover, the implementation of these frozen demands were later assessed. Overall, the demands-frozen step is a first essential step toward ensuring the practice of end-to-end user-centered product development.

Whole Process Walk-through Test

The whole process walk-through test tests products from both a user and operations perspective, looking at all conditions, the whole flow, all functions, and all roles involved. In this way problems are found and products are improved before going to market. The whole process walk-through test should be planned and prepared for at the beginning of product development, but should not be carried out until the whole network joint test and whole network IT joint test are completed. The position of the whole process walk-through test in the product development lifecycle is presented in Figure 5-2. This whole process walk-through test is an internal test, from user terminal to business platform, step by step, to ensure that functionality is complete; the improvement of business operations includes subscribing, billing, charging, etc., which were developed by the different departments. The end-to-end UX is always practiced in a real environment instead of on a prototype to make sure the developed product runs soundly in a real and complex system, including IT, network, and platform. During this stage, all departments should work together.

Figure 5-2 illustrates the product development process conducted on the organizational level, whereas Figure 5-1 focused on the UCD process conducted by the User Experience department. Both figures show the position of the whole process walk-through test in the product development lifecycle. The small-scale pilot (provide the new product and service in one or some pilot provinces), deployment (provide the new product and service on a larger scale or nationwide, including service development, networking building, and new product operation), and total network testing (the end-to-end testing, including network stability testing, functional testing, usability testing, service process testing, and so on) correspond to the product trial process shown in Figure 5-1. Figure 5-3 is an example of the test report used for the whole process walk-through test.

FIGURE 5-2 China Telecom's product development process, using a whole process walk-through test

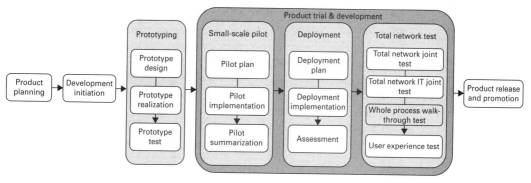

Test Report				
Test item		Test results	Explanation of results	Comprehensive explanation of process experience
1. Users test	1.1 function 1	Pass / no pass		
	1.2 function 2	Pass / no pass		
	1.3 function 3	Pass / no pass		
	1.4 function 4	Pass / no pass		
	1.4 accuracy of charging	Pass / no pass		
2. Internal test	2.1 statistics 2.2 charging 2.3 expenditure 2.4 customer service 2.5 maintenance 2.6 cooperation management 2.7 balance	Pass / no pass		
Test conclusion:			Other explanations:	
Tester:			Time of report:	

Sequence number _____

Problems classification _____

Problems description _____

Reasons for preliminary analysis _____

Settlement _____

Time limit of settlement _____

General interface of settlement (Telecom) _____

General interface of settlement (partner) _____

FIGURE 5-3 An example of a test report for the whole process walk-through test

Establishing an Assessment and Guarantee Mechanism

To ensure that the User Experience process was carried out smoothly in the product development and operations departments, we also clarified and set up the requirements for China Telecom's assessment system. For example, the effects of having final demands versus changing demands were included in the performance assessment system to evaluate how the process was conducted. Moreover, according to the results of the User Experience test, suggestions for improvement could be classified at different levels: very important, important, and common suggestions. User interface–related and information architecture–related problems required a 100 percent improvement in the assessment system. Other companies, of course, set their own standards according to their own situations. The key step here is to ensure that the improvement results requirements are included in the performance assessment for all involved departments, even in the assessment of the product development manager.

Promoting User-centered Ideas to Staff and Making it Part of Organization's Culture

To encourage all staff to carry out product development from a user-centered rather than technology-centered perspective, we saw the need to integrate this thinking into the organizational culture. Many departments thought that User Experience work was just the duty of the User Experience department, so we took several measures to make certain all staff understood that the company had reached a consensus regarding the importance of UX. We took the "sunflower" as the spiritual symbol of innovation centered on users and created a poster (Figure 5-4). The text says: "The wind grazes my eyes; I pursue the sunlight with it. The users' demands are always the sun in our hearts." The posters were put up in working areas to inspire staff to regard users' demands and satisfaction as being the key principle.

FIGURE 5-4 China Telecom's User Experience poster

Results: Benefits of User Experience

The end-to-end user-centered product development process achieves good results, improving the whole User Experience holistically, whether from the terminal, interface, network, platform, or service system. User experience work begins with user research and involves improvement requirements at every stage in the process in the system. The end-to-end UX ensures that improvement is simultaneous and effective.

One service we developed using this process allows users to subscribe and download their favorite music to their cell phones. At first, in the absence of an end-to-end user-centered product development process, the user interface was designed based around the requirements for internal management systems. At the experimental test stage, many people could browse to the product's page and many users wanted to download it; however,

71.83 percent of the people could not download it in the end. By employing a User Experience test, we discovered some standardized requirements in the primary service management system made the interface rather complex, as it included many links. These links made the page difficult for users to understand and navigate, and they were inclined to make mistakes while subscribing. By performing a step-by-step analysis of the test results, we discovered the standards of service and IT systems had led to these problems. We reported these problems to their respective departments promptly. After we improved the user interface and backstage network system, the users' failure rate went from 71.83 percent to 41.11 percent in just one workday, which means the actual download number almost doubled within one day.

	Number of possible downloads	Number of actual downloads	Lose rate	Increase in actual number of downloads in one day
December 23rd	7534	2122	71.83%	94.63%
December 24th	7013	4130	41.11%	

See Figure 5-5 for the original and revised screens.

FIGURE 5-5 The original and revised screens

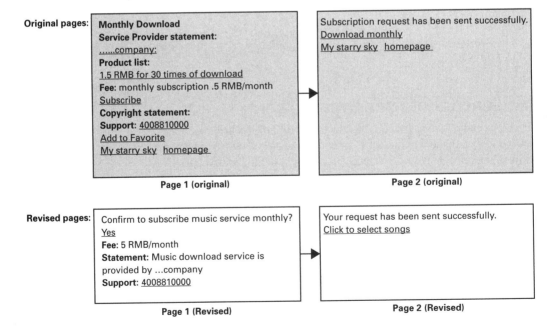

Original pages:

Monthly Download
Service Provider statement:
......company:
Product list:
1.5 RMB for 30 times of download
Fee: monthly subscription .5 RMB/month
Subscribe
Copyright statement:
Support: 4008810000
Add to Favorite
My starry sky   homepage

Page 1 (original)

Subscription request has been sent successfully.
Download monthly
My starry sky   homepage

Page 2 (original)

Revised pages:

Confirm to subscribe music service monthly?
Yes
Fee: 5 RMB/month
Statement: Music download service is provided by ...company
Support: 4008810000

Page 1 (Revised)

Your request has been sent successfully.
Click to select songs

Page 2 (Revised)

Page 1 Revision Explanation

1. "Subscribe" was changed to "OK".

2. "Monthly service; monthly fee, 5 RMB" was changed to "5 RMB/ month".

3. "Service provider statement" was changed to "statement."

4. Deleted the links for "Copyright statement", "Add to Favorite", "My starry sky", and "homepage".

5. Similar revisions for pages for other subscription models based on times were also made.

Page 2 Revision Explanation

1. "Subscription request has been sent successfully" was changed to "Your request has been sent successfully."

2. "Download monthly" was changed to "Click to select songs."

3. Deleted the links to "My starry sky" and "homepage".

The end-to-end user-centered product development model requires an effective system and coordination. The effects of this development model on large operations with independent departments are remarkable, however. As I mentioned at the beginning of this chapter, this process is an effective method for carrying out a "product differentiation strategy focused on users' demands." We established a professional User Experience department that represents users' interests and demands inside the company; this department not only proposes requirements for product development and improvement but also ensures users' demands are considered throughout the process and by the product development department effectively, which contributes to each product's improved quality and usability as well as a wonderful User Experience during the whole process.

Conclusion

The value of User Experience work in the company's product development relies on six essential factors: the development process of UCD products, the company's organizational structure, the UX professional team, the instruments and methods used, the investment of capital and resources, and the seriousness of decision makers. Among these factors, whether the work succeeds is ultimately determined by the seriousness of the decision makers. The implementation of User Experience work asks people to change their ideas, which can only be effectively realized when motivated by top decision makers. What's more, in many organizations, the results of User Experience work may not be adopted by the product development department. When decision makers begin to include the evaluation and suggestions of User Experience into the assessment and performance evaluation of product development they can ensure that product development work centered on users is carried out effectively.

The application of User Experience work can cover the whole flow or just some stages. Companies may establish User Experience work, namely the development of UCD products, which flows through the whole process according to their specific conditions. User experience work is carried out at every important stage of the product development process. This requires good coordination among different product development departments and User Experience teams. Work can also be carried out step by step according to your staff's ability and organizational structure. For example, User Experience work may start with a product usability test and then be applied to other stages such as demand analysis and design gradually.

User experience functions and values vary depending on the stage of the product development process. For example, during demand analysis, User Experience plays an important role in the proposal and pre-research stage; UCD design work can provide more information about users' demands regarding business standardization and interaction processes during product development; usability tests are key to product prototype development and inspections before a product's launch.

After we explored and developed our end-to-end user-centered product development process, we achieved remarkable success by reestablishing the process of User Experience, developing the UX teams' professional abilities, transforming organizational mechanisms, and establishing an organizational culture focused on users' demands. Specifically, the achievements are as follows:

1. In 2010, more than 2,500 usability problems involving key products in mobile Internet services were found, and the improvement rate of valid problems reached 89 percent after follow-up implementation, therefore, achieving a better User Experience of products.

2. After comparing testing data from November and June 2010, we found a steady increase in user satisfaction with external users by 2.3 points and internal users by 7.9 points.

3. User experience contributed to product development and economic benefit directly and effectively, with revenue increased by 60 million RMB in 2010.

Summary

- **What is the business context (e.g., product, customers)?**
  China Telecom's strategic goal is to focus on the information strategy of our clients. We provide them with fixed telephone services, Internet access, mobile services, and online value-added information services with professional experience and quality.

- **Which problem(s) does the UX practice address?**
  UX has solved the following problems to a large extent: lead to the creation of new products and markets, enhanced the proficiency of product development, improved customer satisfaction, allowed us to create unique product features that differentiate use from our competitors.

- **What were prerequisites and constraints?**
  The User Experience team should be established first. Then, the product development process needs to be reformed in accordance with corporate goals, while systematizing and promoting the process and forging transdepartmental cooperation. The main challenge was to formulate a perfect process based on user needs and to guarantee efficient implementation in each department.

- **In which UX development context did you apply your UX practice?**
  Before putting process UX into practice, the company had already established an associated UX team and laboratory. We believe that good customer experience is the basis of business competition and survival, so we will try to apply UX practice in the key process of product development. Currently, we apply UX in main prelaunch testing to optimize customer experience; we achieved significant results from the UX practice that helped us to find usability problems and consistency issues very effectively.

- **What compelling events supported you in applying your UX practice successfully?**
  By comparing, we found that products improved after implementing a user-centered process had a higher success rate than previous ones. We do not regard our UX process as being complete; we are only at the beginning of our success in applying UX across all products.

- **What kind of business or product impact did you achieve through this UX practice?**
  We saw the huge potential and value of User Experience for our current products, as demonstrated by the examples in the chapter. Excellent User Experience has led to a large increase in the rate of users' orders.

Excellent UX can increase downloads and subscriptions, as well as raise customer satisfaction and revenue. After the end-to-end UX, we saw a download increase of 94.63 percent, and a revenue increase across all products by 60 million RMB in 2010. More UX practice means more success.

- **How did you apply this UX practice?**
  We applied five core aspects in our "end-to-end user-centered product development process": First, we restructured the user-centered development process and carried out User Experience work during important stages; second, we optimized the allocation of resources and established professional User Experience teams and laboratories; third, we tested the whole process to establish an end-to-end User Experience test model and coordinated testing with all concerned parties; fourth, we established an assessment mechanism to ensure a product development practice based on User Experience; and fifth, we promoted user-centered notions among the staff, making UX part of our organizational culture.

- **Which recommendations do you have for other companies and departments that want to apply the UX practice?**
  Six important factors influence the value of User Experience on corporate product development: using a UCD product development process, changing the corporate organization and structure, having professional teams in place, developing methods and approaches, investing in UX, and garnering the attention of decision makers. The last factor is a decisive one for success, mainly because implementing UX practice means changing perceptions and only higher officials can effect this.

Chapter 6

User Experience and Agile Development

By Thomas Memmel and
Markus Flückiger
Zühlke Engineering®

Médard Fischer
Swiss Federal Railways®

Usability engineering practice typically focuses on issues related to the user interface (UI), such as ease of use, ease of learning, user performance, user satisfaction, or aesthetics. To design usable software systems, experts are required to have distinct skills, ranging from an understanding of human psychology to requirements modeling and UI design. Usability engineering expertise is behind many terms, such as interaction design, user experience (UX), and graphic design (Belenguer et al. 2003). With a greatly diversified range of interactive products and the growing need to "get the UI right," a variety of roles has emerged (Preece et al. 2002). Usability engineers focus on evaluating products employing usability methods and principles. Information architects are experts in developing ideas of how to plan and structure interactive products. *UX experts* often do all the above, which is why we use this term in this chapter. *UI designers* are people involved in the design of all the interactive aspects of a product. They usually have a different background than UX experts, for example, with regard to their knowledge of design methods and creativity, which is why we distinguish them from UX experts in this chapter, too.

UX adds a new dimension of quality to the supply chain of software development. For many products, it is no longer about how you "use" a piece of software but how you "experience" it. As defined in ISO 9241-210, user experience describes "a person's perceptions and responses that result from the use or anticipated use of a product, system or service. … Usability, when interpreted from the perspective of the users' personal goals, can include the kind of perceptual and emotional aspects typically associated with user experience. … Usability criteria can be used to assess aspects of user experience" (DIN EN ISO 9241-210, 2010). Software engineers are generally trained in programming languages, object-oriented design, system architecture, or database design. Both the software engineering and the UX skillset is essential for the creation of quality products, but no one set is sufficient on its own (Buxton 2003), and the course of collaboration is mostly unclear. In this context, the combination of agile software development and UX is a very promising approach. Especially in projects with very unstable and varying requirements, an agile process based on the philosophy of inspect and adapt is a great starting position. As empirical methods are at the core of both agile software development and UX, both procedures match pretty well. We describe the combination of agile software development and UX know-how as *agile UX*. Such an approach can provide customers with great software, capable of making the difference in terms of product impact.

In this chapter, we report on our experience in developing the software product ALEA (Alarm and Event Assistant) with an agile UX approach. The project was installed by Swiss Federal Railways (SBB), Switzerland's biggest travel and transportation company, and carried out with support by Zühlke, a leading technology and consultancy company providing bespoke software solutions, product innovation, and management consulting. We describe the advantages of the agile UX process as we lived it and how UX contributions positively impacted the quality and success of the final product. For this purpose, we interviewed people from the ALEA team and asked them about their individual project experience. Our main goal was to bring their opinion to you in the most authentic way. We, therefore, provide the answers from the interviewees within the point-of-view (POV) boxes, which are, at the same time, the core of our chapter. In between the different POV boxes, you will find background and contextual information about ALEA.

The Business Context

"There is a fault in the overhead cables at Winterthur. The S7 train will be delayed by five minutes." Before this announcement reaches travelers, several hundred people at SBB and its partners have to communicate intensively. If this communication is slow or ineffective, resolving events takes longer, trains are even more delayed, and passengers lack crucial information about detours and connections. For passengers, this results in longer trips and, generally, a more negative customer experience. For SBB, slow or ineffective communication has a financial impact and damages the company's reputation. Relevant parties thus need to receive information and decisions accurately and quickly. Time is of the essence when disruptions occur.

Until ALEA, SBB personnel communicated via phone, which took more time and led to redundancy and errors. In case of an event, operational staff, referred to as agents in the following, had to struggle with a huge amount of information. Standard measures for handling events mainly existed as paper-based documents. SBB wanted to minimize the effects of rail traffic events with a user- and task-centered software product such as ALEA:

- ALEA is a SBB infrastructure software tool that supports agents in coping with events. With ALEA, the agents get into the driver's seat of operative management.

- Agents can leverage ALEA to decrease the amount and duration of SBB train delays.

- ALEA supports measure management for the complete spectrum of different kinds of disruptions, ranging from small events to complete interruptions.

Problems Addressed and Project Goals

ALEA users are SBB agents (see Figure 6-1), and the software is used particularly in events and emergencies. Such events and emergencies can, for example, be railcar breakdowns, technical problems in a broader sense, track or junction plate damage, or injury to persons. Naturally, failure management always also means stress for the agents involved. Hence, any relevant information must be accessible at a glance and agents must be able to decide on the required steps quickly. If information, which had previously been communicated via phone, is not forwarded properly, passengers have a bad customer experience due to delays and insufficient information about detours. Recall the last time you missed a train or were stranded at a train station due to a train delay or event with no information at hand on how to get home and you can easily understand the importance of information flow at SBB. Moreover, disruptions that last for some time are, as a matter of course, very costly for SBB.

FIGURE 6-1 An agent at the SBB control unit (© Swiss Federal Railways)

ALEA needed to allow for efficient decision making, providing a fast routing of information and filtering mechanisms to get the right information to the right people. SBB was also extremely interested in UX; therefore, ALEA had to have the following qualities and features:

- Offer an efficient and nonredundant flow of information, accessible for all involved operation personnel, minimizing their information overload and allowing them to focus on solving the problem at hand

- Function as a communication tool that allows for easy broadcasting and processing of accurate and complete information, especially because the delivery of incorrect or incomplete information can result in increased costs for SBB

- Allow for a quick assessment of situations to enable faster problem solving through a graphical visualization of events that support a text-based information presentation

- Provide a means for defining roles and assigning tasks for controlled and coordinated measure management, which includes tool-based contacting mechanisms enabling one-to-one, one-to-many, and many-to-many communication

- Be a framework for common conceptualization, planning, and broadcasting of measures involving all important services to improve information accuracy for travelers

- Function as an information terminal for onsite customer support based on live data about traffic disruptions and changes to the time-table

The Development Context

The development of ALEA was part of the implementation of a series of SBB software-development projects. ALEA had to be developed from scratch and was a completely new system. Because we wanted an explorative and iterative project management and development approach, we decided to apply Scrum, which is discussed in the "Scrum" section later in this chapter. Altogether, the ALEA project ran for two years before the first release was published.

POV: Project Manager, Business

The ALEA project was very special compared to other software projects at SBB. We knew that the UI was going to be the key success factor, which is why we recognized the need to consider UX. We already had a rough idea about the UI, but we realized we would need professional support and decided to have an UX expert and a UI designer on the team. Moreover, we had to start from scratch, which was both a chance for innovation and a risk with regard to budget and timing. This is why ALEA also became one of the first Scrum projects at SBB. If I look back on the development of ALEA, I remember the UX expert conducting a lot of interactive workshops. Flipcharts and brainstorming were daily tools. Many people on the project perhaps misconceived usability and expected the UX expert to switch to visual designs and prototypes quickly. The UX expert, however, successfully convinced them that the methods he applied helped to keep the design space open and allowed for a more abstract consideration of alternate solutions. I think the UX expert has to have a very strong personality and a very broad experience in order to make people change their mind about UX methods. Before we started writing code, we had a very important preproject that helped us to shape our vision and express concrete UX needs. In other words, the UX activities at this early stage helped to make ALEA a success. The second most important success factor for project success was the permanent presence of onsite users who had permanent access to the test environment. The onsite customers sat in the same room as the team. By the way, sharing one room was something that developers had to accept in order to make the setup work smoothly.

Team Setup

The project team consisted of eight developers plus the UX expert and the UI designer. The UX expert, who was in charge of keeping the focus on SBB's UX goals, was onsite two to three days a week. He was a full member of the team. We had three onsite users on the team, who were each also available two to three days a week. The onsite users worked closely together with the UX expert and supported him in requirements engineering.

POV: Onsite Users

As onsite users, each one of us was in the team office two to three days a week, working about 50 percent of the UX expert's schedule on ALEA. Our main assignment was to gather and define requirements together with the UX expert. We did this as representatives for all later ALEA users, which is why we felt very responsible for getting the requirements right and getting the right requirements into ALEA. We, therefore, supported the UX expert in writing requirements documents. Although we had to learn a rather technical writing style, we added important aspects about the daily work of later ALEA users. We also created abstract wireframes for expressing requirements visually at times, which supported the development of a shared understanding.

It soon became very clear that we would not be able to cram all requirements into the final product due to budget and time constraints. At a certain stage, prioritizing requirements became a very frequent duty. Naturally, we had many expectations with regard to the implementation of as many requirements as possible. Consequently, it was sometimes very frustrating to remove requirements from the backlog. In addition, the users we represented were not happy about having to delete many requirements, which is why we sometimes were in the line of fire during painful discussions with users. Nevertheless, the project was a positive experience for us, and as end-users, we now know the software development process much better.

Due to the nature of Scrum, we could show the intermediate releases of ALEA to other control unit colleagues (see Figure 6-1). Developers visited the control unit, too, in order to understand requirements better, which, in turn, enabled them to implement appropriate solutions. But we also learned that it is impossible to elaborate on everything in the necessary detail, which meant some ALEA features turned out to be more complex than we all expected. The UX expert tried to ease this situation by, for example, using a prototype to obtain feedback from those working onsite on other projects. However, time pressures, and maybe a lack of enough UX resources as well, forced us to make some premature decisions. The parts of ALEA that we could not optimize due to time pressure will most probably be adapted during the next releases of the software.

Scrum

Scrum is a very popular and modern software–project management method. Scrum is also famous for the variety of Scrum meetings. One important meeting is the daily stand-up meeting called *Daily Scrum,* where all team members report about yesterday's and today's work as well as about problems and obstacles. In a Scrum process, the team releases a new part of the software every two to four weeks, which is called a *sprint.* The *user story* is an important artifact in Scrum projects. Each user story is broken down into tasks. All tasks are summarized in the *sprint backlog.* The effort required to complete a task is estimated in person hours and rarely takes longer than one to two days to implement. One to many user stories can make up a minimal marketable feature, which is just the right size to provide some added value, for example, in terms of increased revenue, work efficiency, or UX. User stories are generally developed by customer or user representatives and written on index cards. Each story has to have enough details to allow for estimation and planning. The created stories receive story points, which give a rough idea of the resources required for implementation. One format of a user story is "As a [some user], I want [to do something], so that [I can achieve some goal]" (Cohn 2004; Nodder & Nielsen 2008).

In ALEA, the Scrum team wrote down acceptance criteria, quality criteria, and success criteria for each user story. The stories were included in the *product backlog*, which was continuously reprioritized according to new and changing requirements. The backlog was on a wall in our team room, where we posted the user stories. In ALEA, each sprint lasted three weeks. Intense meetings were held before a new sprint started. For every sprint, the team extracted certain user stories from the backlog to implement them during the sprint. The *release burn down chart* tracked progress in terms of how many stories were implemented across all sprints. Usually, the horizontal axis of a release burn down chart shows the sprints, and the vertical axis shows the amount of work remaining at the start of each sprint. The *sprint burn down chart* displayed the remaining work in the sprint backlog. The *team velocity* indicated the amount of story points coded during every sprint. After every sprint, the team discussed the lessons learned in a *retrospective meeting* and then held a *review meeting* to gather feedback from the product owner and all interested stakeholders about a presented piece of software.

Applying UX Practice Within Scrum

As with other agile processes, the Scrum philosophy is also grounded upon fundamental agile principles, which were captured in the Agile Manifesto (Beedle et al. 2010):

- Individuals and interactions over processes and tools

- Working software over comprehensive documentation

- Customer collaboration over contract negotiation

- Responding to change over following a plan

These agile principles are very close to the values of UX experts, who usually find themselves in the role between business and development. It's often the duty of UX experts to bridge the gaps between different stakeholders, for example, people with different professional backgrounds, and to prepare the ground for consensus. The importance of communication has always been at the heart of UX methods, whether through moderating workshops, conducting interviews, or communicating ideas with UI prototypes. Due to its iterative nature, openness to change is also at the core of UX. This helps UX experts find their role in the Scrum team.

UX methods can add value to a product developed using Scrum, if the UX expert can bring real end-user requirements into the user stories and into the team's mindset. A user story can, for example, be enriched by the results of previous or new user research and the information from personas. Because there is no time for extensive documentation, user needs and UX issues must also be communicated in the Scrum meetings. User scenarios, storyboards, and prototypes help to connect and prioritize different user stories. The results of usability tests add criteria in measuring the quality of the released software.

Support for UX Practice

Agile UX can only work if the mindsets of both agile- and user-centered worlds are combined in a project. In ALEA, we could successfully apply an agile UX approach because the business project manager and the product owner recognized that UX, especially in terms of user involvement, was required to develop a good UI. The complexity of event and emergency management was the crucial factor in why the UI had to be easy and efficient to use. The integration of UX design methods into classical requirements engineering work packages provided the ground for a consequent and sustainable UX project. If only one UX expert is on the team, the variety of UX-related tasks can quickly put him or her into a very demanding and challenging position. If the UX expert is able to recruit

UX assistants from within the Scrum team, he or she can not only share responsibility but also encourage the proliferation of a UX-mindset: the more team members can meet with users, either personally or through user models, the more developers will think in a user-centered way or even start to apply basic UX concepts and methods themselves.

On the other hand, a dedicated UX team runs the risk of not involving developers early enough. Such a team tends to create detailed sketches of the UI and to throw them at the developers as detailed specifications, which generally results in an expensive solution. On its own, the UX team often lacks the means and skills to know, given the developers' backgrounds, the chosen technology, and the current solution, what is expensive or inexpensive to build. The developers do not learn enough about users and user needs and, therefore, do not build a good solution for users. This means the UX team must constantly take care of all the details. And the UX team will often hear phrases like, "Why didn't you tell us that earlier? The software architecture, software framework, or toolkit we used does not allow for an easy implementation of this feature. It will take several months to build it in the way you need."

Although there is no upfront requirement in an agile UX project, you need to have enough product backlog items to start sprint planning. Accordingly, the UX expert can start shaping the software product by working with the project planning or management team through the visioning stage. An important precondition for the successful application of UX methods in ALEA was the involvement of the UX expert in the visioning preproject, during which he helped the business stakeholders to create a product vision. In terms of UX product impact, the ALEA preproject was perhaps even more important than the UX work during exploration and development. During the preproject, methods of contextual design, for example, resulting in video recordings from field observations, helped the team understand the key issues and major breakdowns in failure management. The presentation of some key figures about how SBB agents communicate was an eye opener for business stakeholders (see "POV: UX Expert" for a detailed report). This presentation was one of the important compelling events that supported the continuous application of UX practice during the whole project.

Applying techniques of contextual design was, in general, extremely helpful for discovering the high-level requirements that were part of a solid product vision for ALEA. Later on, when development had started, the UX expert widened his focus toward the Scrum team and worked with them on product synthesis. This is why UX experts should be able to work in both the software engineering and UX world. Knowing about the business goals as well as user needs strengthens the UX expert's role and helps him or her guide the developers in the right direction.

Thinking Ahead: Aligning Software Development and UX

Certainly, permanent team work is at the core of agile development. Many UX experts do mainly concentrate on current problems and their daily assignments: "I'm a (UX) designer. I work one sprint in advance of the developers. My job is to make sure that when they start a sprint I can give them a design for what they'll develop in that sprint" (Cohn 2010). But UX experts must support the team both in present time and in the future, which is why the work schedule for a UX expert should be more like the following: "I'm a (UX) designer. I'm on the development team, and my primary job is to make sure we finish whatever work we commit to for the sprint. But that doesn't take up all my time, so I spend a good amount of it looking ahead at what we're going to build in the next sprint or two. I then gather data, mock up designs, and do whatever I can so that when we start on a feature in a future sprint, we're able to finish it in that sprint" (Cohn 2010).

The UX expert has to make sure that UI-related issues, for example, related to content presentation, dialog flow, and consistency, are solved before the team starts implementing the respective user stories. Because the UI needs the required backend functionality to show certain features, UX activities need to be synchronized with development tasks and backlog prioritization. To make this work smoothly, the UX expert has to work out which parts of the UI are going to be developed next, for instance, by looking at the UI-related tasks in the backlog. At the same time, the UX expert should be available for spontaneous workshops and discussions. As a result, agile UX, in theory, happens as parallel track development (see Figure 6-2).

FIGURE 6-2 Agile UX with parallel track development (based on Jocham and Memmel 2009)

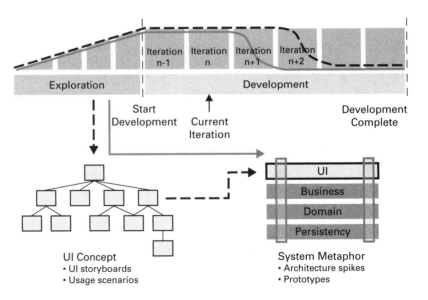

Some agile projects have a *sprint zero,* also called "exploration," but regardless of the term used, there is no time for many UX activities. Rather this sprint is about understanding the main UX goals and the most relevant user needs. During the exploration, the UX expert tries to develop a UI concept, expressed, for example, through means of UI storyboards and usage scenarios (see the bottom-left of Figure 6-2). The main idea of parallel track development is to regularly feed validated UX concepts and UI schemes to the development team and the development backlog. This makes the UI an important pillar of software development, in addition to the business, domain, and persistency layer (see the bottom-right of Figure 6-2). UX activities regularly happen ahead of development: two sprints ahead, user research is conducted; and one sprint ahead, design is developed. This means, for example, that important user studies can be prepared for iteration $n+2$ (see the dashed wave in Figure 6-2), while the UX expert creates concrete UI elements and UI prototypes for iteration $n+1$ (see the solid wave in Figure 6-2). The UI prototypes enrich the user stories with UX information or trigger the development of new user stories that are fed into the backlog. During the current iteration (n), the UX experts work closely with the team and help them make decisions and solve problems. In addition, UX experts conduct usability tests for parts of the software that have already been implemented (e.g., during iteration $n-1$). Working ahead also provides the chance to adapt the acceptance criteria for a user story based on the user research and design work already done by the UX expert (Jocham and Memmel 2009).

POV: ScrumMaster, Software Architect

I initiated the organizational shift of software development at SBB toward Scrum. As the ALEA software had to be implemented from scratch, I chose an agile approach because of the unstable and evolving requirements. SBB knew that the UX of the software would be very important in making the whole project a success. A primary UX goal was that ALEA must be an efficient and effective tool in failure management. Both the change toward Scrum as well as the recognition of UX as a key quality criteria were, therefore, essential preconditions for ALEA's success. Accordingly, we lived the "agile and UX process" in a very interweaved and explorative way. At the beginning, developers tried to build solutions based on their own best guesses. After feedback from the onsite users, they started to meet for discussions and workshops with the users and the UX expert instead of just deciding what to do on their own. Together with the UX expert and the UI designer, we investigated the backlog items. For features that were very closely related to the UI, we made sure the UI concept was available just in time for the next sprint planning meeting. For this purpose, the UI designer used a separate backlog to plan her activities. We had a very UI-driven development process and almost all team members liked it. Those who preferred not to interact with the onsite users or the UX expert worked on the backend. Those who were happy to meet with people and cared more about translating their requirements into a great frontend worked on the UI team. Thinking and working on the UI at least one sprint ahead was very useful in helping us circumvent too much UI refactoring. The UX expert has to have one foot in the present to support the team in solving urgent matters and one foot in the future to prepare the ground for a consistent UI. A solid navigation map should be in place from the very beginning.

To make parallel track development work smoothly, three players have to look ahead and constantly communicate: the product owner, the UX expert, and the developers. The UX expert will care mainly about a great UX and its associated benefits. The developers will want a good quality solution that is not too costly. The product owner will decide upon alternatives and the priority of the user stories, considering costs and benefits. All three players have to understand and agree on why a specific solution is the right one. Especially if a huge amount of UX activities are happening on a parallel track and documentation is reduced to a minimum, communication is crucial. Scrum is a great environment for conversation between the UX expert and the team.

POV: Client Developer, Software Engineer

We had a clear separation of concerns for the client and the backend server architecture. The developers on the team decided which area they wanted to work on, but some of them also changed sides on demand, especially when UI issues impacted the backend architecture and vice versa. A developer should be able to work on all development layers. This eases decision making with regard to software interfaces and components. In addition, knowledge can be transferred if team members switch between the layers. The developers' broad knowledge and flexibility were success factors for ALEA.

During the project, we had access to three real end-users (SBB agents). They were at our disposal for discussing the requirements and alternate solutions. Together with the UX expert, they did the business and requirements analysis. The requirements documents that we received from them did not, in most cases, anticipate a solution. They were usually written in an "agile fashion," with not much detail and as a combination of key points.

In the beginning, some developers complained about this approach because they could not just start coding. Typically, we first had to discuss possible solution variants with the end-users, the UI designer, and the UX expert. Afterward, we often had to wait for the UI designer to create some wireframes, which visually specified the requirements. And even then, some details still had to be refined in further short discussions. Most developers realized very soon that this agile way of finding solutions provided the ground for a collaborative and creative approach, which allowed us to get things pretty right from the very beginning.

Accordingly, the most impressive specialty on this project was that we all acted in a culture of spontaneous meetings and small workshops. It is important to mention that it was not the UX expert who invited us to such gatherings. The developers proactively met with the onsite users, the UI designer, and the UX expert, for example, when requirements were unclear or when a developer needed a decision on the UI design. During such spontaneous workshops and stand-up meetings, ideas were sketched out and refined until everybody felt comfortable with a solution. Our best work results were for those parts of ALEA for which we held such informal meetings. Moreover, it was significant that when a developer did not participate in such discussions, the decisions made were usually subject to later changes because he or she overlooked some important aspects. By bringing team members with different backgrounds and know-how (nontechnical and technical, client-side and server-side, even from different domain areas) together, many great ideas successfully made their way into the final product.

In ALEA, we looked ahead based on the current product backlog. The goal was to have discussions before the sprint during which onsite users, the UX team, developers, and product owner agreed on what functions needed to be built, how the UI should look, how it would be implemented, and what needed to be refactored. For these discussions, the onsite users and the UX expert worked on functions and priorities. The UI designer then created wireframes of the UI. At last the developers reviewed the wireframes and decided how to best implement these ideas. For some user stories, that is, the easy ones, we worked just like this.

For a second kind of user story, the ones in which it was unclear what the technology could deliver when, for example, we had to interface with another system, the UX expert and onsite users created an idea of the desired functionality; the developers drove a spike implementation, i.e., a coding experiment; and together with the product owner, they decided on a possible solution. This then served for the basis for some wireframes and the next sprint. More generally speaking, we solved the task of looking ahead in the following way:

- **Identifying new topics, epics, or user stories** The onsite users and the product owner were mostly responsible for this part. It was based on the product vision, the feedback on current product implementations, and changes in the organization and parallel projects. The UX expert supported this process by providing additional means for getting feedback, using low-fidelity prototyping, workshops, role-playing games, and usability tests.

- **Selecting user stories**   The product backlog served as the basis for more detailed investigations. Depending on its priority, the size of the user story, and the risk associated with it, we chose when and how deeply we as a team would look into implementing a user story.

- **Refining and detailing user stories**   We did not just put the product owner and the team into a room and let them refine the user stories. We made use of the possibilities of UX methods like contextual design, low-fidelity prototyping, and usability walkthroughs, in conjunction with proven design methods like sketching and wireframes, and then combined these with best practices from software engineering like spike implementations and evolutionary prototypes. The results of this work were fine-grained user stories ready for implementation.

POV: Software Architect, Backend

I had previously worked on agile projects, but I had never experienced a setup in which agile development met UX. For ALEA, the customer identified the need and integration of UX methods. This provided a great basis for a successful project. The UI was relevant with regard to all development layers. For example, we developed filter mechanisms for the ALEA users, which were important for failure management and decision making. Although the implementation of those filters was a backlog item especially related to the backend server architecture and the database, the task was very dependent on the UI. We had to know what information was relevant for users in order to create the filters. In addition, knowing how users wanted to filter was important for designing a filter mechanism that could be well represented at the UI layer.

ALEA was a very UI-driven development project. This was a completely new experience for me, because I was used to rather backend or technology-driven development projects, where the UI was too often considered a byproduct or less important. The great advantage of the UI-driven approach was that the backend team could significantly reduce the effort needed to provide the right interfaces. Because we always knew what was required at the UI, we could focus on implementing just the right set of interfaces between our client and server.

The UX expert on the team was responsible for achieving the usability and UX goals. He usually approached the developers with the user requirements and sometimes a few sketchy ideas. Although he often already had an idea about how certain requirements could be implemented, he only presented us with the real requirements, and it was always up to the developers to develop an appropriate solution. Accordingly, we had a high degree of freedom in translating requirements into running code. In this context, we also compared alternatives, and we ran some spike solutions to find out whether a solution was able to cover both simple and complex use cases. In general, ideas and solutions were usually discussed with the whole team or in temporary task forces that met in ad hoc workshops. The overall documentation was kept to a minimum level, and the documents created were seldom written in a prosaic style.

The rough UX concept was often available one sprint ahead, for instance, represented by some wireframes. The UX expert and the UI designer were in charge of thinking ahead, but we tried to support their work with development resources. Hence, in some situations, the visionary work was done by a competent trio, and although the thinking ahead was not an explicit backlog item, we always reserved development time for it. Because the UX expert and the UI designer were physically available most of the time, they could also support us in ongoing development tasks. They did not just live in a future-orientated parallel track, but rather jumped between two timelines. I think it is impossible to plan all usability activities and the whole UI design ahead of time. Accordingly, the agile process is, in my opinion, a very good basis for UX methods. In large projects, I would choose an agile process whenever the UI has a great weight.

Agile UX Methods

During the ALEA preproject, the UX expert mainly applied methods that were based on contextual design (Beyer and Holtzblatt 1997). At the control center in the cities of Luzern and Winterthur, the UX expert made video recordings while the agents worked on disruptions and emergencies. The focus of this recorded observation was to understand how agents communicate with each other. The recordings helped the team understand the nature and dynamics of disruptions and showed that too much time was spent on processing information, rather than on taking care of the disruption itself. The findings were crucial to building the right software application.

POV: UX Expert

As UX expert, I worked closely with the Scrum team. My main assignment was to think ahead, gather and define new ideas and requirements, consider new business processes, and think about the overall potential of ALEA. In this context, I also supported the product owner. Before I advanced to being a UX expert, I worked as a software developer. This helped me when discussing the feasibility of alternate solutions and in estimating the effort required.

I had joined agile development teams as a UX expert previously, but ALEA was the first full-blown agile UX project I participated in. ALEA was also special in that the organizational structure at SBB worked in a classical, non-agile way. Consequently, the ScrumMaster's and product owner's main task was to keep political issues away from us.

I was already involved in the ALEA preproject, during which I helped the business stakeholders to create a product vision. At this stage, I mainly employed methods of contextual design. I videotaped some of the agents while they handled events. From an analysis of the recordings, we drew communication diagrams and cultural diagrams. These recordings and diagrams revealed problems in existing processes, and the diagrams helped us figure out the key issues and understand the types of breakdowns that agents at SBB had to face. Based on our findings, we derived some managerial numbers that estimated how much time users spent in useless communication rather than in solving the problem on the rail racks. Altogether, this brought to light the actual problem in failure management at SBB: ineffective and inefficient communication.

In the course of the UX process, I also methodologically prepared and supervised several role-play games to enable the agents to play through some future-oriented communication scenarios. The role-play highlighted the best communication flow and how breakdowns, disruptions, and jams could be prevented. During roleplaying, we also used rough paper-based UI sketches and index cards to express our vision of future communication concepts. In addition, I worked extensively with storyboards that turned out to be strong eye-openers for all stakeholders, because they externalized the product vision we had created in a way everybody could understand. The storyboards showed how the communication should work and why the new way worked well. In addition, the storyboards also provided the ground for changing existing business processes. In the end, the product vision was complemented with a .NET software prototype I had implemented. The prototype expressed the main features of our vision and was, therefore, subject to some proof-of-concept usability walkthroughs. As an executable representation of our idea, it also worked as a marketing tool for ALEA.

The developers took care of the backlog, but we added the UI-specific requirements and criteria to the user stories and we tried to plan UX activities in advance. During the exploration stage, my assignment was to extend and refine the requirements we identified during the preproject. Because I partly worked onsite with the product owner, I was also responsible for planning and conducting usability tests. The usability tests, however, posed some challenges. Given the incremental and agile character of the ALEA project, we had to wait too long for a version mature enough to actually conduct a good usability test. Because of this, we did not realize early enough that using Eclipse RCP as a client technology would not be sufficient for our application. As a result, we had to add additional software components to solve usability issues with the Eclipse RCP UI elements. We lost a lot of valuable time and money (i.e., user stories). With a few UI spikes, e.g., a functional coded UI prototype, we could have prevented this from happening. Our lesson: If you don't have a solid and feasible UI concept before starting to code, UI development is likely to get very expensive, because you will most likely have to refactor a lot.

We invited users to participate in the usability tests we conducted. The onsite users assisted me, for example, in writing the tasks for usability tests. Defects were reported using the bug-tracking tool. If we had to revise the UI, then the UI designer either changed the existing screens or produced new ones. The new design proposal was then included in the user stories and allocated for implementation. This way, the UI designer was responsible for getting the UI design right and putting issues on a tracked to-do list.

An early sketch of the future user interface, showing one incident

Description of the incident

Selection of different views for this incident, e.g., immediate actions, predefined resolution concept

Incident information: incident end, disrupted line, and assumed end of disruption

Declare an incident as resolved and abort the application of current resolution concept.

Different versions of resolution concept with validity periods

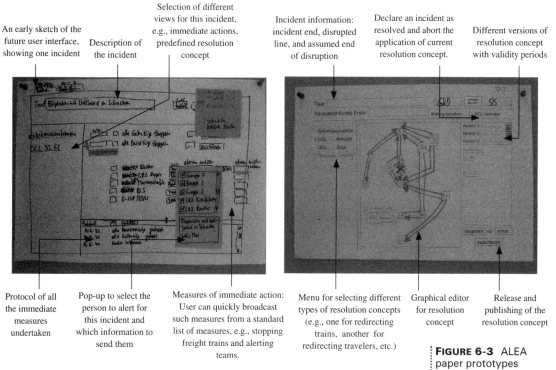

Protocol of all the immediate measures undertaken

Pop-up to select the person to alert for this incident and which information to send them

Measures of immediate action: User can quickly broadcast such measures from a standard list of measures, e.g., stopping freight trains and alerting teams.

Menu for selecting different types of resolution concepts (e.g., one for redirecting trains, another for redirecting travelers, etc.)

Graphical editor for resolution concept

Release and publishing of the resolution concept

FIGURE 6-3 ALEA paper prototypes (© Swiss Federal Railways)

We tested and assessed requirements with storyboards, wireframes, and UI prototypes, which showed how specific areas of the software would look. The main benefit of the ALEA UI prototypes (see Figure 6-3) was that everybody understood them.

Therefore, all stakeholders reviewed requirements before a single line of code was written. In ALEA, the client UI was developed in Eclipse RCP. Unfortunately, Eclipse RCP does not support rapid prototyping. Coding UI spikes or trying out ideas was very expensive. The client technology did not match with the agile principle of embracing change and, therefore, influenced the team's work style. In our opinion, Eclipse RCP is not the optimal choice for UI-intensive agile projects.

POV: UI Designer

Most of the time, I worked with the onsite users and the UX expert. They prepared the requirements, wrote usage scenarios, and created the UI concept. Sometimes they also expressed complex requirements, first written out as text, with the support of wireframes made in Microsoft Visio. Most of the prototyping activities were my responsibility. In the initial phase, I started the interaction design with wireframes, which I created in Adobe Illustrator. At a later stage, I turned the consolidated wireframes into high-fidelity prototypes, for which I used Fireworks as a tool. Naturally, the prototyping activities also happened in an iterative fashion.

Because we used Eclipse RCP as a client technology, we could not realize all design elements as desired. Otherwise, the limitations helped us stay focused and prevented a too-excessive UI visioning. Once I had to push the developers to use an Eclipse RCP widget library, which we needed to implement a user-friendly interactive table design for the ALEA client. After I had done the accompanying wireframes and collected user feedback, the developers coded the table using the prototypes as a kind of visual specification. During later stages of the project, we had a full representation of an agent's workplace as a running system in the team room; the whole Scrum team and the most important business stakeholders were located in this room, sharing workspace and project artifacts. We used the reproduced setup in order to simulate user interaction with ALEA, especially with regards to the many different screens and the other software applications an agent has to use.

My impression is that the overall implementation of ALEA was very quick. The team usually turned ideas into prototypes and subsequently into running code within several weeks. With regards to the UI, we could not solve all parts perfectly from scratch. We also underestimated some user tasks and created the wrong UI and controls for those tasks. Sometimes, the fast speed at which the team worked was counterproductive. As we often had to glue concepts into code so quickly, we did not always have time to refine and consolidate them as required. Because we had to release the initial version at a predefined milestone, some interaction concepts had to be changed during later stages of the development process. Accordingly, some end-users had to change their mental model, which was frustrating and led to some negative feedback. But today, the ALEA UI looks almost exactly as I proposed and designed it.

For communicating with onsite users and the UX expert, we soon had our own UI backlog—a wall with post-its describing UI-related tasks and assignments. This very personal way of working together was sometimes also difficult. For example, some developers approached me with ideas or assignments without having the project manager's approval, which placed me in an awkward position.

Usability testing is a very important method for discovering bugs or issues with software. These tests are also important for UX experts as they lend credibility to a project. It's always better and easier to convince disbelievers with facts from usability tests rather than postulating an individual opinion. You can set up usability tests in an agile fashion. In ALEA, mobile usability labs were used to test the frontend of the application for viability and compliance. The usability test tasks were selected with regard to the priority and relevance of the accompanying user stories in the backlog. Typically, a usability task involved a sequence of several interrelated user stories, i.e., user stories that built a sound usage scenario. Any potential improvements were immediately fed back into the development process. To make this work properly, the development team did reserve some time for fixing found usability issues, which were documented as updated user stories or defect cards during every sprint. This approach is very similar to rapid iterative testing and evaluation (RITE). RITE means that you immediately fix bugs and issues you have found in usability test iteration n, in order to already execute iteration $n+1$ with a revised version of your software (Medlock et al. 2002). If you conduct usability tests in an agile UX project, you may find critical issues that require making changes to already implemented user stories. The ALEA usability tests were conducted onsite. The developers could thus easily join in. However, they were not allowed to just watch; they were assigned the role of an observer and had to watch the ongoing test closely to report on usability issues. Figure 6-4 shows the ALEA as it appeared during the final usability test study.

Areas for which the current user is responsible

Case list showing the incident, including location and the triggering train

Incident resolution measures relevant for the current user. The list shows, for example, redirections, exceptional stops, redirection, cancellations, and more.

FIGURE 6-4 The ALEA GUI during the final usability test study (© Swiss Federal Railways)

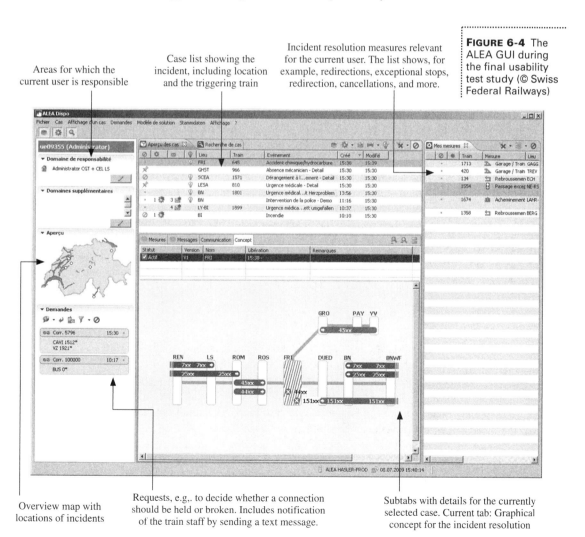

Overview map with locations of incidents

Requests, e.g,. to decide whether a connection should be held or broken. Includes notification of the train staff by sending a text message.

Subtabs with details for the currently selected case. Current tab: Graphical concept for the incident resolution

Product Impact

During the ALEA usability tests, we faced several critical findings with regard to window management, dialog flow, and the look and feel of the tables used to display emergency and procedure information. They additionally helped us to produce a UI that matched the needs and expectations of end-users. After all this, the ALEA rollout at SBB was utterly quiet, resulting in comments such as "the application is a pearl" (business application manager, SBB IT), "the application went live without making any noise" (manager IT projects, SBB infrastructure), and "you are heroes" (project manager, SBB infrastructure). SBB had no problems in terms of user acceptance, and even though many users had nearly no training at all, most users were able to apply the new software in a straightforward fashion.

POV: Project Manager, Business

Although we concluded that ALEA was a great success, the product impact of ALEA is difficult to measure quantitatively. We cannot say in numbers that customers get information faster or that information is spread more efficiently just because of ALEA. We cannot prove the impact of ALEA on the overall number of delays because ALEA was introduced in parallel to other actions. But I am convinced the numbers would be very impressive. We did, however, conduct an employee survey and the qualitative feedback highlighted that the complexity of failure management was significantly reduced. ALEA users felt they now had a much better overview in emergencies and they feel much better informed in less time. The elapsed time between recognizing a disruption and announcing the disruption to passengers was reduced, and the information provided is more accurate. Both are very helpful for our customers. Users mention that they can now focus on solving the problem at hand instead of spending most of their time forwarding information. This supports them in understanding situations much more efficiently and effectively, which, in turn, enables them to make better decisions.

For ALEA, agile software development and UX methods were a valuable combination, which helped to build a bridge between the IT department and the end-users at SBB. The project was a great starting point for developing more user-centered software products at SBB in the future. The product and business impact of the UX methods applied during the ALEA project can be summarized as follows:

- Thanks to UX integration, SBB agents can today focus on solving the problem at hand instead of spending most of their time forwarding information.

- Due to improved information flow, SBB personnel are able to take care of SBB customers in a much better way. The elapsed time between recognizing a disruption or emergency and informing SBB passengers about the disruption was decreased, and the information provided now is more accurate. Travelers are informed about the reason for disruptions or failures and are provided with information about alternate routes and connecting trains.

- The amount of information received by every system user has been significantly reduced. This helps SBB agents and other service personnel recognize relevant information easier and faster.

- Costs have been reduced because SBB personnel are able to prevent many communication errors, users have a more effective understanding of situations, and are, therefore, able to make the right decisions.

- The integration of UX into the agile development practice at SBB helped to build a bridge between the IT department and the users of SBB software. This is a great starting point for developing more user-centered software products in the future.

- The UX spirit spread to the business people; they began to simplify processes and choose pragmatic and effective solutions for the business processes around ALEA.

The way we worked in ALEA impacted other development projects, too. Working with onsite users turned out to be a good idea in many areas. The project managers realized that working closely with end-users and involving important stakeholders in the visioning and design process made many problems disappear, especially those related to user acceptance. Because we highlighted problems through roleplaying, video recordings, and expressive diagrams, management began to reconsider existing business processes. To really address the communication and efficiency issues SBB faces, the business organization has to change as well—and by closely working with onsite users, the business is already changing and will continue to do so.

POV: Onsite Users

From a business impact analysis, we know that users appreciate working with ALEA. We hear a lot of positive feedback about its efficiency and effectiveness. In 2009, the year ALEA was introduced, our trains met a new punctuality record. As with many return-on-investment analyses, we cannot determine ALEA's exact contribution to meeting this record because other parallel activities contributed to the punctuality record. Besides the positives, some business processes must still be aligned with the new software. Some internal business rules still ask users to send separate messages, for example, as e-mails, although ALEA already covered the whole information flow. This causes duplicate work and must soon be fixed to make users happier. In addition, the project management team could sell the software to other railway partners in Switzerland. In some of these companies, the business impact of ALEA would be even more positive and obvious because these particular companies do not have any failure management software. Using ALEA across organizational borders is also an advantage for us, because with ALEA, we can communicate with other railway companies easier and faster.

Because of ALEA, UX methods became a topic in many other projects as well. We think that the proximity of developers, designers, and end-users was a great experience for the whole team. Altogether, the application of UX practice in the ALEA project was based on some important cornerstones, which are summarized here:

- **Farsightedness**   UX people look and work ahead, for example, to develop several alternate design solutions for backlog items (deferred from epics or user stories), which are associated with the software's UI.

- **Focus**   UX people mainly develop the interaction concept; details are filled in later together with developers.

- **Beyond the on-site user**   Domain experts and end-users were continuously available and actively participated in the project. The Scrum team could, therefore, gather critical knowledge. This was fundamental for the project's success.

- **UX driver**   The UX expert could aid the understanding of UX by asking the right questions and demonstrating the impact of (changing) requirements by means of sketching and UI prototyping.

- **UX integration**   Some UX experts tend to work separate from the team. This breaks the feedback loop among the UX expert, team, and users. This is not appropriate because the success of an agile project very much depends on close conversation. The success of ALEA was only achieved because the UX expert and the team had a fully integrated work style.

If UI plays an important role, an approach combining agile development and UX methods are a good fit. It is a great but demanding way to create valuable software products. Incremental and iterative development provides the chance for frequent feedback about whether the team is on the right track. For such an agile process to work smoothly, you need experienced developers who are eager to understand and learn about the end-users. If this knowledge is broadcast to all layers of development and design, the team becomes more and more self-reliant in applying UX methods, which, in turn, frees the limited resources of the UX expert. The UX expert's role is to be an enabler, for example, with regard to providing the right methods and facilitating developers or onsite customers to follow through with UX methods. The UX expert needs the rest of the team to work as UX ambassadors and assistants because he or she can neither do it all alone nor does it make sense for the UX expert to do so. If UX has a high priority, everybody on the team needs to understand the users. And, quite simply, the best way to get to know the users is to work with them. The UX expert should be a full member of the development team. If he or she can partially work as a UI developer at the same time, the communication and decision making within the team is even more efficient.

In ALEA, the agile approach together with the highly qualified, interdisciplinary, and communicative team members was an important success factor in achieving a good UX for the ALEA software application. The ALEA project was shaped by a culture of learning by doing, permanent collaboration among team members, and continuous team enabling. In ALEA, communication among team members worked well. In addition, workshops held to solve problems and brainstorm about the right design solutions were crucial. Certainly, as an UX expert, you work as a go-between, and you have to be able to work with different people.

From our experience with the ALEA product development, we can distill some recommendations for business and project managers, software developers, and UX experts who plan to be part of an agile UX project in the future:

- **Team cooking**   The UX expert should not be the only one to employ user-centered methods; the whole Scrum team should. Enable the whole Scrum team to contribute to usability and design considerations. Make sure everybody talks to each other and asks the right questions, especially when requirements or concepts are unclear.

- **A picture is worth a thousand words**   Use UI prototypes to communicate and consolidate visions and ideas and apply them as visual specifications for developers.

- **UX upfront**   Because UX was integrated as part of the requirements engineering activities during exploration, even early (small) releases of the software (parts) already had a high usability. With regard to usability testing, this allowed us to focus on the optimization of really critical and complex parts of the design.

- **Iterative approach allows for real-world testing**   The complexity of emergency situations and the work context of SBB personnel made it necessary to leave the design room and the lab as soon as possible. Although time-consuming, testing delivered parts of the software in a real-world environment is much more enlightening than testing them in the lab.

- **Knowledge preservation**   Basic knowledge about user needs, task models, personas, and UX guidelines should exist independently from single projects because this kind of knowledge can be reused for years across many different projects.

Summary

- **What is the business context?**
  SBB wanted to minimize the effects of disruptions in rail traffic with a customer-specific software product.

- **Which (business) problems did you address with your UX practice?**
  In case of a disruption or failure, dozens of people at SBB and its partners had to communicate intensively. Flaws in the communication process impacted customer experience, for example, causing delays and insufficient information to be conveyed. For SBB, disruptions that last for some time are very costly.

- **What were constraints and prerequisites?**
  So far, SBB personnel had communicated on the phone, which caused a loss of time, added redundancy, and introduced errors. In case of an event, agents had to struggle with a huge amount of information.

- **In which development context did you apply your UX practice?**
  ALEA had to be developed from scratch, and it was to be a completely new system. ALEA was part of the implementation of a series of SBB software development projects. Scrum was chosen as the development process. After two years, the first release was put into operation.

- **What compelling events supported you in applying your UX practice successfully?**
  SBB had a rough idea about the UI, but realized they would need professional assistance.
  The preproject and the associated visioning prepared the ground for UX. The integration of UX methods into the requirements engineering work and the close cooperation of UX people with developers were important door openers.

- **What was the achieved product and business impact?**
  Costs have been reduced because agents are able to communicate more efficiently and with fewer errors. They understand situations more quickly and are able to make better decisions.

  The elapsed time between recognizing a disruption or emergency and the announcement informing SBB passengers was reduced, and the information provided is now more accurate. Both are very helpful for SBB customers.

- **How did you apply the UX practice?**
  Application of methods were based on Contextual Inquiry during the early stages and prototyping and usability testing during development (Beyer and Holtzblatt 1997). UX practice was tightly coupled with classic requirements engineering activities. UX people looked and worked ahead, separating UI backlog. Domain experts and end-users were continuously available and actively participated during the project.

- **What recommendations do you have for our readers?**
  A picture is worth a thousand words, employ UX upfront, create usability tests for delivered parts of the software in a real-world environment as soon as possible.

References

Beedle, M., A. van Bennekum, A. Cockburn, W. Cunningham, M. Fowler, J. Highsmith, A. Hunt, R. Jeffries, J. Kern, B. Marick, R. C. Martin, K. Schwaber, J. Sutherland, and D. Thomas. 2010. Manifesto for Agile Software Development. http://agilemanifesto.org/ (accessed June 21, 2010).

Buxton, B. 2003. Performance by design: The Role of Design in Software Product Development. In Proceedings of the Second International Conference on Usage-Centered Design, Portsmouth, NH, October 2003, pp. 26–29.

Belenguer, J., J. Parra, I. Torres, and P. J. Molina. 2003. HCI Designers and Engineers: Is it Possible to Work Together? In IFIP Working Group 2.7/13.4, INTERACT 2003 Workshop on Bridging the Gap Between Software Engineering and Human-Computer Interaction.

Beyer, H. and K. Holtzblatt. 1997. *Contextual Design: A Customer-Centered Approach to Systems Designs* (Morgan Kaufmann Series in Interactive Technologies). Burlington, MA: Morgan Kaufmann.

Cohn, M. 2004. *User Stories Applied: For Agile Software Development.* Boston: Addison-Wesley Professional.

Cohn, M. 2010. Succeeding with Agile: Software Development Using Scrum. http://www.infoq.com/articles/cohn-chapter8 (accessed June 15, 2010).

DIN EN ISO 9241-210. 2010. Ergonomics of Human-System Interaction-Part 210: Human-Centered Design for Interactive Systems. Deutsches Institut für Normung e. V. (DIN).

Jocham, R., and T. Memmel. 2009. Agile User Experience. *Computerworld – die Schweizer IT-Plattform für IT-Professionals,* Ausgabe Fokus Software-Entwicklung. IDG Verlag.

Medlock, M. C., D. Wixon, M. Terrano, R. Romero, and B. Fulton, B. 2002. Using the RITE Method to Improve Products: A Definition and a Case Study. Presented at the Usability Professionals Association 2002, Orlando, Florida.

Nodder, C., and J. Nielsen. 2008. Agile Usability: Best Practices for User Experience on Agile Development Projects. NN/g Nielsen Norman Group Report, 2nd edition. http://www.nnngroup.com/reports/agile (accessed June 18, 2010).

Preece, J., Y. Rogers, and H. Sharp. 2002. *Interaction Design: Beyond Human-Computer Interaction.* San Francisco: John Wiley & Sons.

Chapter 7

Focus on Users' Value:
Making User Assessment an Evaluation Indicator for Product-Related Departments

By Yan Chen, Qi Luo, and
Lixian Huang
Tencent®

Internet companies usually evaluate the performance of their product-related departments by using figures such as cardinal user number, active user number, revenue, and cost control. Rarely is overall user evaluation utilized to evaluate a product team's performance and user satisfaction. However, by doing so, we can judge the product team's views on the importance and influence of User Experience (UX) to product development and business decisions. Tencent has created a user evaluation system that considers UX as one of the performance indicators for evaluating product teams: the User Experience Evaluation System (UXES). We have improved the evaluation system step-by-step over the past five years and regard it as a significant performance indicator.

This chapter introduces the background, construction, operation, and impact of the UXES. In addition, the concept of *Focus on Users' Value* for evaluating a product-related department is illustrated explicitly.

About Tencent

Tencent was founded in November 1998 and is now one of the largest Internet providers of integrated services in China. Its main market is in China, and the company has developed quickly and steadily since its inception. Tencent's operational philosophy is *Focus on Users' Value.*

Introduction to Tencent and Its Products

Tencent's mission is to improve people's quality of life using the power of the Internet. Currently, our strategic goal is to provide one-stop online services for life: Internet value-added service, mobile and telecommunications value-added services, and online advertising. Tencent has built a number of leading network platforms in China such as Instant Messaging QQ (QQ-IM); QQ.com, a web portal; QQ Game portal; Qzone, multimedia social networking service; 3G.QQ.com, a wireless portal, Soso.com; Paipai.com; and Tenpay. Based on these products and services, Tencent has created the largest online networking community in China, meeting user requirements for communication, information, entertainment, and e-commerce on the Internet. As of March 31, 2010, QQ-IM was home to 568.6 million active user accounts, with peak simultaneous online user accounts reaching 105.3 million. The development of Tencent has profoundly affected and altered the communication modes and lifestyles of billions of netizens and has created wider application prospects for China's Internet industry.

In September 2009, Tencent became the third-largest Internet company in the world in terms of market value, after Google and Amazon. As of March 2011, it is the fourth largest Internet company.

Tencent's Operational Philosophy

Unlike the revenue models of other Internet companies, approximately 90 percent of Tencent's income comes from fee-based revenue. Users can not only choose a large number of free services but also pay for many premium services such as QQ Membership, QQ Show, Yellow Diamond, and so on, which have more characters, better experience, and higher value. Tencent became the first one among the Internet companies in China to make profits by adopting a business model of providing premium payment services to users. Therefore, users' desire to pay for these value-added services is critical for Tencent, which is why a focus on the users' value is important. Users who pay for services generally require a higher quality product in comparison to those who do not pay for them.

Tencent always pays attention to the users' value and needs in both free and value-added services because we believe business value and users' value are interrelated. Users can stop using our products if they perform badly or are of a poor quality and easily choose other ones, which are also free of charge. Hence, user-centric design and product development is essential to attracting users and maximizing retention rates. And a large user base is one of the key factors in attracting advertisers, which can lower costs and increase the probability of promoting new products and services successfully.

The UX of Tencent's products is a core part of our business model. Tencent is committed to its operational philosophy of *Focus on Users' Value* because we believe that creating value for users is vital to the sustainable development of the company. In summary, a *Focus on Users' Value* consists of four key points:

- Belief in customer-oriented principles, creating value for users and prioritizing users' interests

- Placing high priority on users' experiences and aiming to deliver services that exceed their expectations

- Prioritizing user satisfaction and loyalty and continually strengthening the feedback process

- Maximizing the company's value by maximizing user value

The Reason for the User Experience Evaluation System

Taking overall user evaluation as a performance indicator encourages product-related departments to emphasize UX, thereby benefiting product development. A sense of purpose, sustainability, objectivity, and timeliness are needed to make the system work. Details are given in the sections that follow.

User Requirements Shape Business Decisions

In a company, sustainable development is closely related to users' value; therefore, users should be considered throughout the entire development process for our products and services. Essentially, we should ensure that our customers always have a seat at the table when we make critical business decisions. This is why we have added the UX factor to the overall performance evaluation of our product-related departments.

Each June and December, we assess the overall performance of product-related departments over the past six months. This process is shown in Figure 7-1. First, we set performance goals for product-related departments, including finance, key tasks, UX, and human resource (HR) development. Performance goals are formulated by the performance management department, product-related departments, and evaluation department. Based on the UX performance assessment, the evaluation is

FIGURE 7-1 UX performance as part of the overall performance evaluation of the product-related departments

1. Overall Performance Goal

- Executed by Performance Management department
- Sets the overall performance goal of the product department, including such indicators as finance, key tasks, User Experience, and HR development

2. UX Performance Evaluation

- Executed by Evaluation department
- Makes the plan for the User Experience assessment and assesses the product-related departments. The assessment results will be fed back to the Performance Management department and product-related depatments

3. Overall Performance Evaluation

- Executed by Performance Management department
- Assesses the overall performance of the product-related department, and then gives feedback to the product-related department

4. Product Optimization

- Executed by Product-Related department
- Optimizes the products based on the appraisal results, and the optimized results will be taken as a reference for the next appraisal

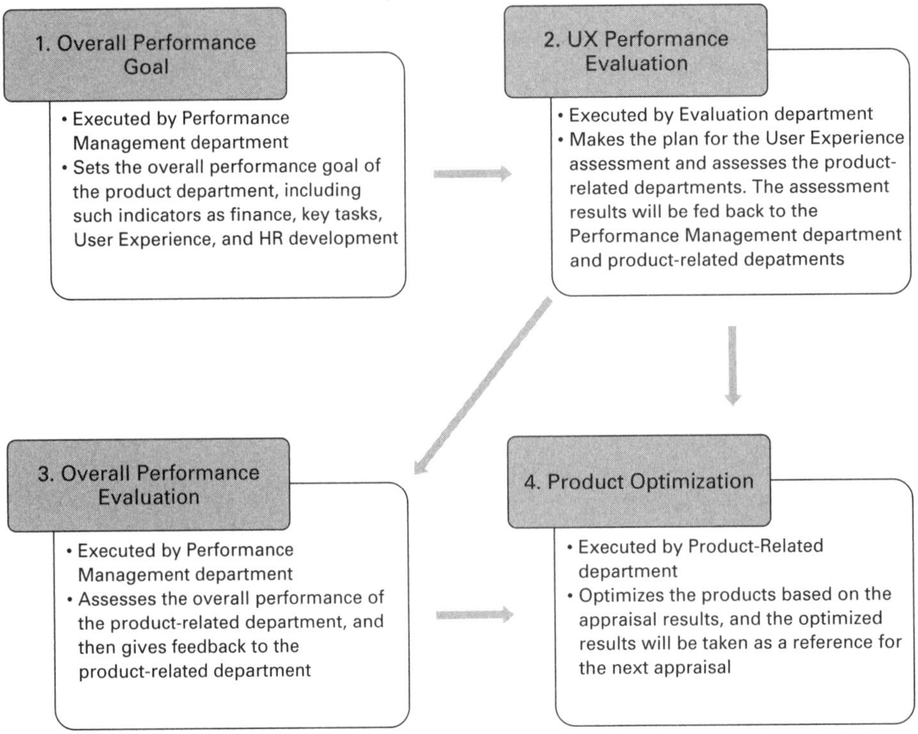

completed by the Customer Research & User Experience Design Center (CDC). CDC is a core department focused on User Experience design and customer research and is responsible for formulating and implementing the UX assessment process. CDC feeds the appraisal results back to the performance management and product-related departments after the process is complete. Next, the performance management department considers overall performance, including the UX assessment, and then provides feedback to the product-related departments. Finally, each product-related department can optimize its products based on the results, which are used as a reference for the next evaluation as well.

Adding the UX assessment to the overall performance evaluation of product-related departments helps ensure that the department understands user perception when making commercial decisions. It also gives the product-related departments a more accurate insight into user demands, creates values for users, and eventually maximizes product value through maximizing user value.

Optimization of Product Development

If a product-related department blindly seeks short-term performance gains but ignores UX for a given product, it is likely that, although short-term growth in the department's performance will increase rapidly, long-term performance will decrease. This development model is not healthy. Here is an example.

In QQ, system notice messages are displayed in the lower right-hand corner of the QQ IM window. Based on the guide for Windows interface design, its functions are to notify users of operations' results, display important system messages, and provide access to useful operational, system, and application programs. However, because QQ has a strong user group, it is a good, low-cost advertising tool for the product-related departments. Thus, they have used a host of tips to promote products and boost the short-term KPIs of their departments. Indeed, it stimulates a short-term increase in product usage but badly impacts UX. For example:

- Users receive up to ten messages each day.

- Message content is random: ads, function publicity, friend messages, payment advice, and hot topics.

- The more services are activated, the more messages are received.

As a result, most users close messages without reading them as they assume these messages lack value. Though benefiting from a large amount of publicity in the short-term, there is no long-term value as users eventually ignore these messages. Such a short-term strategy is bad for UX. Conversely, if a company prioritizes long-term product promotion based on raising UX with useful messages, product promotion would be optimized.

From this example, we know, as the performance management department, that if only short-term indicators are considered, assessing the impact that bad UX has on users is hard. However, by considering UX, the product-related department can strike a balance between short-term goals and the company's long-term vision, and thus we can better develop healthy and sustainable products.

Systematic Appraisal of User Experience Evaluation System

How can product quality, including UX quality, be improved over the long term? The following is an example.

When QQ was fairly new, the R&D team often obtained feedback from forum users and then developed and optimized software features based on this information. Since 2006, usability tests have become the main method for collecting QQ user feedback, and questionnaires have been used to measure user satisfaction. In 2009, the QQ R&D team employed many methods to collect users' overall views, including usability tests, questionnaires, household surveys, prototype testing, backend data analysis, and suggestions from the user service forum. The process progressed through various stages, including product demand discussion, prototype design, development testing, and operation. Evaluating UX outcomes scientifically and comprehensively is difficult, however. For this reason, the CDC established a scientific, systematic, and timely experience appraisal method to assess UX objectively and impartially.

Establishing the User Experience Evaluation System

When the User Experience Evaluation System (UXES) was created, methods for evaluating the UX included expert appraisals of UX work and of experience design quality and feedback from users based on having used the products. Although the first appraisal system added user assessment to performance appraisal, the process was qualitative and subjective, and challenges existed during implementation. After five years of using the system, we have formed a scientific and systematic UXES.

Basic Process

Figure 7-2 displays the basic UXES process.

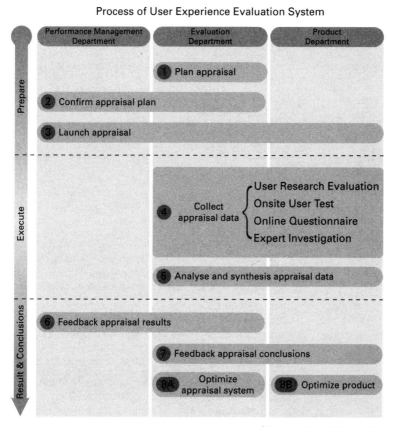

FIGURE 7-2 The basic UXES process

The performance management department, evaluation department (that is, the CDC), and product-related department are involved in this process (Table 7-1).

The procedure can be divided into three stages: appraisal preparation, appraisal execution, and result and conclusions, as shown in Figure 7-2.

The appraisal preparation stage is comprised of three steps: plan appraisal, confirm appraisal plan, and launch appraisal. These are detailed in Table 7-2.

Department	Description
Performance Management department	The overall appraisal of all product-related departments and overall performance comprise indicators such as finance, key tasks, UX, and HR development. The presidents of the company take the lead.
	The UXES proceeds from top to bottom in this department.
Evaluation department	Responsible for planning and implementing the UX appraisal process.
	This is the key department that runs through the whole UXES process.
Product-Related department	Chosen from all product-related departments to undergo the UX appraisal.

TABLE 7-1 UXES Departments

Procedure	Description
Plan appraisal	Planning involves selecting the products being appraised and their related-parameters. These products and parameters may differ from the key products and parameters at certain times.
	Examples: 1. During certain appraisal periods, some popular new functions for existing products or new products emerge. These are likely to be appraised. 2. The company has recently prioritized product safety and functions. These are likely to be appraised.
Confirm appraisal plan	The appraisal solutions differ each time. The final appraisal solution needs to be determined after communicating with the performance management department (led by the presidents).
	The first two steps must be implemented as soon as possible.
Launch appraisal	On the first day of Evaluation, the performance management department delivers a notice including the schedule and other details to the evaluation department. The appraisal department arranges the specific plan and informs the product-related departments to be appraised. Thus, the process runs from top to bottom.

TABLE 7-2 The Appraisal Preparation Stage

Procedure	Description
Collect appraisal data	In order to better and more comprehensively appraise the product-related departments based on UX, we use four methods to gather data: user research evaluations, onsite user tests, online questionnaires, and expert investigations. Each focuses on a different aspect; for example, the online questionnaire emphasizes quantitative data collection, whereas the onsite user test emphasizes qualitative data collection.
	Data collection needs the most people to join in the entire appraisal procedure, which directly affects the efficiency and quality of the evaluation. The four methods of data collection are introduced in detail in the following section.
Analyze and synthesize appraisal data	The collected data is summarized, calculated, and output as a report.

TABLE 7-3   Appraisal Implementation Stage

The appraisal implementation stage is comprised of two steps: collect appraisal data and analyze and synthesize appraisal data. These are described in Table 7-3.

The result feedback stage is comprised of three steps: feedback appraisal results, feedback appraisal conclusions, optimize appraisal system, and optimize product. These are described in Table 7-4.

Procedure	Description
Feedback appraisal results	The evaluation department feeds back the UX results for a product-related department to the performance management department, which are, in turn, added to the overall performance result.
Feedback appraisal conclusions	The evaluation department feeds back the appraisal conclusions to the product-related departments. This comprises a detailed appraisal report in addition to the conclusions. It references problem tracking and optimization suggestions.
Optimize appraisal system	The project summary will be presented and promoted, respectively.
	The evaluation department summarizes the appraisal projects, integrates human resource, time input, and the investment proportion of each component. It analyzes the components that need improvement and collates solutions for unexpected risks. The data play a significant role in optimizing the UX appraisal system.
	After the project summary is output, the evaluation department analyzes common problems and conclusions from the appraisal in more detail.
Optimize product	Based on the appraisal results, the product-related department can optimize its products. The results of the optimization process form a reference for the next appraisal.

TABLE 7-4   The Result Feedback Stage

The process outlined in this section originates from CDC's five years of experience. To create a similar UXES, a company can use its own details.

Data Collection Methods

The data collection methods form the center of the UXES. Selecting a suitable method for data collection requires paying attention to these elements:

- **Time perspective** For assessing the performance of a product-related department, it is better to appraise UX over a long-term period rather than a short-term period.

- **Multiple perspectives** The views of users and experts must be considered. Users focus on individual usability and satisfaction, whereas experts care more about uniform experience and standard product design.

- **Data** Qualitative and quantitative data must be collected and include precisely focused "What and Why'" questions. Quantitative data show the extent of a problem while qualitative data tell us the reasons for the problem.

- **Purpose** This focuses on the changes and development of product-related departments to improve UX. The relative appraisal score is more significant than the absolute score because it can be used to compare with other departments or rival products.

Therefore, the data collection method we apply includes four components:

- User research evaluation

- Onsite user test

- Online questionnaire

- Expert investigation

The results are obtained from the comprehensive appraisal of these four components. Table 7-5 displays appraisal content, parameters, and aim of the four collection methods. The different appraisal methods are both complementary and related.

Appraisal Method	Appraisal Content	Appraisal Parameters	Appraisal Aim
User research evaluation	User research conditions for the product-related department	Quantity Quality Effectiveness Participation level Process and specifications' construction	Assesses product-related department input regarding UX.
Onsite user test	Actual usage conditions and feedback	Task completion Mistakes Times Learnability Efficiency Problem feedback	Assesses whether users can smoothly complete a task, mistake frequency, learnability speed for new functions, and other feedback.
Online questionnaire	Product satisfaction	User satisfaction Product features Competitor products Comparison Brand image	Assesses user satisfaction, confirms other research, and employs spot tests and expert investigation.
Expert investigation	UX problems with a product	Design specifications of Tencent's products Usability norms	Assesses UX based on product design specifications (such as components and unified logo) and usability norms, analyzes problems, and proposes solutions.

TABLE 7-5   Appraisal Methodologies

Statistical Methods

The four evaluation methods give four different results:

User research evaluation = S1

Onsite user test = S2

Online questionnaire = S3

Expert investigation = S4

Each evaluation method emphasizes a different aspect, giving their evaluation scores different weights. The weights of the four evaluation scores are α1, α2, α3, and α4, respectively. Thus, the total evaluation score of S is calculated by the following formula:

$$S = \alpha1 S1 + \alpha2 S2 + \alpha3 S3 + \alpha4 S4$$

When the evaluation scores are reported to the product-related departments, they are compared with the highest, average, or lowest achieved scores of all the evaluated product-related departments. Thus, each department knows the gap between their product and the highest achieved score. This comparison gives the evaluation context. The following figure shows the four-dimensional evaluation of a certain product and the highest scores in each dimension for all the company's products. The lowest score is 0, the highest 100.

The four evaluation methods differ in terms of the calculation methods used. For instance, the final score for the network questionnaire depends not only on the result of this survey, but also on the result of the last survey, which needs to be used for comparison. In addition, survey results for competitors' products are taken into account for comparison as well. Then a final score is calculated by considering all these results.

On the other hand, the statistics for the user research evaluation are more complex as they involve the following subdimensions: quantity, quality, validity, participation, and standard construction.

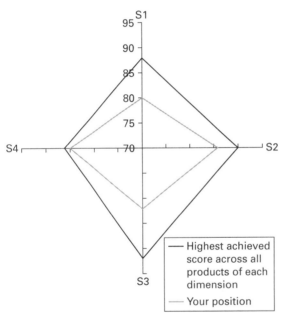

Highest achieved score across all products of each dimension

Your position

FIGURE 7-3
Comparing a certain product's scores with the highest scoring product across the four parameters

Each subdimension is statistically independent; we horizontally compare product-related departments and vertically compare time periods for a certain product-related department. Thus, the user research evaluation score is based on the different weights of the subdimensions. The weights of the subdimensions are determined through the Analytic Hierarchy Process (AHP), as shown in Figure 7-4. The AHP is a structured technique for dealing with complex decisions. Rather than prescribing a "correct" decision, the AHP helps decision makers find the one that best suits their needs and their understanding of the problem (More details are referred to at http://en.wikipedia.org/wiki/Analytic_Hierarchy_Process). Similarly, the four weights—α1, α2, α3, and α4—that form the total evaluation score can be determined through the AHP.

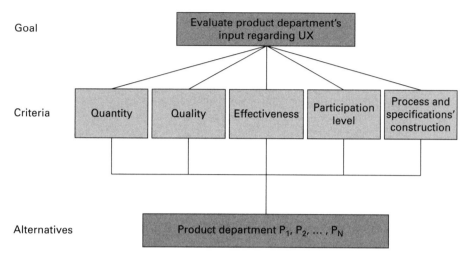

Goal — Evaluate product department's input regarding UX

Criteria — Quantity | Quality | Effectiveness | Participation level | Process and specifications' construction

Alternatives — Product department $P_1, P_2, \ldots, P_N$

FIGURE 7-4 Schematic diagram for user research evaluation statistics

We output a detailed evaluation summary report that integrates obtained data, discovered issues, user feedback, proposals from the network questionnaire survey, user observation and interviews, and the expert investigation. These assist the product-related departments in better tracking the results and optimizing their products and their UX.

Operating the User Experience Evaluation System

To develop a better problem-solving methodology, operational execution is particularly important. Tencent has many products, so the number of statistics that we collect and process during the evaluation phase is huge, and this huge number increases the difficult of operating the evaluation system. In practice, we've concluded that the four operational elements discussed in this section are essential. Through this operation, the User Experience Evaluation System has been effectively promoted and implemented, reflecting its value.

Top-to-Bottom Promotion

Tencent's corporate philosophy is user focused. MA Huateng, our Chief Experience Officer and Chief Product Manager as well, believes that enterprises can only survive if they win the hearts and minds of their customers. David Wallerstein, the Vice President of Tencent, says that "Customer Engagement," or what we now commonly call "CE," has been a core part of our product development cycle since Tencent's early days.

When we launched our QQ-IM service in the late 1990s, we regularly communicated with our users, built relationships with them, and regularly monitored our Bulletin Board System (BBS) for user input. We had no specific name for this user interaction, however; we just considered it to be a crucial part of our product development work. Ultimately, CE is a core principle of Tencent and a key driving force of our corporate growth. The desire to satisfy users with leading Internet services and products and continuously improve our offerings based on user demand is crucial to every member of the Tencent family.

Guided by a business philosophy that focuses on users' value, Tencent's leaders strongly support the UXES. At the beginning of the evaluation period, the leaders of the company propose the products to be evaluated, which are generally our most popular products. At the end of the evaluation period, they hold meetings to report the evaluation results and propose solutions for the most serious problems. For example, in the 2009 UX evaluation, one proposal was that videos about the key issues for the R&D team should be made and publicized at the annual strategy conference. This idea was well supported.

Due to the top-to-bottom execution initiated by the leaders, the results of UX evaluation are easily disseminated.

Prompt and Efficient Implementation

We introduced the UX evaluation project process in "Establishing the User Experience Evaluation System," earlier in this chapter. Because multiple roles and phases are involved and multiple product-related departments are evaluated, the project process is complex and needs to be completed in one month, which means prompt and efficient implementation.

Effective project management is thus crucial to meeting this deadline, minimizing risks, and maximizing resource sharing and utilization. A template exists for each step, as detailed in Table 7-6, which keeps documentation consistent and reduces staff workload.

Project review is thus smooth and personnel can be trained during the UX evaluation process. At the beginning of the project, some quality issues can necessitate reworking tasks. If appropriate HR and time are invested in project review and personnel training, the amount of reworking needed can be reduced.

Evaluation Result Feedback

The evaluation score only means that the performance evaluation is complete. We hope that the evaluation system urges product-related

User research evaluation	*User Research Material Statistical Template*
	User Research Evaluation Score Template
Onsite user test	*User Test Plan Template*
	User Test Records' Template
	User Test Post-Test Questionnaire Template
	User Observation and Interview Score Template
Network questionnaire	*Network Survey Questionnaire Design Template*
	Network Questionnaire Data Analysis Code Template
Expert investigation	*Experience Expert Walkthrough and Evaluation Report Template*
	Expert Walkthrough and Evaluation Score Template
Evaluation summary	*UX Evaluation Total Score Template*
	UX Evaluation Summary Report Template
Project management	*Project Progress Management Template*
	Project Summary Report Template

TABLE 7-6   Templates for the UX Evaluation Project

departments to value and improve UX; therefore, the evaluation system can fulfill its inherent value. The following experiences must be shared:

- **Identifying the requirements of product-related departments in advance**   When collecting materials, we identify the survey requirements of the product-related departments, use them as evaluation references, and include the relevant conclusions in the final report. Thus, we can ensure that the evaluation results are in line with the expectations of the product-related departments. Product-related departments tend to accept proactive assistance easily and welcome the evaluation project.

- **Outputting evaluation results in detail and clearly**   By "in detail" we mean that the evaluation results should include not only the evaluation scores, but also the evaluation summary report, which elaborates on the data, discovered issues, and proposals. This information helps product-related departments obtain valuable conclusions and solutions to most issues.

    By "clearly" we mean that the evaluation results should be intuitively displayed and stated and easy to understand. Using only data and boring theories makes evaluation results difficult to digest.

● **Conducting effective communication of reports**   After the evaluation summary reports are e-mailed to the product-related departments, conferences are set up with the product-related departments as a communication platform. Generally, product managers, designers, development engineers, and operation engineers are invited to the conference. Various participants can easily propose solutions and include these solutions in the optimization plan.

In summary, we should consider how to maximize the value of the evaluation results at all stages of the evaluation system's implementation. It is of great importance to deliver feedback results effectively, both to product-related departments and evaluation departments.

Continuous Optimization of the Evaluation System

Historical data and experience are very important to ensure subsequent projects are free of unnecessary mistakes, losses, and failures. At the end of each evaluation project, we summarize what should be continued and what should be improved. The summary also serves as evidence for subsequently optimizing the evaluation system. We dynamically update and continually optimize the UXES, enabling it to advance with the times.

For instance, we outputted a project summary document that includes 45 key points about effective communication based on a recent evaluation project, including the content of each link to the user observation and interview process, network questionnaire design, and report writing, which is vital in guiding future UX evaluations.

The Value and Influence of the User Experience Evaluation System

The UXES not only assists the performance evaluation department, but also has great value and a profound influence throughout the entire company.

First, the UXES urges product-related departments to pay close attention to UX and improve product quality. The company has various product-related departments that, in the past, have focused different levels of concern toward UX, and the evaluation system motivates them to pay greater attention to UX. For example, one year ago, a product-related department was examined by evaluating one of its products, "Mobile-phone Browser." Several problems were detected, such as confusing interface contents and poor guidance for new users. And others, like the high cost of main operations, inconsistent interaction logic, and visual performance, were also found through the experts' investigation.

Further details about these issues follow:

- **The problems detected through onsite usability test**   In practice, many times users could not open web pages because they did not understand the explanations due to unreadable text and did not know what to do next after they failed to open the current page. Users were also confused by the inconsistent interfaces of error alerts. These problems resulted from designers' providing poor operational guidance and their failure to design a consistent interface for displaying error alerts. Therefore, it is important to use clear wording so users quickly understand what's wrong with the browser and what to do next. And ensuring the consistency of various error alerts will help users read the contents quickly and correctly and help to decrease the error rate.

- **The problems detected through expert investigation**   Users found inputting suffixes like ".com", ".net," or ".org" when trying to access a website troublesome. One solution is to use an automatic matching system so users are able to choose the domain name suffixes instead of having to type them.

We provided evaluation reports listing detailed problems that had been detected through the data collection methods discussed earlier to the product-related department, so these problems could be solved and product quality greatly improved accordingly.

Second, the UXES helps product-related departments establish a system for regularly tracking user satisfaction. Previously, some product-related departments paid attention to user demands during product design and development. However, most of the user feedback information came from the product Bulletin Board System (BBS), which was rather dispersed and qualitative, although it had certain value. Other product-related departments carried out a user satisfaction survey after a product was launched, which they subsequently discontinued. Therefore, they could not make vertical comparisons. The UXES is sustainable, however, and outputs comprehensive, quantitative, and qualitative evaluation reports for regularly tracking user satisfaction.

We can also make a horizontal comparison of user satisfaction for each parameter of the evaluated products within the same period. By doing this, we can analyze what current users are satisfied with and identify what needs to be improved. Figure 7-5 shows the horizontal comparison of user satisfaction with client software. It is clear that current users are satisfied with the interface skin of the software, but dissatisfied with performance (including access speed and stability), and this deserves attention from the product-related department.

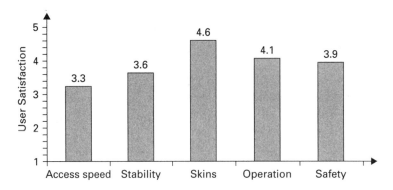

FIGURE 7-5 User satisfaction with the client software for each parameter (sample size N = 1589). In Figure 7-5, value 1 is the lowest score showing extreme dissatisfaction, whereas value 5 is the highest score indicating the greatest satisfaction.

We can also compare our products with competing products using a horizontal comparison for user satisfaction. Figure 7-6 compares user satisfaction for our mobile phone software with other competing products. The survey covers eleven subdimensions, such as global scale, access speed, mobile traffic, and application support. These are ranked from left to right according to importance. You can see the differences between our products and the competing products for all parameters. Again, 1 is the lowest score showing the most dissatisfaction, whereas 5 is the highest score, indicating the highest satisfaction.

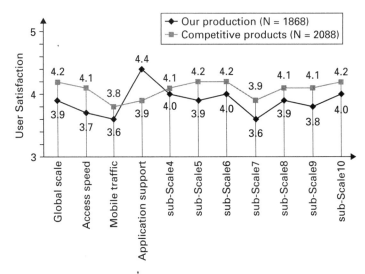

FIGURE 7-6 User satisfaction comparison between our mobile phone software and competitive mobile phone software

After the data from several evaluations are accumulated, vertical comparisons are conducted to help product-related departments understand the development trends for user satisfaction. Vertical comparisons can be used for improving overall user satisfaction and certain parameters as well. For instance, during the first and last six months of 2008, we found that a web product had a low score for advertisements, meaning that the quantity and mode of advertisements disturbed users.

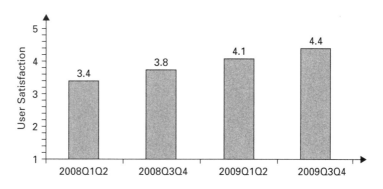

FIGURE 7-7 User satisfaction with the web product in terms of advertisement disturbance

In the first half of 2009, the product-related department adjusted its advertisement sales strategy, and the following evaluation showed UX rose. In Figure 7-7, 1 is the lowest score showing the greatest dissatisfaction, whereas 5 is the highest score indicating the greatest satisfaction.

Third, the UXES urges product-related departments to solve problems and enhance UX.

Through the sustained tracking of user satisfaction, user observation, and interviews, along with expert investigations, product-related departments can identify the aspects of products with which users are satisfied and dissatisfied and which aspects are causing problems. This way, they can solve specific problems directly. The solutions provided by the UX experts can quickly and effectively help product-related departments to enhance UX.

FIGURE 7-8 The UXES helps product-related departments solve problems and enhance UX.

The UX system helps us discover UX problems in each evaluation period and helps the product-related departments to solve these problems in a timely fashion, optimize the product experience, and verify the optimization effect in the next evaluation, as illustrated in Figure 7-8.

During one UX evaluation performed during the second half of 2008, we discovered that many players of one game complained that cheating was easy. Through further analysis and comparison, we output

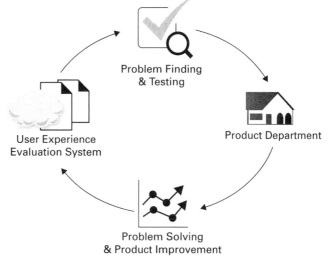

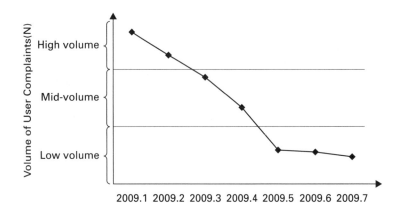

FIGURE 7-9 Number of complaints of cheating from the players of one game

a detailed report for the product-related department so they could solve this issue. With a series of improvement measures implemented in the first half of 2009, complaints dramatically decreased. As shown in Figure 7-9, in January 2009, the number of complaints about cheating was high, but by July, the number of complaints had decreased significantly, dramatically improving UX.

Another product that has been tracked for many years is Qzone. Qzone is a product developed in 2005 by Tencent. It is like a personal space or blog. Users are able to write logs, upload pictures, listen to music, and do customized decoration. We started to evaluate the UX of Qzone from 2007 and have kept on doing so. In the beginning, a number of problems were discovered—the registration and decoration process was too complex, many of the decoration elements were garish, and there was an insufficient number of free decorating services, and so on. We reported these problems to the product team so they would clearly understand these problems at an early stage and so they could better optimize the product. After that, we continued to evaluate this product and track these problems to see if product quality and user satisfaction had improved in regards to those problems. Each evaluation outcome indicated the team was moving in the correct direction and offered some effective suggestions for sustainable optimization of the product, for instance, the addition of accurate navigation of the global positioning system for driving. After a few iterations, we found in the most recent evaluation that the problems had been completely solved. Figure 7-10 shows that the process of new registration became simpler after a few optimizations and that UX has been improved as well. These points show that the product has been significantly improved:

1. The entire new registration can be completed on one page.

2. Four decoration styles, which are suitable for various classes of users, can be selected directly and easily from this page in one mouse click.

3. A user's data such as QQ account, gender, and the date of birth are provided on the registration page. This helps to decrease registration time for user operations and increases the user's sense of identity on this website, which means this user can complete registration without inputting any other data.

4. The system provides clear tips or guidance when invalid data are input.

Finally, the UXES can promote the establishment of fundamental research projects that have universal significance for the company and that drive the application of research results into specific products.

The UX evaluation has shown us that different products have common problems that have not been effectively solved. Where possible, research projects on these problems are being carried out and the results applied. For example, one UX evaluation revealed that users had different sharing and privacy demands when using multiple Social Network Services (SNS) products. These demands were increasingly personalized and diverse. Based on this, we investigated user information and relationship chain management and applied the results to various products.

FIGURE 7-10 The current version of registration page for a new Qzone account (URL: http://imgcache .qq.com/qzone/reg/ reg1.html)

Final Thoughts

The UXES balances short-term performance and long-term goals to achieve sustainable and healthy product improvement. Through the top-to-bottom approach and continuous publicity by the evaluation department, the CD design concept has been integrated into each product-related department, and each employee understands its importance, thus fully reflecting the corporate philosophy of user value.

FIGURE 7-11 Peak simultaneous online user accounts for QQ IM over the past decade

Guided by a business philosophy that focuses on user value, Tencent maintains its stable and healthy development path. For instance, the Tencent QQ IM platform has developed solidly over the past decade. On March 5, 2010, peak simultaneous online user accounts for QQ IM reached 100 million, as shown in Figure 7-11. The advertising potential for other products and their probability for success is phenomenal, helping us to realize a more profitable business model.

Any company wanting to establish such an evaluation system should consider these four points:

- If your company values the UX of its products, you have a strong advantage. Otherwise, strive to set up such an environment. The companies that attach importance to UX are more likely to value and promote the results of evaluating UX, thus strengthening the evaluation system.

- You can establish effective methods for collecting data based on resources and the conditions of your company. For instance, in Tencent, through such platforms as the network questionnaire, background databases for products, and the user Bulletin Board System (BBS), we can collect satisfaction statistics and feedback from a large sample base quickly and cheaply.

- Emphasize publicizing the evaluation results, thus making the UXES more influential. In addition to evaluating performance, consider how to assist product-related departments effectively, so as to improve product quality continuously.

- You should establish a database to accumulate evaluation data for subsequent comparison and analysis.

Summary

- **What is the business context (e.g., product, customers)?**
  Tencent was founded in November 1998 and is now one of the largest Internet providers of integrated services in China. Tencent always pays attention to users' value and needs in both free and value-added services because we believe business value and users' value are interrelated.

- **Which (business) problems did you address with your UX practice?**
  The User Experience Evaluation System can judge the extent to which the product team views User Experience (UX) as important to their product. It can also evaluate the UX level of our products and the difference between our products and other competitive ones. This system helps us sustainably develop products and it provides scientific support for making business decisions.

- **What were (organizational) constraints and prerequisites?**
  The process depends on how a company's management board views the importance of UX to its product.

- **In which development context did you apply your UX practice?**
  We have improved the evaluation system step by step over the past four years and regard it as a significant performance indicator.

- **What compelling events supported you in applying your UX practice successfully?**
  Based on a business philosophy that focuses on user value, Tencent's leaders strongly support UX evaluation work. Before 2006, the R&D team collected user feedback from forums to evaluate and optimize product features. To improve the effectiveness of UX evaluation work, in 2006, we brought in UX engineering experts, which enabled us to conduct UX evaluation work systematically, and as a result, we created the User Experience Evaluation System (UXES). Up to the present, the UXES has already been taken as a key performance indicator for product-development departments.

- **What was the achieved product impact?**
  The UXES balances UX and short-term performance of products to achieve sustainable and healthy product improvement. Through the top-to-bottom approach and continuous publicity and promotion by the evaluation department, the CE design concept has been integrated into each product-related department and each employee understands this, thus fully reflecting the corporate philosophy of user value.

- **How did you apply the UX practice?**
  We apply the UX practice by promoting the UXES through a top-to-bottom approach, with prompt and efficient implementation, by encouraging participation and valuable feedback, and by continuously optimizing the evaluation system.

- **What recommendations do you have for our readers?**
  First, establish a set of effective and agile methods for collecting data based on the condition and business stage of your company. Second, try to promote UX from top to bottom. Third, establish a database to accumulate evaluation data and the product's value points for long-term analysis and optimization.

Chapter 8

Redesigning My Yahoo!®:
Using Prototyping to Facilitate Communication

By Junius Gunaratne

Yahoo!®

My Yahoo! is a personalized start page used by more than 34 million people worldwide every month. When redesigning the page, the My Yahoo! team used several types of rapid prototyping methods as tools to test its redesign with users. The prototypes also served to convey design ideas to product managers and engineers in the form of working specifications. This chapter discusses the competitive landscape of personalized start pages, how prototyping helped the My Yahoo! team better understand its users and demonstrate ideas to various stakeholders, and how this affected the design and engineering process of developing My Yahoo!

The My Yahoo! team overhauled the design of its existing product in an attempt to create a user experience exceeding that of its competitors' sites. The updated product better integrated with the recently redesigned Yahoo! homepage as a way to increase *user engagement*—the amount of time users spend on their pages, a measure directly related to product revenue and monetization. The team addressed user engagement in My Yahoo!'s redesign by introducing compelling new features, addressing usability concerns, and upgrading its frontend implementation to support more dynamic web technology. The bulk of the redesign work took place over the course of a year and laid the foundation for extending the product more easily in the future. Throughout the product design process, the team made extensive and innovative use of prototypes to convey ideas, explore proof-of-concept ideas, and test their concepts with users.

The majority of Yahoo!'s products are available to the public at no cost, thanks to advertising revenue generated by display advertising such as banner ads and inline page advertising. Display advertising has obvious implications on a user's experience. For some products, such as Yahoo! Mail, users can choose to pay for an advertisement-free version of the product; however, display advertising supports the vast majority of Yahoo!'s products. Advertisements generate revenue in two ways: impressions and click-throughs. *Impressions* are the number of people who see an advertisement on a page. An advertisement on a page that is viewed by millions of people costs more than an advertisement on a page that is viewed by thousands of people. *Click-throughs,* as the name implies, are the number of people who click an advertisement to visit the resulting page. Each time a user clicks an advertisement, the advertiser pays Yahoo! a small amount for the traffic generated.

User experience is core to Yahoo! because it has direct implications on the company's revenue. Because Yahoo! depends on advertising as its main form of revenue, it is crucial that users continue to revisit Yahoo! websites to generate impressions and click-throughs. A good user experience also enhances Yahoo!'s brand and reputation. For example, a user who has a good experience on Yahoo!'s homepage is more likely to try My Yahoo!

because the user already has an expectation of product quality and ease of use. Although Yahoo!'s web pages link to many different websites outside of Yahoo!, links between Yahoo!-owned websites often receive more clicks. Market and user research have shown that this is due to some degree of brand loyalty; users also trust Yahoo!'s brand and expect that any Yahoo! website offers a high-quality user experience.

Redesigning the Product

My Yahoo! is a personalized start page. Personalized start pages allow users to add custom content to a page and make changes to the look and feel of that page. My Yahoo! debuted in 1998 as one of the first personalized start pages on the Internet. My Yahoo!'s pages have inline display ads that generate income, and My Yahoo! directs users to other Yahoo! products that also include display advertising on their pages. There is a fine line between the right amount of advertising and too much advertising. If a page has too much advertising, or if an advertisement is poorly placed on a page, users may react negatively and stop using the product. Many users request that advertising be removed entirely, but these same users are also unwilling to pay for a product when other free alternatives are available elsewhere.

My Yahoo! consists of a page with default content, including weather, news, e-mail, and a variety of RSS feeds suggested by My Yahoo! algorithms based on a user's interests. Figure 8-1 shows an early prototype of the My Yahoo! page. A set of content on the page is referred to as a *module.* A user can add more modules to the default and recommended sets by visiting a section of the product referred to internally as the Content Store. The Content Store includes a variety of modules on topics including entertainment, sports, and technology, to name just a few. Each module supports multiple media types such as RSS feeds, podcasts, photos, and video. Modules range from static news feeds to highly interactive games.

Personalized start pages are growing in popularity and an increasing number of websites offer such pages. Users can now choose from dozens of personalized start page websites, ranging from sites dedicated to personalized start pages to traditional news and information sites that have branched out into personalized start page experiences. Yahoo!'s chief competitors, which include Google and Microsoft, offer personalized pages. Beyond iGoogle and My MSN, smaller personalized sites, such as NetVibes and YourMinis, are growing in popularity. More traditional media brands such as *The New York Times,* Fox, and ESPN are also branching out into personalized start pages with their own versions of "My" products.

Many newer websites and most personalized start pages make use of dynamic web page technologies commonly referred to as Asynchronous

FIGURE 8-1 Users can configure their My Yahoo! page to display customized content of their choosing. This early prototype enabled researchers to gather preliminary feedback from users before the final product was released to the public.

JavaScript and Extensible Mark-up Language (AJAX).[1] These dynamic web page technologies make extensive use of JavaScript and client-side browser technologies to create rich user experiences that approach the quality of a desktop application within a web browser. Newer personalized start pages are more like web applications rather than static web pages. Users can manipulate the content on a page using drag and drop, and page updates no longer require a web browser refresh. Adding content and customizing the look and feel of the page is done inline without having to visit other static pages.

The redesign of My Yahoo! is an attempt to design a product that better suits the needs of users in a new personalized start page landscape. With the competitive landscape of personalized start pages becoming more application-like, customer feedback and user research suggested many original My Yahoo! users thought of the product as inferior to alternatives. However, the wide selection of content and users' trust in Yahoo! as a quality brand kept many My Yahoo! users loyal to the product. User research data and customer feedback provided the My Yahoo! team with a strong motivation to make significant upgrades to the product.

The original release of My Yahoo! did not use any AJAX technology. Subsequent incremental releases added some dynamic page behavior, such as the ability to drag and drop modules, as an afterthought. Upgrading the My Yahoo! platform to fully incorporate dynamic web technology involved considerable effort. Supporting a dynamic web application frontend required a major overhaul of the underlying backend database and content technology. My Yahoo!'s large existing user base created product migration and upgrade challenges not only in terms of technology but also in terms of how best to convey the migration process to end users.

With much of My Yahoo!'s application state maintained on the client-side in the web browser, frontend engineers are very sensitive to user interface changes. Introducing dynamic web technologies into the user experience greatly affects interaction with the product. As such, designing a dynamic web application requires a deep understanding of user interaction. Effort invested in building backend technology can quickly be nullified if even minor changes are made on the frontend. In other words, design changes have a high cost. While this has always been true in web development, it is even more so with dynamic web applications because of the number of layers involved in the product's architecture.

User engagement is crucial for a product as highly trafficked as My Yahoo! Because revenue can be directly correlated to user engagement, it follows that usability and user interface design can directly impact revenue. Increasing user engagement is not trivial. My Yahoo! users are familiar with the existing product and have spent a great deal of time adding modules to their pages and customizing their look and feel. Users are accustomed to specific workflows. Changing a page's theme (a predefined scheme of colors and images), manipulating content, or adding RSS feeds is done in a specific way. Modifying these workflows can be disorienting and frustrating to users. There is a risk that users will find a new design confusing, frustrating, or irritating and stop using a particular feature—decreasing their engagement—or, much worse, stop using the product. Listening to users is crucial, as is weighing design and engineering effort with users' concerns. For example, the My Yahoo! team chose to continue to support legacy themes from the original product due to user demand even though this created complications in designing the theme-selection user interface. The team felt that preserving older themes in the product would help keep users loyal and maintain their current levels of engagement.

To measure the success of a redesign for the short term, the team needed to conduct testing to get feedback from new and experienced My Yahoo! users to gauge what they thought of the product in terms of the overall user experience and to assess if users could complete common tasks on My Yahoo! more easily. Success is demonstrated with quantitative, empirical data from surveys with Likert scales[2] and also qualitative data reflecting positive user feedback. However, in order for My Yahoo!'s redesign to be considered successful in the long term, it needed to show measurable increases in user engagement over time. Usage data from server log files showed an increase in hits to My Yahoo! after its redesign and longer user engagement time, which means users are spending more time with the product.

Initial Design Process and Brainstorming

With the many challenges involved with upgrading My Yahoo!, the team could have easily become overwhelmed with all of the potential problems and constraints. Instead of focusing on constraints, during the preliminary product design stages, the design team focused on creating an engaging user experience without any technical or logistical constraints imposed by either business agreements or engineering limitations. This "blue sky" approach consisted of thinking about what the product could be in an ideal world.

Wireframes are basic schematic diagrams used to illustrate page layouts on a web site. The team used these extensively in the blue sky concept phase of the project. Blue sky concepts began with a series of brainstorming sessions that resulted in designers sketching and creating wireframes of conceptual designs for the new product. These brainstorming sessions involved the design team and some of the core stakeholders, including product managers and directors. Though developers were not directly involved with brainstorming blue sky concepts, the design team's prototypers did have discussions with developers so they understood the technology that would be used for implementation. Competing products with desirable features and technology were shown to all team members, including designers, product managers, marketing managers, and developers. The discussions about competing products and desirable features helped frame discussions about the product's future. Interaction designers created screen mockups in Adobe Illustrator, detailing views of new layouts of information displayed in the product. Visual designers iterated through a series of rough designs showing product themes. The design team also worked with external firms to get some fresh input on the product. The design team and the external design firm established several potential directions in which to take My Yahoo! in the future. Working independently from the design team, the marketing team did comprehensive reviews of competitors' products. Yahoo!'s global market research group collected data and studied My Yahoo! user demographics. The user research team created basic personas to help drive design. Marketing and user research provided useful quantitative and qualitative data on people using My Yahoo! The marketing group helped give the My Yahoo! team a good sense of which of the dozens of competitors the My Yahoo! team should examine seriously. These data served well to help the team understand the specific product features they should concentrate on improving.

The design team then presented several of the blue sky conceptual designs to the product managers and group directors. Product managers and group directors worked with designers to create new concepts for generating revenue, such as customized content or branded content, in a departure from traditional display advertising. Working with product managers and based on data from marketing and user research, the design team selected designs to concentrate on further, eliminating several earlier design alternatives. A number of feature requests also came from the My Yahoo! team at large, including software engineers, product managers, designers, and quality assurance testers. The team tried a variety of competitors' personalized page products to gain experience with both good and bad features in these products.

Using Prototyping in Product Design

Following the conceptual design phase, the design team began to concentrate on the approved core design and specific product features. Although the team used a variety of tools and methods to document information architecture, interaction design, and visual design, perhaps most noteworthy is how the team made use of extensive prototyping to communicate ideas. The team did a great deal of exploration with animation and used high-fidelity prototypes to demonstrate animation within a My Yahoo! page. Some concepts such as exposing page navigation and innovative ways of displaying content were shown using click-through wireframes.

Within the human-computer interaction (HCI) community, there is a widespread notion that prototyping is expensive in terms of development time and resources and that prototypes do not accurately gauge user needs.[3] The My Yahoo! team addressed development time and resource issues by using ready-made code libraries to develop prototypes. The team targeted specific types of prototypes to product managers, engineers, and users to get a broad understanding of the user experience.

By using the Yahoo! User Interface (YUI) JavaScript libraries,[4] the design team could rapidly prototype a design in a matter of hours. The YUI libraries offer a variety of tools to handle animation, JavaScript events, and application state. The simple, but powerful APIs allowed the design team to concentrate on refining a design instead of spending time focused on the details of technical implementation. In many cases, the team created working prototypes within a matter of hours after discussing ideas based on wireframes.

The team used three types of prototypes throughout the design process:

● Proof-of-concept prototypes

● Feature-specific prototypes

● Comprehensive prototypes

Proof-of-Concept Prototypes

Proof-of-concept prototypes are used as tools for exploring a generalized idea. Dynamic web pages enable a wide variety of page interaction and animated behaviors. Proof-of-concept prototypes are useful for exploring what is possible with dynamic web pages. For example, a designer or product manager may question if a particular type of animation is appropriate, what a pop-up's timing should be, how layout should behave at varying screen resolutions, or how a carousal widget's interaction should be implemented. These questions do not necessarily deal with the in-depth details of a product feature, but instead are focused on issues of product behavior that broadly relate to the product as a whole. Proof-of-concept prototypes are explorative prototypes created by both frontend engineers and designers that help drive design decisions about features. Such prototypes can show how a page behaves when content is added, deleted, or changed. These prototypes demonstrate components of more complex page interactions at a more atomic level.

In the initial stages of product development, the team used several proof-of-concept prototypes in conjunction with static visual design mock-ups and wireframes to convey ideas. The prototypes created tended to be lightweight—built in a matter of hours and with limited functionality. These lightweight proof-of-concept prototypes demonstrated simple tasks like drag and drop and animation sequences.

Feature-Specific Prototypes

Feature-specific prototypes are used to convey a feature's design and behavior. Several months into product development, product managers and the frontend engineering team began to ask detailed questions about interaction sequences and product behavior. Static visual design, wireframes, and proof-of-concept prototypes did not adequately describe how the product should be built. The feature-specific prototyping began with in-depth discussions about a product feature with a product manager. The feature-specific prototypes built were used to explore directions in product interaction and then used as interaction specifications. Once interaction was defined in a feature-specific prototype, a visual designer created a final, polished static visual design for the frontend engineering team to complement the feature-specific prototype. Feature-specific prototypes were used to demonstrate inline page customization options, modifications to a module on a page, or page navigation. Each of these feature-specific prototypes was guided by a use case, in other words, a scenario of how the feature would be used, to define a specific workflow.

The My Yahoo! team created several feature-specific prototypes to show how the RSS reader worked, how users could add personalized pages, or how they could change page themes. Yet problems surfaced when user testing feature-specific prototypes, as users occasionally tried to perform an action with the prototype that was not implemented. During the My Yahoo! rolling studies, when such cases occurred, the researcher told the user the feature was not implemented and directed him or her to another prototype with the feature implemented.

Comprehensive Prototype

User testing a series of feature-specific prototypes can be a disorienting experience for test subjects because users have to jump among prototypes. For this reason, the team began to use a comprehensive prototype after completing the design of the major product features. The comprehensive prototype bundled all of the feature-specific prototypes together into a single prototype. This gave test subjects a seamless experience in user testing. Test subjects were asked to do a variety of tasks spanning several product features, without having any artificial limitations placed on them by the researcher.

Using a comprehensive prototype also simplified testing by allowing "Wizard of Oz" tests. Prior to user testing, the researcher asked the user about his or her interests and web-use habits, simulating data collected from personalization algorithms and usage data. Researchers were then able to configure the prototype quickly before user testing in the lab to simulate what a personalization algorithm would display. The personalization features of My Yahoo!, used by several modules in the product, were tested before personalization algorithms had been fully implemented in the live product. The comprehensive prototype mimicked personalization algorithms by demonstrating to the user how My Yahoo! selected content based on the user's location and Yahoo! usage habits. This ability to modify personalized data in the comprehensive prototype gave the researcher more relevant and compelling data about user testing.

While effective in user testing, as feature-upon-feature was added, eventually the comprehensive prototype became bloated. Making a change to the behavior of one feature in the prototype broke other features. The complexity of the prototype began to approach that of the live product, making debugging the prototype laborious. Thankfully, in the final stages of product development, as My Yahoo! entered alpha and beta releases, the live product began to serve in the role formerly taken by the comprehensive prototype. Designers, engineers, and product managers began to use the live product to communicate ideas about product behavior. The team began to use feature-specific prototypes and static mock-ups to communicate refinements in visual and interaction design.

The comprehensive prototype built by the My Yahoo! design team slowly fell out of use as the live product incorporated features formerly only demonstrated in the prototype. The cost of adding features to the prototype increased as its complexity increased. In contrast, the cost of refining the product's design decreased as it matured. Once the product reached a mature state, the amount of time it took to modify the product was minimal and prototyping became redundant in describing behavior and interaction.

One of the risks of using high-fidelity prototyping is that stakeholders are susceptible to thinking of a high-fidelity prototype as the final product. The comprehensive prototype built for My Yahoo! had many of the features and functionality desired for the final product. To clearly distinguish the actual product from a prototype, the My Yahoo! team designated prototyping to the design team and production software to the engineering team. The design team owned conceptual designs, such as the comprehensive prototype. The code base of the comprehensive prototype was kept separate and distinct from production code. Certain prototype coding techniques were not to be used in production software without discussion with the engineering team. The design team owned the conceptual product and its code, and the engineering team owned the final product and its respective code. Product managers understood this distinction, and this helped keep prototypes from being confused as production code products ready to be released to the public. This also helped separate conceptual ideas to be tested from features to be implemented in the final product. With this understanding of the separate goals of the prototype versus the goals of the final product, the design team could implement conceptual features quickly in prototypes for user testing, and software development engineers did not have the burden of implementing conceptual features that might be taken out of a product and could, instead, concentrate on optimizing the performance of the final product with a well-defined feature set.

Communicating with Prototyping

In the design team's design process, prototypes became more effective in explaining use cases to other team members than *product requirement documents (PRDs)*, which are verbose documents with a litany of specifications. Use cases could be explained quickly through demonstrations and granular features understood simply by looking at a prototype instead of going through the tedious process of combing through a PRD. Prototypes also became effective in helping sell designs to stakeholders who made final decisions about a product's direction. Often, a working prototype described a product feature in terms that were impossible with language. In a number of cases, directors, product managers, and engineers changed their minds about the usefulness of a feature and reassessed its feasibility of implementation after seeing a prototype. Figure 8-2 shows prototypes of several content modules. For example, as My Yahoo!'s inline personalization feature neared completion,

FIGURE 8-2 The My Yahoo! design team prototyped several content modules to demonstrate functionality to stakeholders before having them user tested in a lab environment.

the design team showed several static mockups proposing dramatic changes in design to improve usability. The engineering team initially objected to the changes. The design team quickly built an inline personalization prototype and conducted user testing on it in a series of rapid rolling studies. With overwhelmingly positive user data from rolling studies and a clear representation of product interaction demonstrated in the prototype, product management and the engineering team decided to adopt the new inline personalization model even though it would delay the product's release.

The design team used prototypes as artifacts to help facilitate discussion. This simplified discussing product design issues with respect to visual design, interaction design, and frontend engineering implementation. Designers addressed specific issues raised by engineers more thoroughly. For example, My Yahoo! designers advocated using extensive animation in the product, whereas engineers wanted to drop most animation due to product performance issues and ambiguous state conditions. Prototypes showed when animation could be useful or superfluous, and helped designers and engineers reach consensus before animation was implemented in the live product.

Agile software development uses short time frames, usually spanning two weeks or so, to make quick, iterative, incremental changes and updates to software. Using such methods, software development teams can set short-term goals that can be assessed after an agile cycle is complete, rather than making the assessment over a longer timeframe, where there is greater likelihood that milestones, objectives, and requirements may change. The engineering team used agile software engineering methods. Prototyping fit well in the agile two-week cycles. The My Yahoo! team's frontend engineers expressed great appreciation when interaction and visual design were expressed explicitly in a prototype. It greatly simplified the difficulty of understanding how a feature should be implemented during short development cycles.

The My Yahoo! team also worked with external contractors at several points in the project when the workload became too heavy for the design team. Prototypes helped bring contractors up-to-date with the product when functionality could not be demonstrated directly in the live product or by reading a PRD. My Yahoo!'s interaction designers created highly detailed PRDs specifying interaction detail at length, but product managers commonly referred to prototypes to demonstrate product behavior and discuss refinements with designers and other stakeholders. Detailed specification documents became less useful when comprehensive high-fidelity prototypes existed. This was particularly true when illustrating use cases with respect to their interaction and visual design. However, in some cases, such as where content should be accessed from and when documenting many *edge-case uses* of the product—software usage scenarios that are possible, but are less likely to occur in everyday use— PRDs were more comprehensive and helpful.

The team did not find prototypes advantageous in all circumstances. The design team found prototyping to be more time consuming in simple cases where changes in visual design or simple interaction were needed. Static mock-ups or short product requirement documents were generally faster to produce and just as expressive as a prototype. In the final stages of My Yahoo! product development, product managers would frequently ask for minor tweaks in color or content module layout. For those tasks, the designer only needed to give a product manager and an engineer a static mock-up.

Final Thoughts

The My Yahoo! team redesigned the site using a design process that made extensive use of three types of prototyping. The team found that prototypes better expressed and more accurately documented the behavior and interaction of dynamic user interfaces than static mock-ups. By matching the fidelity of prototypes to the demands of engineers and product managers, designers used prototyping as a tool to facilitate communication among team members. This served not only to enhance the design process and make user testing easier, but also to help reach consensus among team members in design, engineering, and product management.

The redesign of My Yahoo! served to reinvigorate the product by increasing user engagement. The use of prototypes challenged standard product management and business practices, such as building a product from product requirements documents (PRDs), providing a mechanism to more quickly and efficiently disseminate product requirements in a clear and comprehensive fashion. Product managers and software engineers responded positively to prototyping and, in many cases, preferred its use to standard practices. By using prototyping, product development cycles could be completed more quickly thanks to a better understanding of the product's requirements. Prototyping also enabled product features to be user tested quickly, prior to the actual product's release. Although prototyping is sometimes considered time consuming, utilizing it strategically can help save a great deal of time elsewhere in product development and allow a team to iterate quickly through ideas without having to go through a full-fledged product lifecycle. Teams can then learn quickly from their mistakes and ultimately create better products that users will find more satisfying and enjoyable.

Summary

- **What is the business context (e.g., product, customers)?**
  My Yahoo! is a consumer-oriented product that helps people discover and organize information from the Web through a personalized home page. Yahoo! generates revenue from the product through advertising on the personalized home page.

- **Which (business) problems did you address with your UX practice?**
  My Yahoo! had become outdated compared to its competitors both in terms of the design and the underlying technology. The redesign of the product aimed to make the product cutting-edge, more usable, more attractive, and faster, and to improve the underlying code. Through these changes, the team hoped to change perceptions of the product and increase the user base.

- **What were constraints and prerequisites?**
  Constraints affecting the redesign of My Yahoo! included dealing with a code base that limited the types of technologies that could be used to build the product, upgrading existing users and catering to their needs, mitigating product upgrade migration issues in terms of usability, and communicating design ideas effectively to all involved stakeholders.

- **In which development context did you apply your UX practice?**
  The My Yahoo! team used agile development methods in the production of software. The design team applied agile methods when coordinating with the development team's agile lifecycle.

- **What compelling events allowed you to apply your UX practice successfully?**
  Highly positive feedback from key stakeholders and from customers in user research demonstrated enthusiasm for the product. Upon the product's release, an increase in product usage showed users were spending more time with the product, allowing the company to generate more revenue from My Yahoo!

- **What was the achieved product and business impact?**
  The prototyping techniques used in product development helped define new, more effective ways to communicate design ideas to all involved stakeholders. These techniques are now applied in other Yahoo! products. End-users benefited from these prototyping techniques by having a better-designed product released in a shorter time frame than in the past. From a product standpoint, the redesign led to increased

advertising revenue, more positive feedback from users, and higher user engagement reflected by measurable increases in time users spent on My Yahoo!

● **How did you do apply the UX practice?**
User research helped inform what parts of designs and prototypes could be refined. User experience techniques such as rapid prototyping, iterative sketching, and ideation helped create a better product more aligned with stakeholder and user needs.

● **What recommendations do you have for our readers?**
Often businesses have particular processes they use to create a product and this affects how design can be practiced and what design methods can be conducted. However, by demonstrating business value through some of the prototyping techniques described in this chapter, the My Yahoo! design team showed Yahoo! at large how to better design a product by not necessarily following standard business practices. Prototyping helped expedite communication, thereby decreasing the amount of time it took to design and develop a product. Strategic types of prototyping can help better inform stakeholders about design constraints and encourage the exploration of many ideas quickly. The cost of making design mistakes in prototypes is much less than the cost of making them in a final product, so designers should encourage stakeholders to use prototyping to experiment when design or usability questions are looming. Prototyping is not always the right solution, but it can be a highly effective way to communicate ideas quickly, particularly because other methods of communicating ideas are often interpreted differently by all involved stakeholders.

Endnotes

1. See Jessie James Garrett, Ajax: A New Approach to Web Applications, February 18, 2005, www.adaptivepath.com/publications/essays/archives/000385.php.

2. *Likert scales* capture users' feelings by enabling them to specify their level of agreement or disagreement on a symmetric agree-disagree scale.

3. W. Jones, J. Spool, J. Grudin, V. Bellotti, and M. Czerwinski, Interactive Session: "Get real!": What's Wrong with HCI Prototyping and How Can We Fix It? *CHI '07 Extended Abstracts on Human Factors in Computing Systems,* CHI '07, San Jose, California (April 2007) ACM, 1913–1916.

4. Yahoo! UI Library (YUI), developer.Yahoo!com/yui/.

Chapter 9

User Interface Patterns:
Sustainable User Orientation

By Sonja Sander and Anke Richter

Siemens AG

When money is tight and resources are limited, efficiency—without compromising product quality—becomes an increasingly important factor in software development. Today, user expectations go beyond an optimized user interface for a single product or application. Users expect software to follow common User Experience principles, especially if the software is from one provider and if it is applied in one working context.

The practice of user interface (UI) patterns enables sustainable user orientation in software products. With the help of UI patterns, the proven principles from one product are extracted and systematically reused in other products.

The UI pattern practice at Siemens AG was started in 2000 in the Corporate Technology and Research Center. Further development lead to an in-house UI pattern library with up to 350 patterns containing UI mechanisms for software used in healthcare, industry, and energy domains for diverse target platforms such as desktop and web applications or mobile devices. This chapter will describe how the outcome was successfully transferred to the Energy Automation business unit in 2008 and the unit's specific challenges.

The challenge for User Experience design at Siemens Energy Automation is not to optimize one single application, but to improve the User Experience of the whole product family without causing extra effort for development. As different technologies are employed, Siemens Energy Automation needs a means for communicating efficiently common UI principles, thus reducing inconsistencies between applications. An additional challenge exists because Siemens Energy Automation employs only a few usability engineers, and they cannot design and specify every single screen that is needed.

Key questions concerning User Experience at Siemens Energy Automation include:

- How can UI quality be increased?

- How can development efforts be reduced?

- How can developers be enabled to build usable applications?

The following chapter outlines how UI patterns can be applied for achieving consistent User Experience principles and a common look between applications at Siemens Energy Automation. Additionally, the authors will discuss how UI patterns can increase efficiency in software development by describing the best practices of Siemens Energy Automation. Last but not least, the authors will show how they transferred their usability knowledge within Siemens Energy Automation by establishing a UI pattern library.

Business Context

Siemens Energy Automation is an internationally operating company that addresses an organizational market with specific challenges concerning the types of products offered and customers.

Products

The Siemens Energy Sector helps the world's economies achieve sustainable development thanks to a reliable, economical, and environmentally compatible power supply. The Sector develops efficient technology along the entire chain of energy conversion—from the extraction of oil and gas via power generation to the transmission and distribution of electrical energy (Figure 9-1). Energy Automation develops medium-voltage equipment and systems as well as solutions for energy automation protection and control. The primary goal of these products is to provide reliable and economical electricity supply to consumers.

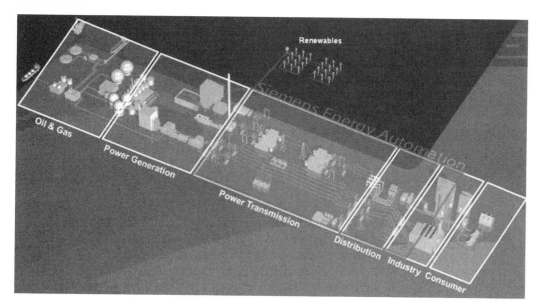

Hardware devices such as protection devices and power quality devices play an important role in Siemens Energy Automation business. Additionally, various supporting software applications are offered for engineering and monitoring. Software is an integral component of Siemens Energy Automation business.

The product range covers software for small displays on protection devices, conventional monitors, and large display systems such as in

FIGURE 9-1 Siemens Energy develops products, systems, and solutions across the complete energy chain. Energy automation products mainly support power transmission and distribution.

control rooms (Figure 9-2). Technical prerequisites are very different. Despite this—one common look and feel for all user interfaces is an important aspect of the Siemens product strategy for communicating a clear brand message.

FIGURE 9-2 User interface design and usability for a wide variety of products and solutions at Siemens Energy Automation—from protection devices to control center solutions

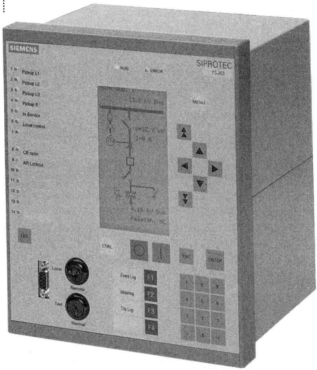

Customers

Siemens Energy Automation customers are power supply companies, public utilities, power plant operators, and industry. The business context requires highly complex applications for different user groups (such as operators, engineers, and commissioners) and working conditions (such as control center, back office, and field work). Users have to cope with highly critical tasks concerning the safety of workers and security of energy supplies.

Market

Siemens Energy Automation offers products, systems, and solutions across the complete energy chain, providing many options to evolve, modernize, expand, and build energy networks and generate revenue in different ways. The business covers the supply side and the markets for equipment and components servicing these industries. Siemens Energy Automation offers its products to organizational markets. In contrast to consumer markets, organizational buyers consist of companies or governments. Although the number of potential customers is limited, the purchase orders are large. Customers make purchase decisions based on technical specifications and expect the products to have a high level of quality; this includes reliability and usability.

Because product lifecycles at the energy supplier side are long—typically 10 to 30 years—an important part of revenue comes from extensions of installed systems. All aspects of energy automation and system integration, even in a multivendor environment, will be handled by Siemens Energy Automation. Such projects need specific customization to modernize and expand systems for many different elements in the Energy Automation portfolio. This type of business, the so-called project business (e.g., power control centers and turnkey projects), is usually very customer-specific, whereas Energy Automation's product business is off the shelf, where large quantities can be sold (e.g., protection devices, including supporting software solutions). Usability activities at Energy Automation have to handle these different preconditions.

Organization

The Siemens Energy Sector currently deploys more than 85,000 employees worldwide. With six divisions, the Energy Sector covers a broad range of solutions, from power generation to distribution and transmission. Energy Automation is a business unit within the Power Distribution division, but it also serves other divisions of the Energy Sector such as Power Transmission.

The organization spends more than 1,200 person-years in research and development per year; of those, nearly half are spent in software development. Software development is an integral part of the Energy Automation organization at Siemens. About 800 software developers work in Germany and other European countries, North America, South America, India, and China. As part of the software development group, three strategic usability experts take measures to deploy usability in the software development process and train developers to increase their usability expertise with the help of user interface (UI) patterns. Additionally, a usability network of 32 representatives of all job roles, products, and locations has been created. Network members meet at regular intervals with the goal of enhancing user-friendliness and easy-to-use functionality across products and projects.

Business Problem

An internal, unpublished survey conducted at Energy Automation in 2009 showed that of the ten most important aspects of customer loyalty, three usability-related issues were ranked in the top four. Easy-to-use is no longer a "nice to have" requirement but a key success factor for Siemens' customers. This is why management takes measures to implement usability within the development process.

The fact that there are only 3 usability engineers compared to 800 developers is a huge challenge. Employing more usability engineers would increase costs. Furthermore, hiring enough qualified usability specialists would be difficult. Therefore, developers have to take over more responsibility for usability. The three usability engineers focus on transferring usability know-how to developers. Introducing UI patterns and building a UI pattern library for developers are promising approaches to improving the usability of products without having a lot of experienced usability personnel.

Today operators monitoring the power grid are under extreme pressure. This pressure is caused by several circumstances: Operators have to cope with the ever-increasing complexity of the electrical system and its operating software. In the last few years especially, the increase in renewable energy sources and feeding them into the grid has added to this complexity. Particularly in critical situations, operators have fewer possibilities for redirecting loads because electrical lines already run close to their capacity limits.

A possible outcome of poor user guidance occurred on November 4, 2006, when the electrical grid collapsed in various parts of Europe. Fifteen million people were without power for almost two hours. An analysis revealed human failure as the cause. Operators working under deadline pressure at a power system control center in northern Germany failed to use all the available technical tools for a comprehensive assessment of the situation (E.ON, 2006).

In most cases, operators use multiple applications for different tasks. For example, it is annoying for users to deal with three different Print dialogs. Different representations of functionality lead to errors and increased time needed to accomplish tasks. A consistent design among applications used at one workplace enables high usability. The definition of a common look and feel facilitates consistency, reducing training costs and preventing operating errors. Additionally less-experienced users can catch on more easily when the operating philosophy for all applications follows the same principles. Users who have applied Siemens Energy software before are familiar with its operating principles and will benefit from this experience when they use other Siemens Energy applications. Working with a common look and feel, tasks can be fulfilled faster and people in charge can make the correct decisions more quickly in an emergency.

Besides improved system usage, a usability methodology and a common look and feel help to reduce software development costs. Budget cuts and limited resources put additional pressure on software development, increasing the need for greater internal efficiency and sustainable outcomes at Siemens Energy Automation. The authors will demonstrate that a usability methodology and UI patterns are powerful tools for optimizing development efforts while improving software usability by establishing sustainable User Experience practices such as the deployment of a domain-specific UI pattern library. Especially in organizations such as Siemens Energy Automation, where development tasks are split among multiple continents and several software development projects operate in parallel, UI patterns enable a consistent branding message by supporting employees to share their knowledge with less effort.

Constraints and Prerequisites

The following constraints had to be faced to establish a UI pattern practice at Siemens Energy Automation:

- A variety of products and applications belonged to different product families within the organization. Different groups and stakeholders were in charge of the development of these products.

- Product development was under extreme time pressure. The description of UI patterns and their review took additional effort because all development stakeholders need to participate.

- Because of long product cycles, a consistent look and feel across products could only be achieved over the long term. Products at Siemens Energy Automation had a history that had to be taken into account in order to meet the requirements of existing customers.

- Only a few usability experts worked in the organization and they could not design and specify every single screen.

- The budget was tight. There was not enough money to describe all 142 identified patterns either simultaneously or in quick succession. This was critical since the acceptance and the usage of a repository depends heavily on the fact that the content is exhaustive, reliable, and up to date.

At Siemens Energy Automation, usability is a task for the whole organization, not just single usability experts. As the organization owns a large number of highly complex applications, its aim is to enable developers to perform basic usability work such as detailing UI concepts. The goal is to reduce the amount of usability defects identified during system tests. By using UI patterns, developers are empowered to elaborate detailed UIs following usability rules. In general, usability engineers act as mentors and strategists, providing guidance to developers and ensuring concept quality through continuous reviews and inspections. As developers are empowered to elaborate detailed UIs based on the UI pattern library, the need to rework concepts and correct usability defects is reduced.

Management support and the utilization of an existing UI pattern library as input facilitated the implementation of pattern practices. The following prerequisites provided a good starting position:

- Siemens Energy Automation already had an established and well-organized development process.

- An integrated usability process had been continually built up and applied within major software development projects over the last five years, with the involvement of all internal stakeholders such as the project manager, product manager, developers, and architects.

- Management had always promoted and supported usability. A common branding message and high usability was seen as an important requirement within Siemens Energy Automation. Management had already introduced initial measures, such as the development of an Icon Database, Style Guides describing a common look, and the programming of reuse components. Management realized that the present development practice did not encompass the integrated approach required to achieve a sustainable user orientation, however.

● The UI pattern approach had been applied by the authors over many years working in the User Interface Design department of Siemens Corporate Technology and Research. We could employ our experience and knowledge of five years of pattern practice for building an Energy Automation–specific UI pattern library. Management was convinced by the fact that the effort could be reduced to a minimum by reusing existing UI pattern descriptions. The description effort was limited to domain-specific adoptions and extensions.

Development Context

Software development at Siemens Energy Automation faces several challenges. First, Energy Automation has a large number and diversity of software products, including a variety of different technologies (web applications, MFC, .NET, Qt). This mix makes it difficult to transfer knowledge between applications and project teams. Additionally, software developers work in several globally distributed development locations in the U.S., Europe, China, and India. This setup requires efficient tools to prevent misunderstanding and double efforts. Therefore, Siemens Energy Automation set up a strict software development process for facilitating efficient collaboration. The process describes the different phases in product management (definition of requirements) and software development (analysis of requirements from a development point of view, implementation, validation). The process covers the assigned tasks for the involved stakeholders from product management, project management, development, and system testing. Clearly defined milestones and deliverables ensure a common language within the organization. The process was originally based on a typical waterfall model concerning the sequential processing of the development phases. However, management launched activities to include agile elements such as sprints to increase flexibility in the process.

Whether software development is driven agile or waterfall, in both cases all involved stakeholders from architecture, development, system testing, and product management need to come to a common understanding of the future system model and customer needs. To reach this common understanding, the usability engineers integrated usability methods in the Siemens' specific development process. The key success factor at Siemens Energy is to involve all relevant stakeholders in usability activities from the beginning to ensure sustainable commitment for usability throughout the development process. Figure 9-3 illustrates the integration of usability activities in the different development phases.

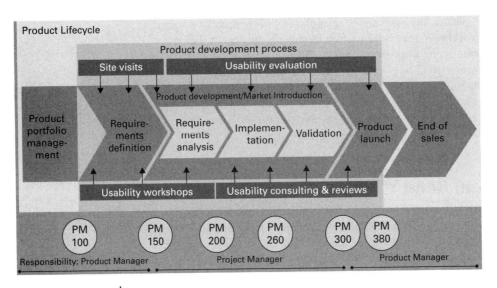

Siemens Energy Automation installed four major usability activities, which are shown in Figure 9-4. The core parts are usability workshops for accumulating the available knowledge about users and their tasks and creating a usage model of the future system. Site visits and usability evaluations take place in between usability workshops. Site visits are performed during early development phases for increasing knowledge of the core users and their tasks. Evaluations are done once the workshop team has created the first UI sketches. The results of site visits and evaluations are fed directly into the next usability workshop for completing the system model and resolving defects. After the workshop phase, generally usability consulting and reviews take place. Again, in this late phase, evaluations are applied for identifying usability defects.

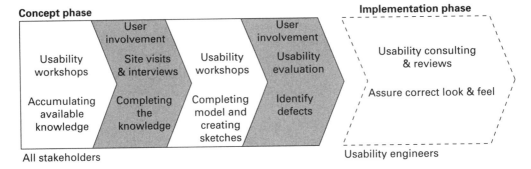

- **Usability workshops** The goal of the workshops is to reach a common understanding of the requirements and software model for avoiding misunderstanding among stakeholders and reducing the time needed to analyze requirements. The *implicit* (experience, domain expertise) and *explicit* (available documentation, competitor products) knowledge of the user and customer requirements are needed for the workshop. Therefore, all relevant internal stakeholders participate, including domain experts, product managers, project managers, developers, architects, usability experts, and testers. The participation of all stakeholders ensures that all existing knowledge in the organization is accessible. Additionally, the presence of developers, architects, and testers facilitates the spread of knowledge as these stakeholders gain a deeper understanding of users and their tasks. Usability engineers drive the workshops to ensure efficient collaboration and a high-quality outcome. Workshops follow the Usage Centered Design process developed by Constantine and Lockwood (1999). The results of the workshop are the creation of the system model of the future software and development of the high-level UI design in terms of sketches of the future user interface. Workshop output is integrated into the requirement specification (description of user tasks and requirements) during the requirements definition phase and the development specification (UI sketches) during the requirements analysis phase; see Figure 9-5. Initially, workshops are set up for three sessions for three full days. However, the number of workshop days depends on the software's complexity. Although workshops are costly in terms of money and time, they have become an established and well-accepted practice in the organization.

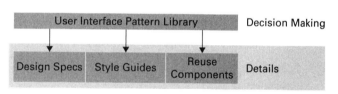

FIGURE 9-5 The UI pattern library as a central access point to existing documentation

- **Site visits and user interviews** The only way to identify the genuine needs of users is to visit real users and watch them work. Therefore, the usability workshop team, including all stakeholders, visits actual users at their workplace to learn *what* users need and *why* they need it. Site visits and interviews serve as a means for closing any gaps identified in the usability workshop. In preparation, the workshop team creates a questionnaire consisting of all open questions that the team could not answer. Additionally, the team decides on which user roles are the focus for the visit. Preparation ensures that the limited time spent at the customers' site is used efficiently. As a result, the team gains invaluable insights into customer needs. Besides this implicit outcome, open questions are closed and the elaborated system model is verified and completed. All insights are fed directly into the system model during the next usability workshop. Again, it is crucial that all stakeholders join the site visit to ensure that results are transferred immediately within the team. The involvement of stakeholders also reduces the need for long reports and, therefore, speeds up usability work.

● **Usability evaluation** Nothing is perfect; usability evaluations allow the team to identify any deficiencies early in the process. Evaluations at Siemens Energy Automation follow the Collaborative Usability Inspection methodology developed by Constantine and Lockwood (1999). The session includes typical users, a typical set of tasks, and a prototype. The user is asked to perform the tasks with the prototype, expressing loudly any concerns, expectations, and thoughts, while stakeholders listen and identify defects as well. In comparison to conventional usability tests, usability inspections involve *all* stakeholders (architects, developers, product managers, project managers, testers, usability experts) in the inspection process. The effort needed to conduct the evaluation is reduced as there is no need for lengthy documentation. The results are immediately visible to all stakeholders. The goal of the inspection is to identify as many deficiencies as possible. Based on the list of all found defects, the project team decides, depending on defect severity, which defect will be solved, when it will be solved, and who will solve it. Inspections are done at early stages in the development process and during several iterations. The first inspection may use a simple paper prototype, others clickable mock-ups in PowerPoint or ready-to-be-implemented software versions. Regardless, the earlier in the process inspections occur, the fewer costs arise later for correcting defects.

● **Usability consulting and reviews** These are ongoing activities conducted by usability engineers for ensuring that the workshop result is implemented correctly. Additionally, the development results are checked for Style Guide compliance.

It is important to note that all usability activities are integrated parts of the software development process. Instead of producing separate usability documents, the outcomes are included in established process documents. For example, the requirements specification describes the basic system model; the development specification specifies the basic UI structure and interaction concepts.

How does this relate to UI patterns? The described development process and usability methodology provide the context for applying UI patterns.

Previously, the definition of UI concepts was focused on individual products. Usability experts had the task of synchronizing concepts, but did not have a means for fulfilling this task. The diversity of technical platforms additionally hindered reuse of available concepts. Consequently, the use of concepts varied among and within products, resulting in a high level of UI inconsistency. The size of the development department and the geographical segregation of staff formed additional obstacles. By introducing UI patterns, usability experts received a tool for analyzing and aligning UI concepts. The creation of new UI sketches was streamlined, leading to a higher level of consistency among products. Additionally, UI pattern descriptions are now accessible to all developers worldwide and serve as references for implementation.

The next section will provide insight into how we built the UI pattern library for Siemens Energy Automation.

Building the UI Pattern Library

The authors suggested supplementing existing processes with UI patterns for tapping the full potential for the organization concerning reuse. As the diversity of technologies prevents reuse of code between projects, the technology-free description of UI patterns allows specifying standards and, therefore, enables consistent interaction mechanisms across product families and projects.

Ensuring Commitment

Before we started working on the contents of the library, we focused on convincing management and relevant stakeholders of the benefits that UI patterns would bring to the organization. We demonstrated how patterns could increase internal reuse and, therefore, reduce development effort. Another compelling argument was that UI patterns could be used to spread usability knowledge throughout the organization, enabling developers to create higher quality UIs and reducing the number of usability defects.

We introduced the idea of UI patterns by demonstrating the UI pattern library we created for Siemens Corporate Technology and Research in 2003 as a best practice and discussed the achieved benefits in terms of higher UI quality and reduced efforts needed to create UI concepts. Additionally, we met with architecture and UI development to achieve more commitment within the organization. We used the meetings to define goals for using UI patterns. For example, UI patterns should support the conceptual phase in usability workshops and the development of reuse components. Additionally, we identified the scope and relevant contents for the UI pattern library (e.g., which products should be included). Finally, we discussed the integration of UI patterns in existing processes and documents. We agreed that the UI pattern library should be a comprehensive repository of all UI principles and controls that are relevant for Siemens Energy Automation software. In contrast to existing Style Guides and product-specific UI specifications, the UI pattern library should be a central access point to concepts, allowing usability engineers and developers to gain an overview of available solutions and linking them to existing detailed documentation such as color definitions in a Style Guide or Reuse Components containing code (Figure 9-5). The engagement and commitment of internal stakeholders has proven its worth as we gained important support in terms of budget and time.

Defining the Library Structure

The next step consisted of setting up the library. Based on our experience with UI patterns, we defined an initial structure for the UI pattern library based on generic user intentions. The concept of employing generic user intentions was developed by the authors in 2003 and proved to be valuable for concept work at Siemens. The advantage of structuring UI patterns by user intentions is that library users gain access to a fast overview of available solutions for a specific problem. In contrast, an alphabetic sorting of patterns does not provide any guidance and information on how patterns are related. The library user might find a pattern quickly but could not ensure that she was selecting the most appropriate pattern for her UI problem. Based on our experience over the past years, comprehensive groupings of patterns by generic user intentions (viewing, changing view, editing, selecting, doing/executing) provide a clear, flexible structure for assigning any UI principle.

Subintentions (e.g., attracting attention) supplement the structure by providing fast access to the pattern of interest. One subintention contains all available—competing—patterns for a specific problem. Based on "use when" criteria, the library user can identify the appropriate pattern for a specific conceptual problem (see Figure 9-6). For example, when the library user is looking for an UI pattern that gives the software user feedback, she would navigate to "Viewing," as this intention represents what the software user would do in a generic sense, and then she would verify based on the listed "use when" criteria what subintention relates best to her problem. Once she decides on a subintention, e.g., "Attracting Attention," the library would list all available patterns such as Alarm Summary or Thermometer, including their specific "use when" criteria. Additionally, "do not use when" criteria prevent common mistakes in pattern usage by linking to alternative solutions. Therefore, the user intention structure supports library users in identifying the appropriate UI pattern.

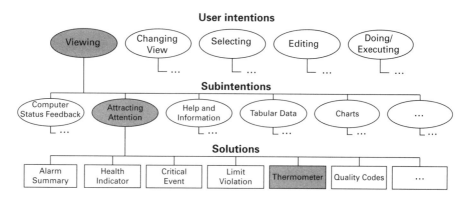

FIGURE 9-6 Structure of the UI pattern library

The final structure of user intentions and UI patterns was evaluated in usability inspections with developers to ensure the UI pattern library had a high level of usability. Colleagues from development asked to automate the decision process for identifying the most suitable UI pattern for a specific situation. However, based on our experience, this process cannot be automated, as the library user needs a detailed understanding of the software context for assessing available patterns concerning their appropriateness. This detailed knowledge cannot be represented in general decision criteria. However, as user intentions have a high degree of abstraction, UI patterns can be transferred between software products having a specific application context (e.g., control center or field work) and independently of the technical implementation.

The description of UI patterns follows a common format, which is based on the original pattern format of Christopher Alexander (1979). For achieving a high level of efficiency in pattern description and usage, we adjusted the format to the needs of Siemens Energy Automation by adding the following categories:

- Examples (screenshots of pattern implementations)

- Used in (lists all software applications that already use the pattern)

- Evaluation (outcomes of usability evaluation sessions concerning the pattern's usability)

- Owner (contact person in the organization responsible for the maintenance of a specific pattern), further information (includes links on detailed documentation available as Style Guides, Reuse Components, or Development Specifications for individual products)

- Maturity level (indicates how established the UI pattern is in the organization)

Table 9-1 shows the complete UI pattern description format.

UI Pattern Name	
Example	Screenshot of typical example
Link reuse component \<optional\>	Link to reuse component (code), if available
Definition	Description of the pattern—what is it and what function(s) does it serve
Use when	Description of usage
Do NOT use when	Not recommended usage (if there is an alternative solution it will be listed)
Wireframe	Style Guide compliant, positioning of elements
Solution specification	Short instruction on how to create the layout, what range of layout variation is acceptable, and what purposes the layout elements serve
Other examples	Screenshots of the pattern as used in projects or products
Used in	Projects or products that use the described solution
Evaluation	Outcomes of usability evaluation sessions concerning the pattern's usability
Checklist	Lists questions for verifying proper pattern usage
Extension \<optional\>	Short instruction about usage and example
Owner	Contact person
Further information	Links to more information (Development Specifications, Style Guides, Reuse Components)
Applicable for	Indicates in which basic conditions the UI pattern is applicable, e.g., web application (mouse, monitor), multimonitor, hardware devices (hardware keys, small monochrome display)
Maturity level	e.g., proven, new
Change history	Author name and date
Comments	Room for questions, additions, concerns (editable by all library users)

TABLE 9-1 Pattern Description Format

Identifying UI Patterns

For building the UI pattern library, we analyzed eleven major software products for Energy Automation, focusing on pattern usage as well as existing Style Guides and Reuse Components. As the number of examples was quite large, we clustered all patterns by user intentions for identifying patterns solving the same problem. Based on the grouping by user intentions, we were able to identify similar patterns (same UI principle for the same problem) and inconsistencies (the same underlying problem is solved by different UI principles). As a result, more than 200 UI concepts could be harmonized to 142 patterns. All identified inconsistencies were marked as "usability construction site" for defining a common, application-spanning UI principle. For example, we identified several navigation mechanisms on the UI. Based on the analysis output, we evaluated the found mechanisms and defined "use when" criteria for the individual navigation patterns (such as portal, tree, tabs, banner) based on their specific characteristics. Some mechanisms were evaluated as "nonsuitable" and excluded from usage. The analysis supported us in identifying inconsistencies in existing software and in initiating the needed changes in the involved applications for achieving a common look and feel across all Energy Automation products. Therefore, besides being the starting point for building the UI pattern library, the analysis output also gave valuable input toward future usability work. Additionally, we used the discovered inconsistencies to communicate the necessity of patterns and usability to management for assuring the necessary budget for future usability work.

The analysis of the major software products and associated documents provided us with a comprehensive overview of currently used UI concepts. The analysis output listed all identified patterns and related examples. For filling the UI pattern library initially, we prioritized the patterns together with internal stakeholders, focusing on their impact on the organization. Patterns having a high reuse potential within the organization (e.g., navigation, status display) were prioritized as more important than patterns solving a specific UI problem (e.g., alarm list).

The UI pattern library contains "simple" UI patterns like checkboxes or radio buttons as well as "complex" concepts, for example, for import and export of data, consisting of combinations of several simple patterns. Though complex patterns have increased benefits for consistency, simple patterns are needed because the requirements of multiple applications often differ in detail. For example, several applications deal with "analysis" at Siemens Energy Automation. However, the analysis tasks and requirements differ concerning needed information and urgency. For example, the analysis of a blackout requires immediate action while the analysis of power quality is done, in retrospect, at regular intervals. The availability of "simple" patterns allows the creation of UIs that support the specific requirements of the task. For identifying patterns, we weigh the advantages of complex, task-specific patterns and the flexibility of simple patterns that could act as building blocks for supporting specific tasks.

Describing UI Patterns

The pattern library contains UI patterns as textual descriptions including screenshots and sketches. The description informs the library user about available technical implementations for the pattern (reuse components). However, the description does not contain implemented code per se. The decision for extending existing platforms for supporting new UI patterns depends on the responsible architect's assessment.

Patterns were described by pattern experts like the coauthor from Siemens Corporate Technology and Research. As we benefited from colleagues' expertise with UI patterns, the effort needed to describe patterns was reduced to a minimum. (Depending on the pattern's complexity, we needed between 4 to 12 hours to add a new pattern to the library.) For maintaining internal support, we motivated colleagues from all development locations to become pattern owners. Pattern owners support the description of patterns by providing examples and verifying the pattern description in internal reviews. Currently, various internal roles such as developer, project manager, product manager, architect, or usability engineer act as pattern owner. Outcomes of usability evaluations are fed into the pattern description. This includes positive as well as negative results. The notification of evaluation outcomes facilitates the application and possible improvement or extension of the pattern.

Reviewing UI Patterns

Reviews follow a defined cycle for ensuring pattern description are of high quality. First, one of the usability engineers at Siemens Energy Automation previews the description. Based on comments, the pattern description is updated accordingly. Second, the reworked pattern is reviewed by a core team consisting of usability engineers, selected UI developers, and the pattern owner. The preview increases the efficiency of the review process as the core team receives review input that already meets high-quality standards. Review efforts depend on pattern complexity (5 minutes to 15 minutes). The total effort to describe and review patterns takes about 5 hours to 10 hours depending on pattern complexity. All pattern description activities are coordinated by Sonja within the Siemens Energy Automation organization.

Publishing UI Patterns

To ensure UI patterns are available for colleagues from all development locations worldwide, the UI pattern library uses wiki technology. The advantage of using a wiki is easy extensibility for new patterns and maintenance of existing patterns. The wiki language is straight-forward and easy-to-ease without any special skills. Additionally, the installation and maintenance of the wiki server is simple and does not require any licenses. The library is integrated in the development Intranet at Siemens Energy Automation and, therefore, accessible to Siemens Energy Automation employees without extra login or installation requirements. Meanwhile, the UI pattern library contains 55 descriptions of UI patterns. Figure 9-7 shows an example UI pattern in the Siemens Energy Automation library.

FIGURE 9-7 Example UI pattern

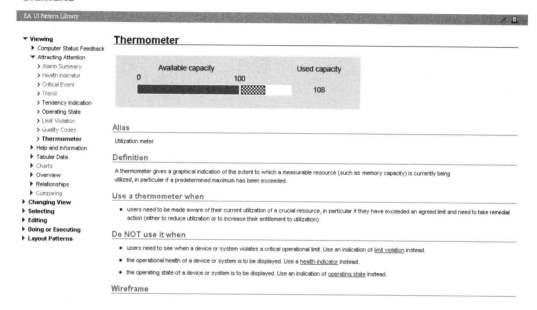

Using UI Patterns

UI patterns support the identification of appropriate mechanisms on the UI such as tab cards for structuring contents, especially when the conceptual model and visual design of the future software is specified. UI pattern activities at Siemens Energy Automation are aimed toward reducing efforts. Therefore, the UI pattern library and its usage have been integrated into existing organizational processes. The following sections outline how UI patterns are used in the software development process. As Figure 9-8 shows, UI patterns are mainly used in the requirements analysis phase for creating UI sketches and in the implementation phase as reference for developers. As the dashed lines indicate, new UI patterns can be added during both phases,

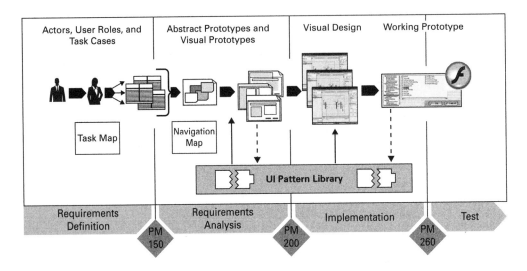

FIGURE 9-8 UI patterns as an integrated part of the usability process

if requirements cannot be fulfilled by available UI patterns from the library. The decision for adding new UI patterns to the library depends on the relevance of the pattern for other software products. When the expected level of reuse is high, the pattern is added to the library. Table 9-2 summarizes how UI patterns support development phases.

As mentioned previously, Siemens Energy Automation bases its usability activities on the Usage-Centered Design Process developed by Constantine and Lockwood (1999). The methodology provides a comprehensive means for supporting all development phases. The purpose of this chapter is to describe the basic principles of usage-centered design as it is practiced at Siemens Energy Automation. The authors do not want to preach this specific methodology as the one and only usability approach as there are many different approaches for achieving good usability results. However, we want to outline how UI patterns can be integrated into existing usability activities. Usage-centered design methodology has

Development Phase	Usability-specific Goals	Use of UI Patterns
Requirements definition	Ensure consistency among different applications	Reference for requirements
Requirements analysis	Create UI sketches (navigation and visual prototypes)	Support decision-making
Implementation	Implement UI sketches	Support detailed UI design Reference for developers

TABLE 9-2 Use of UI Patterns in the Different Development Phases

proven its worth for Siemens Energy Automation over the past years as the methodology is very comprehensive and easy to understand for internal stakeholders who do not have any usability expertise.

Requirements Definition

All usability activities at Siemens Energy Automation start with analyzing the actors and the tasks they need to perform with the future software. Referring back to Figure 9-8, *actors* are persons using the future software, for example, network operators. *User roles* describe the relationship between the software and the actor, for example, "monitoring energy network." The identification of actors and roles allows us to verify that the requirements are complete and enables us to decide on the essentials needed for the future system. *Task cases* are performed by the actor in roles. The task case models the "what" and "why" of the software use rather than the "how." Task cases are comparable to essential use cases as they focus on the essentials of the requirements. Each task case describes what the user wants to do in order to fulfill the task (*user intention*) and what the future software needs to do to support task completion (*system responsibility*). Task cases are abstract, simplified, and technology-free. The description allows the project team to focus on the essential user needs resulting from the task. The technical feasibility is examined in later steps for enabling innovative solutions. The knowledge of the actors and their tasks is the foundation for discussions related to the software requirements and functional scope. Product managers integrate this output in the requirement specification, which serves as input for architecture and software development.

Pattern Use: Requirements Definition

In this early phase, patterns are used as a reference for requirements. For example, if the task analysis reveals "import" as a task for the user, the requirements specification can link the functional "import" requirement with the existing import UI pattern for ensuring that the import functionality of the new application is in line with import mechanisms already implemented in other software. As mentioned previously, the diversity of technologies often prevents reusing the code for the implemented pattern. Therefore, UI patterns are an important tool for harmonizing UIs across multiple software products.

Requirements Analysis

Usability activities in this phase focus on building a model of the future software based on the knowledge of actors and tasks. For identifying a suitable software structure, the usage-centered design uses a *task map* consisting of all essential task cases. The task map clusters task cases into navigation contexts. The goal is to represent the user workflow adequately in the software for reducing navigation efforts and facilitating an easy orientation when using the software. Another tool, the *navigation map,* illustrates the navigation flow between the different navigation contexts identified on the task map.

Pattern Use: Defining Navigation

The UI pattern library supports the conversion of the navigation map into mechanisms on the future UI. The UI pattern library supports this step in listing several UI patterns for the user intention "changing view." The library user can pick the most suitable navigation pattern by reviewing the listed "use when" criteria for each pattern.

After the navigation map, the project team creates a sketch for each individual navigation context. Based on the task cases, the team examines what data (*system responsibility*) and actions (*user intentions*) are needed within the specific navigation context and how they are related to one another. As a result, an abstract prototype visualizes the basic structure of the future UI (Figure 9-9). *Abstract* means that the prototype does contain the pure information on data and actions; it does not show, however, the actual appearance or behavior of the UI. Abstract prototypes help to bridge the gap between task cases and visual design. They serve as a pre-stage for UI design. Based on the abstract prototypes, the future UI is defined and sketched on paper as a visual prototype (Figure 9-10). *Visual* prototypes transfer the abstract information on data and actions into actual UI principles such as drop-down boxes and buttons.

Pattern Use: Visual Prototyping—Drawing Sketches

UI patterns support creating visual prototypes (sketches). Visual prototyping requires a high degree of experience and knowledge of UI principles as well as creativity. The UI pattern library supports creating visual prototypes by giving an overview of available, already established UI principles. As the task cases contain a generic and solution-free description of user intentions (actions) and system responsibilities (data), the library user can map the concrete application context of the software. Because the UI pattern library uses user intentions as well for structuring UI patterns, the user intentions detailed in the concrete task case can be linked easily to existing UI patterns, which are mechanisms for representing the user intention on the UI. For identifying the appropriate pattern, the library user has to

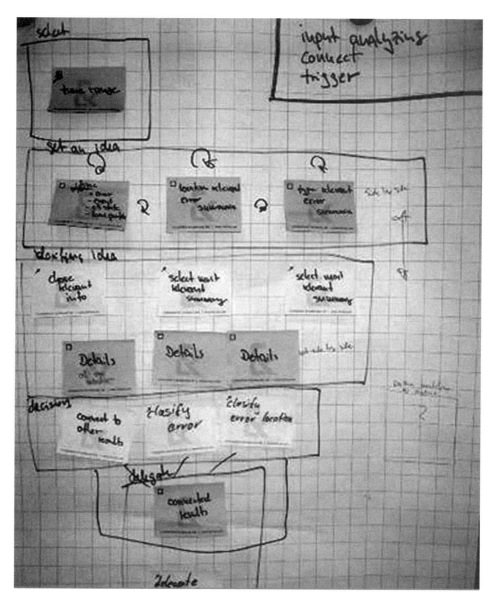

FIGURE 9-9 Abstract prototype

follow a three-step approach (Figure 9-11). First, he needs to determine the user intention based on the knowledge of the user task. Second, he needs to identify the subintention based on knowledge of the user task. Third, he needs to decide on a specific UI pattern based on the listed "use when" criteria. Figure 9-12 details the process of identifying the appropriate pattern for the task "setup software."

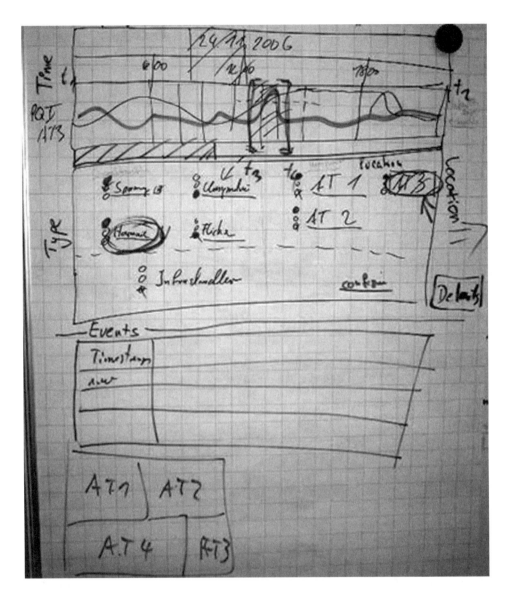

FIGURE 9-10 Visual prototype

Implementation

As the project progresses, visual prototypes are detailed and adjusted to existing standards concerning coloring and sizes as described in Style Guides. Several visual prototypes (static screens) can be combined into a clickable PowerPoint slide with very little effort. As a result, a low-fidelity

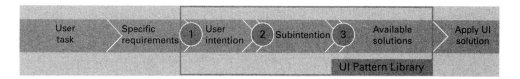

FIGURE 9-11 User intentions, subintentions, and available solutions guide library users in identifying the appropriate pattern

prototype reflects the UI and basic interactions of the future software. This output delivers an optimal performance in practice because the prototype communicates the usability goals in an easy-to-understand way. The prototype and the underlying concept are then integrated into the development specification during the requirements analysis phase.

Pattern Use: From Concept to Implementation

In this phase, UI patterns serve as input for detailing UIs and as reference for developers. As the UI sketches become more detailed, appropriate mechanisms need to be identified for representing these details adequately. For example, based on our experience with UI design, we noted that a common problem is arranging information in a way that provides the future user with a good overview. The more information that is added, the more crowded the screen will be. By using the UI pattern library, mechanisms for adjusting information display (such as tabs or filters) can be identified for increasing usability. Besides the applicability for conceptual work, developers at Siemens Energy Automation use the UI pattern library as

FIGURE 9-12 Example for identifying the appropriate pattern for the task "setup software"

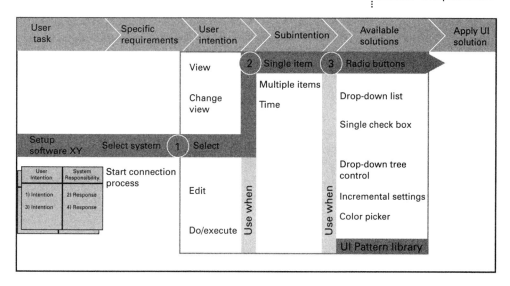

a reference during implementation. Therefore, the UI pattern library also provides a method for creating a common language within a diverse and geographically split development team.

The UI pattern library provides a fast overview of available UI principles that can be applied to the problem at hand. Usability work is accelerated significantly as the library provides a single entry point to information that was previously spread among various documents or, even worse, only available as implicit knowledge. As the UI pattern library also includes a wireframe for each pattern, the information in the library can be linked 1:1 on the paper sketches for the visual prototypes. Consequently, the use of patterns opens up new possibilities for increasing efficiency in conceptual work and ensuring consistency of future UIs.

At Siemens Energy Automation, the UI pattern library is used mainly by usability engineers and developers during usability workshops. However, as the organization consists only of three usability engineers for several hundred developers, the library also supports nonusability experts in development in applying UI principles correctly in order to improve UI quality and reduce the efforts needed for error corrections during late development phases. Therefore, another important success factor is the integration of UI patterns and their application in training sessions. Usability engineers at Siemens Energy Automation provide regular training sessions for UI developers in all development locations. UI patterns are an integrated part of usability trainings. The goal is to familiarize developers with the UI pattern library so they can use the library for detailed concept work such as defining the contents of a dialog. The training includes basic information about UI patterns, an example of how the UI pattern library is used (similar to Figure 9-12), and a hands-on part. Based on a given task case (receiving trouble calls), developers draw a sketch for a UI that represents all listed data (system responsibility) and actions (user intention). Participants are explicitly asked to use the UI pattern library for identifying suitable UI principles, as they will have to represent their results and explain why they chose particular mechanisms. Training participants are split into groups of three to four. Each group has a laptop for accessing the UI pattern library. After 30 minutes, the groups present their UIs to the other groups and defend their decisions. The training gives developers a familiarity with the pattern library. Additionally, they gain confidence in the library being a helpful way to reduce usability defects.

Compelling Events

The introduction of UI patterns and the UI pattern library was supported by several events creating a fertile soil within the organization:

Importance of reuse in the organization   Siemens Energy Automation had already established activities to increase the code reuse within development. Reuse is necessary because Siemens Energy Automation offers multiple software products to its customers. By reusing code, the organization saves money and time in development. The authors demonstrated to management and architecture (the group owning the reuse process) that UI patterns are a powerful means for increasing reuse potential in the organization. Besides the traditional reuse of code, UI patterns additionally enable the reuse of concepts and ideas, thus reducing the efforts needed during concept and design. Furthermore, UI patterns enable developers to implement more usable software. As UI patterns extended the existing reuse activities (code) established by the architect group, management was convinced to invest effort and budget to establish UI patterns in the organization.

Visualization of pattern benefits in the training sessions   The integration of UI patterns in the usability training schedule allowed us to demonstrate the benefits of patterns to developers. In training sessions, several groups of developers are asked to build a UI concept for the same task based on the UI pattern library. The output of different groups has a high rate of consistency because participants identify UI principles based on the "use when" criteria in the library. This high consistency of training output demonstrates to participants that the UI pattern library is a reliable tool for achieving consistency. Additionally, the descriptions in the UI pattern library enable developers to explain why they decided on a specific UI principle. Decisions in UI design are based on patterns rather than the discretion of an individual developer. Therefore, the solution is more stable—the number of defects and the need for changes in later phases is reduced.

Achieved Product Impact

Establishing a common look and feel   UI patterns have a high impact on the consistency of the User Experience and enable intuitive use of software. By applying UI patterns, all applications follow the same principles. Therefore, the user expectation of consistent behavior among Siemens Energy Automation applications is fulfilled, leading to decreased learning effort and error rates for the software user.

UI patterns enable the development of more consistent and generic solutions across teams and locations. For example, for creating the UI pattern "Import/Export data," requirements from different products were synchronized by a team culled from different projects and locations.

According to the development process, project teams work by themselves. This example showed using cross-product teams to develop UI patterns could have an even greater impact. The solution subsumes a broader spectrum of requirements and, therefore, is applicable in even more products. The UI pattern "Import/Export data" will be used at least in four products. Because of different software development cycles, the pattern has not yet been implemented in every product, but the solution is available in the UI pattern library and can be accessed and referenced easily during development. Thus, the UI pattern library is a good means for achieving sustainable user orientation. In the long-term, UI patterns ensure that Siemens Energy Automation products will be consistent in their look and feel. Additionally, the pattern approach follows a long-term strategy: new user interface concepts across product families are being harmonized one by one. By grouping the application examples based on generic user intentions (such as "view," "change view," "edit," "do/execute"), inconsistencies became obvious immediately. The UI pattern library makes the identification of inconsistencies much quicker and simpler than it would be without such a repository. As one of the initial improvements, we harmonized 200 to 142 user interface solutions among Energy Automation applications. Siemens as a company achieves branding benefits because users recognize and experience that Siemens applications follow a common look and feel.

In-house Benefit

Saving costs through reuse　By establishing user interface patterns and a global UI pattern library in the organization, we've achieved several benefits. First, the development process across the organization is more efficient. Instead of reinventing the wheel repeatedly, knowledge is readily available for reuse. The pattern library is an efficient means for exchanging solutions between products and technologies and strengthens cross-departmental collaboration and knowledge exchange among projects, organizational units, and sites at Siemens Energy Automation. The UI pattern library is seen as a common best practice sharing tool among the individual stakeholders in product management, development, architecture, and usability.

Furthermore, project managers now have comprehensive overview of existing solutions and code. With reuse, they can lower development costs. Especially in the requirements analysis and implementation phases, agreements between all stakeholders are reached more quickly by using established and proven solutions. If an adequate solution does not exist within Energy Automation applications, this is very obvious and the newly developed solution can be documented quickly as a new pattern or as an extension to an existing pattern so that colleagues can access this information before software release. Double efforts can be avoided, thus lowering development time and costs.

Therefore, the UI pattern library provides a powerful foundation for applying common UI principles. At Siemens Energy Automation, the major software products are based on UI patterns. These products serve as best practice for other applications. On average, each pattern is used in about three to five applications. However, because of the fact that development cycles are long, the exact return on investment from the UI pattern practice is not quantifiable at this time, which makes it difficult to acquire new budgets for patterns within the organization.

Transferring usability knowledge   Having a central UI pattern repository brings usability up to the next level of quality. In addition to Energy Automation Style Guides containing details about measurements, spacing, colors, and fonts, UI patterns give guidance about usage of a specific user interface solution. The way the UI patterns are structured in the library and the brief description of "use when" and "do not use when" criteria support the design decision process. The interface solution, which fits best in a specific context, can clearly be identified and the design decision can be justified by contrasting similar user interface design solutions. By using UI patterns, less experienced employees can achieve higher quality user interface concepts more easily, thus reducing the number of usability defects. Because not every screen can be specified by the usability experts, developers are supported by the UI pattern library, when they have to decide on details concerning user interface implementation. Additionally, the UI pattern library supports product managers in the requirements phase in deriving user requirements. Furthermore, UI patterns help to preserve knowledge in the organization by providing a stable reference point and worldwide accessibility.

Recommendations

Ensure involvement of stakeholders   The key success factor for usability activities at Siemens Energy Automation is the commitment and support of internal stakeholders from product management, project management, development, and architecture. Involving stakeholders puts usability on a firm footing. We used different means for convincing and involving stakeholders in UI patterns. First, we gave examples of the UI pattern library we created for Siemens Corporate Technology and Research to illustrate our understanding of patterns. Of course, most readers do not have an already existing pattern library to use as reference. In this case, readers could use one of the pattern libraries available on the Internet (see "Pattern Libraries on the Internet" for examples). Second, we outlined the benefits of UI patterns to stakeholders. By integrating UI patterns in the existing reuse strategy, stakeholders were able to understand the advantages of UI patterns and dedicate budget to UI patterns. Last, we ensure continuous involvement by splitting tasks related to identifying, describing, and maintaining UI patterns. Pattern ownership and integration in reviews are two means for involving colleagues.

Pattern Libraries on the Internet

Jenifer Tidwell   http://designinginterfaces.com/
Martijn Van Welie   http://www.welie.com/patterns/index.php
Infragistics   http://quince.infragistics.com/

Establish usability processes first before introducing UI patterns

Another success factor in establishing UI patterns at Siemens Energy Automation is the integration of UI patterns in existing development and usability processes. UI patterns supplement existing methods. When you do not have a usability approach installed in your organization, you should not introduce patterns first as a usability tool, as colleagues will not be able to make use of UI patterns without having basic usability knowledge. It's better to start with basic usability methodologies, such as task analysis and user interviews first, before thinking about UI patterns.

When you already have a usability process in place, the integration of UI patterns will be smooth because the established usability methodology contains possible links to UI patterns. In our case, the Usage-Centered Design methodology provided a good foundation as task cases are described as user intentions, which we used as links to generic user intentions in the UI pattern library. These direct links helped colleagues in development understand the usage and benefits of UI patterns. Additionally, we integrated UI patterns into the usability training for developers to ensure a broad knowledge of UI patterns in the organization.

Establish an UI pattern description process

Writing UI patterns takes time and experience. Generally, colleagues do not have experience in writing UI patterns and cannot spend extra effort in addition to their regular work in product management or development. For this reason, we established a core UI pattern team of seven people who were already engaged in usability or were motivated to increase their usability knowledge. One person was responsible for writing the first draft of a UI pattern and for the reviewing process. Make sure this person has enough time for the task. This will ensure consistency and quality among the UI patterns and will accelerate their production. We also installed a UI pattern library owner who coordinated all pattern activities. This person has a good overview of all Energy Automation products and has a long-term experience in usability engineering and UI pattern practice. The UI pattern library owner does the first review and gives feedback to the UI pattern writer. After developing a reworked draft, the UI pattern is sent to the pattern owner and the core team. Within 14 days, comments are returned. Comments are taken into consideration and clarified. These reviews across projects are necessary to develop a common understanding about the pattern and to increase acceptance and publicity in the organization. The finalized UI pattern is published in the internal UI pattern library, which is based on wiki technology, providing a fast and easy way to make changes and additions. However, identifying and describing a UI pattern is only one part of introducing UI patterns into an organization. Even more important is to ensure that UI principles as described in the UI pattern library are implemented correctly.

Keep the pot boiling   UI patterns are not a one-time task but afford opportunities for continuous effort. As long as there is innovation, new patterns have to be described in the UI pattern library. Therefore, you will need to constantly budget money and time for maintaining patterns. Best practice examples and pattern success stories will help you to convince management to allocate the necessary budget. Additionally, a newsletter informing colleagues about the latest patterns helps them remember the UI pattern library. Furthermore, individual engagement can be achieved by motivating colleagues to participate in pattern efforts. At Siemens Corporate Technology and Research, we provided "pattern awards" in terms of chocolate to all engaged colleagues. Another possibility is for management to define pattern-related goals for employees.

Summary

- **What is the business context (e.g., product, customers)?**
  Siemens Energy Automation is selling technology along the entire chain of energy conversion for providing a reliable and economical electricity supply. Typical customers are power supply companies, public utilities, power plant operators, and industry. Customers make purchasing decisions on technical specifications and expect the products to have a high level of reliability and usability. Siemens Energy Automation is a global player. Headquartered in Germany, the business sector employs around 800 developers in Europe, the Americas, and Asia.

- **Which (business) problems did you address with your UX practice?**
  Customers expect a high level of usability and consistency across
  Siemens software. Usability becomes more and more a unique selling
  proposition as it prevents human errors in controlling the power grid.
  However, there are only three usability engineers for 800 developers
  within the Energy Automation business unit. UI patterns address both
  business problems. They increase usability and consistency in the
  software and support the transfer of usability know-how to developers.

- **What were constraints and prerequisites?**
  Major constraints were extreme time pressure and budget cuts in
  software development, leading to a high expectation concerning return
  on investment for UI patterns. However, long product cycles hinder an
  immediate return on investment. The most important prerequisites for
  a successful integration of UI patterns were management support and
  high usability awareness in the organization.

- **In which development context did you apply your UX practices?**
  The usage of many different technologies and globally distributed
  development locations afford tools for preventing misunderstandings
  and doubling of efforts. Siemens Energy Automation follows a
  defined software development process that integrates four major
  usability activities: (1) Usability workshops for achieving a common
  understanding of the requirements and software model among key
  stakeholders; (2) Site visits and user interviews for understanding what
  users need and why they need it; (3) Usability evaluation for identifying
  any deficiencies early in the process; and (4) Usability consulting and
  reviews for ensuring correct implementation of usability outcomes.

- **What compelling events supported you in applying your UX
  practice successfully?**
  Siemens Energy Automation had already established activities to
  increase code reuse within development. UI patterns supplement reuse
  activities by providing a means for reusing concepts with ideas across
  different technologies.

- **What was the achieved product and business impact?**
  UI patterns have a high impact on the consistency of the User
  Experience and enable intuitive use of software. By applying UI
  patterns, all applications follow the same principles. More than 200
  UI concepts could be harmonized to 142 patterns. On average, each
  pattern is used in about three to five applications. This reuse leads to
  decreased learning effort and error rates for the software user.

- **How did you apply the UX practice?**
  The key success factor for usability activities at Siemens Energy
  Automation is the commitment and support of internal stakeholders from
  product management, project management, development, and architecture.
  We used different means for convincing and involving stakeholders in
  UI patterns. First, we gave best practices to illustrate our understanding
  of UI patterns and to show their potential outcome. Second, we involved
  colleagues to take over UI pattern ownership and to participate in reviews.
  Additionally, the use of the UI patterns was part of the usability training
  schedule. Hands-on training demonstrates to developers the advantages of
  UI patterns in terms of consistency and stability.

- **Which recommendations do you have for our readers?**
  Establish a usability process first before introducing UI patterns. When
  you already have a usability process in place, the integration of UI
  patterns will be easier because the established usability methodology
  contains possible links to UI patterns. In our case, the Usage-Centered
  Design methodology provided a good foundation as task cases are
  described as user intentions, which we used as links to generic user
  intentions in the UI pattern library. Consider that building up your
  own domain-specific UI pattern library is a long-term investment that
  takes time and money. Therefore, it is very important to ensure the
  commitment of management. The more complete the UI pattern library,
  the higher the rate of acceptance in the organization and the greater the
  achieved benefit of reusing concepts.

References

Alexander, C. 1979. *The Timeless Way of Building.* New York, NY, USA:
Oxford University Press.

Constantine, L., and L. Lockwood. 1999. *Software for Use: A Practical
Guide to the Models and Methods of Usage-Centered Design.* New York:
ACM Press.

E.ON. 2006. *Fehleinschätzung in komplexer Netzsituation wesentliche
Ursache der Netzstörung vom 4. November.* Retrieved from http://www
.eon-energie.com/pages/eea_de/Presse/Pressemitteilungen/Aktuelle_Presse/
Pressemitteilung.htm?id=87373.

Chapter 10

Rapid Testing System

By Jian Wu

Haier®

Haier is a global leading brand of major appliances and the most valuable brand in China. Along with its 29 manufacturing plants, 8 comprehensive R&D centers, 19 overseas trading companies located around the world, and more than 60,000 global employees, Haier has become a multinational corporation. In 2010, Haier's global revenue was 20.7 billion USD with a brand value of 12.9 billion USD.

According to the latest data released by Euromonitor, with a market share of up to 6.1 percent, Haier ranks first among brands of major appliance globally in terms of market share. This was the first time that a Chinese company was the number-one brand in the major appliance industry. At the same time, the market share for Haier's refrigerator and washing machine is 10.4 percent and 8.4 percent, respectively, with both ranking first in the industry. Moreover, Haier leads smart-home solutions in Asia.

By the end of 2010, Haier had applied for 9,738 patents, 2,799 of which were invention patents, ranking first among Chinese appliance enterprises. Haier is the most involved appliance company in raising international, national, and industry standards. Haier is the only Chinese enterprise to be a member of the management decision-making team of the International Electrotechnical Commission (IEC) and was selected to be the first "Practice base for standard innovation" globally by the IEC in June 2009.

Why Haier Values User Experience

In the 1980s when Haier was still a startup, the company had already set up a regular workflow driven by the market. At that time salespeople promptly gave feedback to the R&D department. This process was useful and effective for a midscale company as we were close to market and surviving the competition among thousands of players in a planned economy was easy. As time passed, however, sales-driven R&D topics did not work well because demand for greater variety grew in China. Consumers throughout each region had different consumption habits. Even the salespeople, who were face to face with consumers every day, could not figure out what consumers really wanted as their demands were too diversified. We came to believe that the solution lay not only in getting feedback from salespeople but also from end users. Therefore, we attempted to bring end users into this interesting process, letting them tell us what they preferred using in day-to-day life and play a more active role in a new product development process, as shown in Figure 10-1.

FIGURE 10-1
Haier's old development process

As we've entered the twenty-first century, network and digital technology has changed life tremendously. Before they knew it, consumers suddenly found themselves confronted with a number of new products equipped with touch screens, fancy features, and other dazzling interfaces. Consumers felt these products were interesting but they could not operate these new products as easily as they could current models. For example, we received a letter from a science professor who told us he could not understand the logic needed to operate the control panel of a washing machine. He was puzzled about the brand-new design. Our biggest concern is to make our products easy to use, presenting consumers with a uniformly good experience. This drove us to set up a User Experience platform based on user research and user interface design.

The User Experience Design Process at Haier

As a home appliance manufacturer, Haier has always been focused on end users, both in terms of our corporate strategy and operation, as well as in advocating for comfortable living solutions. After performing long-term global lifestyle tracking, we discovered that consumers want core services more than just the hardware itself. For example, people want a hole on the wall instead of a drill itself, consumers need fresh food not a cooling box. As a result, providing consumers with intuitive solutions is Haier's ultimate goal. We, therefore, seek to provide fresh food storage, fabric cleaning, hot water, and family entertainment solutions rather than just a single refrigerator, washing machine, water heater, or television. To implement this corporate development strategy, the Global User Research department aims to create new user experiences that lead to comfortable living. In everyday operations, the Global User Research department set up a number of channels that we can utilize to communicate with defined consumer groups and invite them to participate in panel discussions and to actively take part in design activities throughout the entire development process.

In the current information age, personal knowledge is more readily available via social networks as hot topics and tasks can be accomplished in short time spans by people located worldwide. Haier has introduced the fundamental philosophy behind Wikipedia into its R&D process to encourage target consumers to join in new product development from the very beginning, and all employees are part of an open, sharing, and global operation via a distributed network. Open innovation is Haier's goal in pursuing research and development as an organization. That's why Haier has introduced consumer involvement into its overall development processes to deliver full-process User Experience.

Each step in the user-centered design (UCD) flow (shown in Figure 10-2) is co-designed by users. By considering all factors of general User Experience when designing home goods and services, Haier follows the flow and approaches of traditional UCD, so as to enhance convenience and increase user satisfaction, shown in Figure 10-3. Haier emphasizes users not only in procedures like sales and after-sales services, but also during the elementary stage of product development and even at the stage of concept creation.

FIGURE 10-2
Haier's standard Product Line Management (PLM)

Phase 0	Phase 1	Phase 2	Phase 3	Phase 4	Phase 5	Phase 6
概念與定義	調研與計畫	開發設計	驗证與測試	交付與上市	成熟營運	產品退市
Concept & Definition	Investigation & Planning	Development	Validation	Delivery	Mature Operations	Support Life

Haier always focuses on two main objectives during the overall process. One is to identify unspoken consumer needs; the other is to understand contextual experience. However, User Experience research among the various product lines within the corporation has not been conducted concurrently: the major appliance groups, including refrigerators and washing machines, began implementing user research and User Experience design much earlier and have gained more experience and maturity because this category of appliance is now mostly driven by consumer demands; whereas the digital product groups, including mobile products and consumer electronics, have been driven more by technology so they are relatively late to User Experience and are just now including end users in validating final concepts and gathering ideas to augment design.

FIGURE 10-3
Haier UCD flow

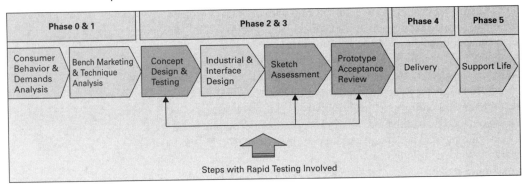

Why Rapid Development Is Important for Haier

While agile development is no longer a new concept for the Internet or telecommunications industries, the home appliance industry has a longer product development cycle and tends to feel less anxious at the passing of time.

However, in China today, the competition within the home appliance industry has been more intense than in other locations around the world, where the major home appliance industry is a developed industry and there have been few disruptive innovations that greatly impact the market over the past decade so most companies focus on sustaining innovation. For example, a refrigerator developed by a European competitor takes two to three years to develop, and one model will be on the market for seven to eight years. In China, refrigerators are developed and go to market within one year because many manufacturing companies skip many steps in the development process, and one model only lasts three years before a new one takes its place.

The more traditional UCD development process, in which a new model goes from planning to development to market, lasts approximately two years. Such a long cycle leads to more risks because customers may be lured by products developed by competitors catering to customers' tastes more quickly. On the other hand, it's difficult for us to gain a competitive edge without tested products.

As a result, a rapid development and testing process is very much needed. By conducting a rapid testing system, we've shortened the development cycle by 20 to 40 percent, and that's why, in the best case scenario, Haier can launch a brand-new User Experience–quality product in eight months.

How Rapid Testing Works

The rapid testing system is part of the standard flow in Haier user research in Product Line Management (PLM). The team sets up a contextual environment and validates the main findings from consumers' comments or from interactions with target users. The rules for testing are similar to those for usability tests but we emphasize accessibility, satisfaction, and joy over use. We generally measure overall satisfaction by recording Aesthetic, Instinctual, Value, and Subjective scores. As mentioned previously, by conducting tests using our rapid testing system, we've reduced development time by 20 to 40 percent. We attribute this to two factors.

Standardized Materials

Standardized materials, including standard research plans, standard questionnaire outlines, and standard report frameworks, are not only prerequisites of the rapid testing system, but also a main factor in shortening the time needed for testing. Standardized materials allow us to reuse documents from the database. At Haier, we began focused User Experience work in 2002 and have accumulated plenty of experience and documents for almost every stage of UCD. The advantage of using a standard question framework is to establish a historical database that is built from many various product development cycles, so as to provide a data decision-making platform for planning.

Standardize research planning is created and classified in detail according to research category, product class, product permeability, among other categories (see Figure 10-4 for the standardized research plan format). Utilizing standard research plans and sample designs can save time during project implementation.

While the test is being conducted, standardized questionnaires are culled from the database and adjusted according to fit the special character of the product. The time spent doing this is significantly less than having to create brand-new questionnaires from time to time. Creating questionnaires is time-consuming and problematic, especially when UX team members have left or been assigned new responsibilities that prevent the reusing of personal experience not to mention sharing with other team members. At another level, unified designs ensure the consistency and reliability of later research, and standard reference values can be accumulated over the long run, which is convenient for comparing future research and making accurate judgments. By using standardized questionnaires, certain standardized

FIGURE 10-4
The format of a standardized research plan

Type	Product Type	Product Price	Local Permeability	Approach	Sample Size	Research Object	......
Validation of Working Sketch	......	......	......	......	......	......	......
Model Test on Real Machine	......	......	......	......	......	......	......
......	......	......	......	......	......	......	......

report formats can easily be reused as well. As a UX practitioner, you have most likely spent time discussing which index should be included or how the report should look, or perhaps, you and your team have discovered you missed something important during field work and you are faced with either incomplete results or several hours of re-interviewing users. Because the various report formats were created and saved along with the various questionnaires, redundant work is reduced, saving a great amount of time during testing.

In addition, it has also enabled us to make a full comparison between each product concept, working sketch, or model, and evaluate its value in order to develop a scoring system. Using this database platform, designs that have standard scores enter the project development process; designs that fail to meet development standards will be improved and tested for a second time. User Experience changes the traditional project development model, in which decisions were made mostly based on personal experience of market sensitivity to reduce market risk. Though the results of consumer preference testing cannot predict the market performance of products completely, this scientific decision-making model improves the chances of success for single-type products based on user demand.

Meanwhile, we also set up a database that stores consumer complaints and ideas. Once the technology and cost are feasible, we can integrate this feedback into our innovative designs so they go to market faster, bringing more added value to consumers. Satisfied consumers strengthen the Haier brand over the long run, greatly upgrading our brand image, which allows us to keep our leading position in the appliance industry.

However, one of the prerequisites for successful rapid testing is to have plenty of experience with all of the documents, and to summarize and refine the documents for re-using purposes.

Making Good Use of Outside Resources

Besides all the standardized documents just mentioned, we also save time during fieldwork by making good use of resources outside of our own company. We have signed confidential agreements with a local leading user research and sourcing company that has qualified hardware facilities, professional staff, and the experience of long-term cooperation with giant research companies at home and abroad.

This is especially important for the home appliance industry, and particularly when the home appliance company sells products to Chinese users. Because China is wide both in terms of longitude and latitude, Chinese users have totally different lifestyles from north to south and from east to west. For example, people in Guangzhou province rely on refrigerators even in winter since the average temperature is 9°C (48°F) in January. Food can spoil in one night without refrigeration. But for people living in Heilongjiang province, the average temperature in January is minus 18°C (0°F), which means the outdoors is a natural refrigerator, and you may find that when many people leave home, they turn off their main refrigerator.

As a result, we usually need to conduct tests in multiple locations in China, which could be very time consuming since it requires many experienced personnel to conduct tests at the same time in several cities, and it takes time to prepare a proper lab or test context in each city. This is where outside resources provide help. In our case, we have an eight-year cooperation business partner, Beijing ISAR User Interface Design, which owns standard usability labs in over six cities around China. By fostering long-term cooperation with them, they not only have participated in most stages of our UCD flow and properly understand our needs, but also they provide resources that save time in preparing facilities and recruiting users in each city.

Major Steps in the Rapid Testing System

We introduced the rapid testing system in three steps of the UCD process: concept testing, sketch assessment, and prototype acceptance review. Both material standardization and outside resource utilization were used in all three of these test steps.

Concept Testing

In the process of inspiring user innovation, several practical product concepts gradually emerge from analysis of the market, the customer, and strategies of the company itself. These concepts usually concern information about concept names, major function points and profit points, sources of demand, communication points with consumers, and even some hand-painted design drafts (Figure 10-5 shows one example).

Although the product concepts at this stage are somewhat vague and probably subject to further changes, early assessment of these concepts is necessary. The aim is to get early feedback and thus make necessary corrections and adjustments before more resources are invested and proceeding to the next stage. As a result, the following categories shown in Figure 10-6 are always included in the questionnaire framework for all product concept tests and the results interpreted in detail.

During the rapid testing system process, feedback and suggestions from target consumers about product concepts are collected. Target user recruitment for rapid testing is based on our user resource database, and questions are adjusted within the framework questionnaire to meet the needs

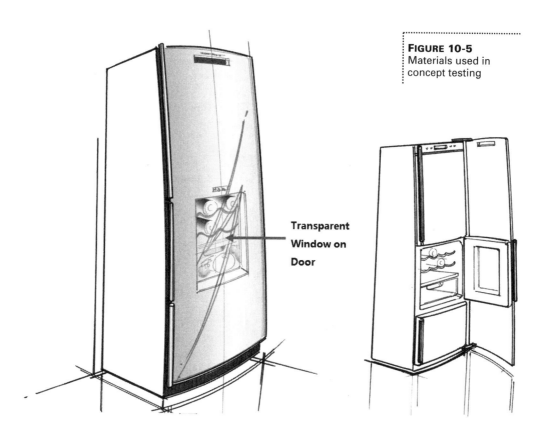

FIGURE 10-5
Materials used in
concept testing

**Transparent
Window on
Door**

of the test. Electronic interviews and recordings enable us to input data right after the interview and begin the data processing stage. By using standard report frameworks, key conclusions can be generated and quickly sent to other departments for further processing such as planning for designing or improving the product, instead of having to spend long periods of time polishing the report itself. Normally, reports can be finished and issued in about two to three weeks, which saves at least half the time of a traditional test cycle and improves efficiency.

FIGURE 10-6
Categories considered
in concept testing

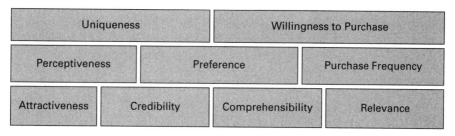

Uniqueness		Willingness to Purchase	
Perceptiveness	Preference		Purchase Frequency
Attractiveness	Credibility	Comprehensibility	Relevance

Sketch Assessment

After user participation in the initial design process, designers complete the product's structural design and finalize its appearance according to the information collected and then create a full-size sketch. Figure 10-7 shows one example. When the design passes internal review and assessment, assessment with user participation begins.

FIGURE 10-7
The full-size sketch

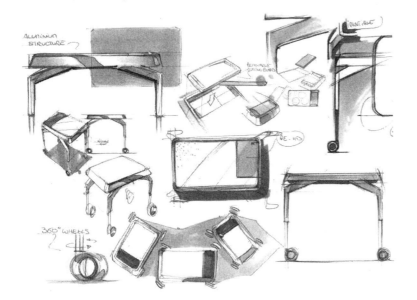

This stage comes after the concept design and testing stage to assess the concept's visual appeal. The main aim at this stage is to select the most appealing product appearance design or to improve the product's appearance. Initial tests include user acceptance and assessment of appearance factors like color, material, line, consistency, and pattern, as well as the visual effect of the operation interface. In addition to drawings, 3D animation is added in some cases to make concepts more active. A Flash display can sometimes be more effective in assessing an interface.

User assessment approaches may differ in actual projects. If the design requirements are clearly stated, quantitative tests are likely to be conducted, focusing on appearance, attractiveness, and user acceptance; if the design framework needs to be improved, user participation at this stage is important so that problems are revealed and corrected.

As in concept testing, the basic operation of this stage in the rapid testing system is similar. Although at this stage, you must decide whether to conduct qualitative or quantitative tests according to different situations.

The general cycle needed to complete and issue a report is also two to three weeks, which can save half the time of traditional test cycles and improve efficiency.

Prototype Acceptance Review

At this stage, accurate quantitative data is acquired through user assessment of models similar to real machines. This assessment provides guidance for marketing and sales strategy of products (Figure 10-8 shows an example of one prototype review).

FIGURE 10-8
Models used in a
prototype review

In this process, we normally recruit 200 consumers composed of present customers and potential targeted customers with the proportion determined by product category. This is the most expensive part of the full User Experience design process.

At this stage, our goal is to obtain quantitative feedback about the high-fidelity prototype, thus helping to guide decisions about which prototype should be developed and to obtain suggestions for improving prototypes. The following factors, including marketing, acceptance, and usability, as detailed in Figure 10-9, need to be considered during this stage.

Each User Experience test is prepared in advance to save time costs. Following the assessment, we further classify user feedback and ideas for innovation into medium- and long-term improvement suggestions in order to help marketing and the product team understand the product development priorities.

At this stage, designs and prototypes are more complete than they are in the previous stages. We often use a quantitative approach in our rapid testing process to allow customers to make final choices quickly. By referencing standard comparisons in the database and the success rate

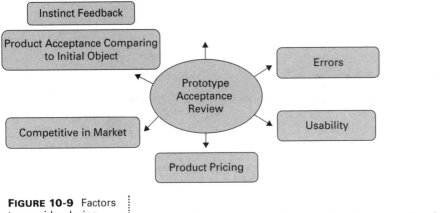

FIGURE 10-9 Factors to consider during prototype review

assessment of products going to market, the general cycle to complete and issue a report is also two to three weeks, which, once again, saves half the time of the traditional test cycle and improves efficiency.

Achieved Impact

Rapid testing is usually a core contribution from the Haier Global User Research center, which completes the project proposal, interview outline, interview operation, data analysis, report writing, and report interpretation independently. The User Research center communicates with the business division directly about the project's requirements and goals, and outsources work like venue rental, customer invitations, and quantitative interviews to external companies. Utilizing a rapid testing system can greatly shorten product testing steps. In addition, due to the standardized materials derived from the database summaries of Haier's previous testing experience, any changes to material, especially reports, require no effort for the product department to learn, and so don't cost extra time for other groups in the product development process. As a result, shorter product testing steps lead to a shorter development cycle using the UCD process, satisfying the needs of business division to promote products into the market and maximizing the probability of meeting customer preferences and gaining customer acceptance.

Since the trial implementation of our rapid testing system, the efficiency of User Experience in all testing steps has been largely improved, and the whole development cycle has been reduced roughly about 20 to 40 percent. The saved time varies by product and situation.

The shortened development cycle does not come at the price of compromising product quality in terms of Users Experience. Not only does this process ensure a match between product and consumer demands, but also it sustains innovation. A close User Experience chain has been formed to create quality products that customers need.

The rapid testing system is now used to regulate working sketch testing and implementation process for sample machine/model testing in Qingdao, one of Haier's locations. Later, we will promote this process to the whole country. Haier will promote user-centered product design broadly, as well as rapid and accurate design plan testing and cost-savings. Together, these factors ensure we will keep providing products in accordance with user demand and improve user satisfaction at the same time.

Summary

- **What is the business context (e.g., product, customers)?**
  Our company is a global home appliance manufacturer of major appliances, consumer electronic, and small appliances as well as smart-home solutions that are oriented to customers all around the world. Haier is committed to creating a new lifestyle—inspired living for the global consumer.

- **Which problem(s) does the UX practice address?**
  To survive in a market with intense competition but, at the same time, sustain the UX quality of our product.

- **What were prerequisites and constraints?**
  A rapid testing system needed to be integrated into our UCD process using standardize research plans, questionnaires, and report formats, which we prepared first. Enlisting the help of business partners with good reputations, abundant resources, and deep insight into our corporation was also important.

- **In which UX development context did you apply your UX practice? (at the beginning or mature application)**
  UCD processes have been about 70 percent integrated into the product development process.

- **What compelling events supported you in applying your UX practice successfully?**
  Two factors regarding the Chinese home appliance market compelled Haier into utilizing a rapid testing system. The first one is the importance of User Experience; the other is the importance of a relatively short development cycle.

- **How did you apply this UX practice?**
  We have established a local laboratory, partnered with a powerful subcontractor, standardized test plans, questionnaires, and report formats to test new products and gain acceptance of those products quickly.

- **What kind of business or product impact did you achieve through this UX practice?**
  We shorten development cycles, which has allowed us to launch products early to market with a high customer satisfaction. In this way, we took the preemptive opportunity to obtain a large market share and considerable profits.

- **Which recommendations do you have for other companies and departments to apply the UX practice?**
  Since testing is just one part of the whole user-centered design process, in addition to standardized research plans, questionnaires, and report formats, other UCD criteria should not be forgotten on any level. For example, defining target users is also crucial to guaranteeing a product's UX quality. Otherwise, you are just conducting a fast but incorrect evaluation that will have no beneficial effect.

Chapter 11

Design Thinking:
Expanding UX Methods Beyond Designers

By Aline Baeck and Peter Gremett

Intuit®

As User Experience professionals, we employ our user-centered design methods (UCD) on many types of products and services. As businesses have recognized the important role design plays in product success, we have been included in the earliest phases of development.[1] Our role now exceeds traditional deliverables such as workflows and page designs; we also increase product innovation, processes, and the business bottom line. Design Council research found that design can directly and significantly improve sales, profits, turnover, and growth. Using and valuing design brings bottomline benefits, and those who understand and act on this insight have a competitive edge over the rest.[1] Intuit is one such company that is leveraging design within a wider business context, a practice called *design thinking*. By sharing our design thinking experiences at Intuit, we hope to inspire other designers to broaden their approach and influence other companies and institutions.

Design Thinking

Design thinking—in the last few years this phrase has appeared everywhere, from Wikipedia to *Harvard Business Online,* from Stanford University's D-School to *BusinessWeek*. But what is it?

Design thinking is a method of solving problems that is fluid and open for the duration of the problem it is applied to. The heart of the method is understanding the customer: all ideas and subsequent work stem from knowing the customer. Design thinking defies the obvious and instead embraces a more experimental approach. And it is broader not only in approach, but also in scope. Often, when people hear the term "design," they think of a page layout or web page components such as buttons. However, design thinking is applied not just to design problems, but is often used to explore and define business problems as well as to define products and services.

Herbert Simon, one of the founding fathers of artificial intelligence and a cognitive psychologist, defines design thinking as

> ... a process for practical, creative resolution of problems or issues that looks for an improved future result.[2]

Tim Brown, founder of IDEO and an advocate for design thinking, defines it as

> ...a discipline that uses the designer's sensibility and methods to match people's needs with what is technologically feasible and what a viable business strategy can convert into customer value and market opportunity.[3]

What these definitions and many other design thinking definitions have in common is that unlike analytical approaches that focus on narrowing the choices, design thinking focuses on going broad.

In fact, design thinking is a more creative and user-centered approach to solving problems than traditional design methods. As a methodology, it combines empathy, creativity, and feedback to generate a solution that meets user needs while also producing revenue.

To understand design thinking, it helps to understand the core attributes of the methodology:

- **Ambiguity** Being comfortable when things are unclear or when you don't know the answer

- **Collaborative** Working together across disciplines[3]

- **Constructive** Creating new ideas based on old ideas, which can also be the most successful ideas

- **Curiosity** Being interested in things you don't understand or perceiving things with fresh eyes

- **Empathy** Seeing and understanding things from your customers' point of view[3]

- **Holistic** Looking at the bigger context of use for the customer

- **Iterative** A cyclical process where improvements are made to a solution or idea regardless of the phase

- **Nonjudgmental** Creating ideas with no judgment toward the idea creator or the idea

- **Open mindset** Embracing design thinking as an approach for any problem regardless of industry or scope

Design thinking is not only a combination of these attributes, but also a cyclical progression of activities. This progression is perfect for solving problems and discovering new opportunities. The steps used in design thinking aren't linear, but rather overlap, and they may be used more than once. "Businesses are embracing design thinking because it helps them be more innovative, better differentiate their brands, and bring their products and services to market faster."[4]

Consider healthcare provider Kaiser Permanente, which sought to improve its healthcare workers' and patients' experiences through design thinking. After several months of coaching and participation in design thinking workshops, the nurses, doctors, and administrators were inspired to generate many new ideas. One new idea addressed nursing-staff shift changes at four Kaiser hospitals. The cross-disciplinary project team (a technology expert, a process designer, a union representative, and a former nurse) worked with nurses to identify several problems with the way shift changes occurred: inefficiencies of time, how patients responded to medication, and the patient's overall well-being. Armed with information gathered through interviews and observations at the hospitals, the team explored potential solutions through brainstorming, which led to rapid prototyping. One of the designs that emerged had nurses pass on information about the patient in front of the patient and also included an application to capture this information throughout the shift. The new design reduced the transition time between nurses by over half, improving the quality of the caregiver's experience, and, in turn, improving patient care of the patient.[3]

Design thinking is nothing new to designers. Designers learn these skills in school and on the job. It is part of who designers are and how they work—a fundamental part of the creative process. The real challenge is to take a designer's instinctual way of working and share that within an organization. But to teach design thinking, more is needed than the set of attributes we listed in this section. Understanding how these attributes manifest themselves in traditional product development phases such as problem definition, inspiration and ideating, prototyping, and soliciting user feedback will help communicate these attributes by placing them in a framework that an organization can understand.

Define the Problem to Solve

If you don't know what you are solving, how can you solve it? This key question seems basic but is often overlooked. The best way to begin this phase is to write down what you believe to be the problem. The act of committing the problem you want to solve to paper helps make it more concrete and adds clarity. After you have written a concise description of the problem, share it with the team to see if it resonates with them. By getting different points of view on the problem, you have a better chance of arriving at the true problem and reducing the effect of your point of view. These alternative views will help you hone in on what problem you are attempting to solve; ultimately, engaging users to provide their point of view and insights is paramount in defining the problem.

Look for Inspiration

For my part I know nothing with any certainty, but the sight of the stars makes me dream.

—Vincent van Gogh[5]

Inspiration means taking in your environment—colors, feelings, music, textures, and the way things work. You store this information in an inner reservoir to be drawn from almost unconsciously when solving problems.

You have to maintain an open mind and be observant to the things around you while letting ideas flow in without a critical attitude.

Although inspiration can come from many places, try observing the people using your product. This leads to the discovery of new connections, people's needs, and key insights. Don't be fooled into thinking that focus groups, surveys, or customer complaints are the way to do this. By going to users instead of bringing them to you, you can observe their daily routines and processes directly. These customer visits are extremely valuable and can be conducted in many ways. In some cases, the observer stays in the background and lets the user lead the discussion. In other cases, the observer employs activities to draw out information from the user. Although there is some preparation involved, the customer visit is a gold mine of inspiration and information that often leads to big breakthroughs. These breakthroughs often reframe the problem that is being solved. That is one reason why it is important to have some fluidity throughout the design-thinking process.

Ideate Multiple Ideas

To have a good idea you must first have lots of ideas.
—Linus Pauling (Two-time Noble Prize winner)[4]

After spending time with your users and getting inspired, it's time to synthesize. The rich information you have collected should be organized and distilled into digestible takeaways that can be shared with the team. These key insights can then be used to generate ideas. At this stage, the focus should be on the quantity rather than quality of ideas. This can be difficult because most people have a tendency to edit themselves before they speak. The obvious and incremental ideas will come out first. Keep pushing to get as many ideas out no matter how ridiculous they may sound.

Design thinking is most successful when you have multidisciplinary groups of people coming together to brainstorm and generate ideas. This collaboration from different points of view generates great ideas and, according to Tim Brown, is "indisputably a catalyst for innovation."[6]

Generate Prototypes

This phase is all about making the ideas real. Concrete ideas are more easily manipulated and revised. Technologies can also be explored and discussed at this phase and are manifested through tangible prototypes. The importance of this phase is to generate multiple prototypes to explore different ideas. Relatively inexpensive prototypes enable you to get a feel for what you are solving. Another benefit of prototypes is that they help get your team moving in the same product and design direction.

Solicit User Feedback

Bringing the prototypes to users ensures that the product is user-centered. There is a rich set of existing methodologies that are effective ways for eliciting feedback from users (such as usability testing and group task analysis). We can't cover those methodologies in this short chapter given that they are the primary subject of many books. It's enough to note that letting users utilize the prototypes is an important step in uncovering unforeseen issues, reframing the problem, and refining the solutions. These relatively inexpensive prototypes are extremely valuable to the product-creation process and give the product a better chance at success.

Benefits of Design Thinking

In order to stay ahead of their competitors, beat Wall Street, and engage customers in a new way, many companies are turning to design thinking to drive new ideas. We are in a world where advances in manufacturing, globalization, and technology have leveled the competitive playing field, and most products in mature markets have feature parity.

This environment has given consumers a healthy appetite for design as companies adopt it as a differentiator. You see designers as spokespeople in commercials; you see design highlighted in mainstream magazines. As consumers have more buying power, they are choosing in favor of beauty, simplicity, and design over just functionality.

A 2007 survey by Kelton Research for Autodesk found that when 7 in 10 Americans recalled the last time they saw a product that they just had to have, it was because of design. The survey found that among younger people (18 to 29 years old), the influence of design on their decision to purchase was even more pronounced.[7]

Wall Street currently believes that innovation (often fueled by design thinking) is a leading indicator of future growth of a company. In Britain, design is at the top of the list for 16 percent of businesses as a key success factor, and it's at the very top of the key success factor list among 47 percent of "rapidly growing" businesses.[7] This is a significant shift from previous years and bodes well for the industry as a whole.

Business Context

Intuit Inc. is a leading provider of financial management, tax, and online banking solutions for consumers, small- and mid-sized businesses, accountants, and financial institutions. Intuit's 2010 revenue topped $3 billion. Intuit has been recognized as America's most-admired software company and is ranked by *Fortune* magazine as one of the country's best places to work. We solve important problems by taking the customer's perspective and focusing on ease-of-use.

Intuit has historically employed various methodologies to foster new product ideas. For example, the founder, Scott Cook, has driven the development and use of Customer-Driven Innovation (CDI) to promote both an understanding of user needs and a methodology to develop products that creatively address real customer problems. Intuit's focus on and understanding of our customers has contributed to the company's success in our market space. And like many companies, Intuit encourages an environment of continuous improvement.

In the last several years, Intuit has recognized that elements of design thinking in some groups have contributed to their success. For example, employing design thinking has enabled Intuit to speed up the process of defining customer problems as well as imagining a broader range of solutions for our small-business customers. As designers and researchers, we play an important role in this initiative, and, in this chapter, we will show how these methods and activities have helped this movement gain momentum within the company. As Cindy Tripp from Proctor and Gamble noted in a recent *BusinessWeek* article, "design thinking can be applied everywhere, everyday."[8]

Company Culture

Intuit has long been recognized for its focus on customers; Scott Cook, Intuit's founder and Chairman of the Executive Committee, directly engaged with customers to understand how they managed their personal finances during Quicken's development. This tradition has expanded and become standard practice on project teams throughout Intuit.

A project often begins with a hypothesis about a customer problem that needs solving. One of the first steps that the cross-functional team takes (these teams usually consist of product management, design, and engineering) is to visit customers and better understand what the customers do and how they think about their tasks. By visiting several customers in their work environment, teams learn about users' difficulties, whether users recognize those as difficulties, how they work around them, and what relationship the work processes have to the users, their work, and their environment. This gives the team a shared understanding of the customer and the problem to be solved. Regular project checkpoints with management test the team's understanding of the customer. This means that teams are less likely to waste time in the later, more expensive phases of development because of a poorly defined problem.

Design Thinking Activities at Intuit

We've looked at how design thinking is manifested in product development steps such as problem definition, inspiration, ideating, prototyping, and user feedback. Intuit also took several actions to increase design thinking in the broader context and to instill design-thinking principles so that they are becoming a natural part of the product development processes.

Executive Sponsorship

Management and other key influencers are important if design thinking is going to be adopted by a company. Key influencers within a company who promote the value of these practices speed up the adoption of these practices. At Intuit, several executives were involved in initiating and promoting the design-thinking initiatives. Due to their high-level participation and sponsorship, design thinking rapidly gained visibility throughout Intuit. The executives' participation has ranged from sponsoring a series of external speakers to mentoring a group of design-thinking "catalysts" who were chosen due to the widespread recognition of their design-thinking skills.

These catalysts have continued to train others and roll design thinking out to the broader organization. This has disseminated design practices at Intuit much faster than if the movement had been purely a grassroots effort. This has also given the core group of design thinkers a clear focus—design thinking in service to the business goals of the company rather than just design metrics.

Inspirational Talks

The design-thinking initiative at Intuit began with inspirational talks, which continue to be a cornerstone of the program. The 90-minute talks are primarily given by outside speakers who demonstrate how their companies applied design thinking to specific problems. These talks create excitement about design thinking and how it can be applied to projects.

One of our most inspirational talks was given by a key leader at Apple. He spoke about how design played a key role in the customer experience for retail stores. Retail stores are not something that people traditionally identified with Apple; most people thought of the iPod or laptops. He described the harmony of design and level of precision that went into the creation of the underground New York Apple store. The store experience both inside and outside mirrors the physical products that Apple's customers love. After the store was completed, customers lined up for blocks to get into the store, and it is still an icon in New York City.

Guest speakers like this are utilized nearly every quarter to maintain awareness of and inspire design thinking in all employees. Recently, these talks have included internal speakers who show how they applied design thinking within our company. These talks are valuable because they provide examples of the application of design thinking within our own culture and processes.

One drawback to these lectures is that finding inspirational speakers can be difficult. The problem with internal speakers is that they sometimes lack the clout and charisma of many external speakers. External speakers, meanwhile, can be hard to find and expensive to hire. We believe, however, that if you get the right people for inspirational lectures it will pay off in terms of generating excitement and opening employees' eyes to a different way of thinking.

Workshops

Workshops are another method we used to familiarize our organization with design thinking. These are companywide events open to all employees and widely advertised by our corporate sponsor. These hands-on workshops provide examples and foster discussions on how to implement design thinking within the corporate culture. These events typically take place quarterly and are broadcast to all campus locations. The workshops are well attended by the various roles (engineering, QA, design, marketing, operations, tax specialists, etc.) in the company.

The 90-minute workshops start off with an attention grabber and an introduction to the topic. The next 30 minutes of the workshop consists of the guest speaker discussing a case study. The next phase of the workshop is interactive. It usually starts off with an exercise completed either in advance or in the workshop. This phase is usually followed by some sort of sharing or discussion in pairs or in small groups and then by a whole group discussion. Any new concepts and conclusions are introduced and the session ends with a question-and-answer session.

One of the most successful early workshops was a practical example of design thinking. An expert who teaches design thinking at a nearby university facilitated this session. During the session, he taught design thinking to hundreds of employees in multiple locations. His approach in the workshop was to have employees think broadly and design a product from scratch. The initial designs were followed by multiple iterations and customer feedback that allowed employees to create a design that would work well for the customer. Attendees were then asked to come together as a larger group and debrief about the exercise. The questions presented during the debriefing led to a very interesting discussion on design thinking and the product development process.

This workshop was successful because it created a situation for employees to actually design a product using design thinking methods. It was fun and engaging for participants, which created a lot of excitement and "water-cooler" talk about the design-thinking initiative.

We have found that workshops provide a safe environment for trying design-thinking activities before having to apply them to a real project. Participants have found it easier to relate to a broad theory of design thinking when it was applied to a specific activity.

Hackathons

Hackathons or *jams* are another activity that Intuit uses to drive design thinking within the company. Hackathons are essentially full-day sessions where employees can work intensely on a project of their choosing. The projects might be company priorities, features, or new ideas that employees have come up with on their own. Hackathons are independent of the company production cycle, which is quite liberating for attendees. Employees can either work by themselves or as a team. Attendance is completely voluntary and is in addition to any other work they have going on. They are not allowed to miss a deadline to participate in the session since it is outside current project development commitments. However, hackathons provide a good opportunity to take something you wanted to work on during the day but can't and turn it into something tangible.

The beauty of a hackathon is that it produces actionable and specific ideas. Conceivably, these could be big strategic concepts, tactical features, or completely new lines of business. The time constraint becomes an asset because it forces people to get to the core of the idea and get something done rather than get it done perfectly. What starts off as a rough idea ends up being more refined after working on and discussing the idea with other participants. This is fairly easy since a lot of people participate and teams utilize each another throughout the day to gather feedback and improve their ideas. At the end of the day, projects can be pitched to key executives to glean recognition, cash prizes, and funding to take the project to the next level.

More recently, customers have joined the executive team during the pitch phase. Customers are given the opportunity to provide input on which projects should move forward. The work and energy created among the participants is impressive. Projects may not make it live and into customer's hands. But that's not the point, the point is for employees to see an idea become a reality in one day and, therefore, inspire more action within the regular product development cycles.

These sessions are great at empowering employees and getting people involved in solving problems. Since teams can form organically, the projects serve to build comradeship across organizational boundaries. Inherently, these sessions generate many new product ideas that might be future projects or new markets. The successful application of design thinking at these sessions is due to the creation of a safe environment and management support.

Quick Experiments

A final key component to design-thinking practices at Intuit is *quick experiments.* Quick experiments are the practice of getting design solutions out of the development process and into users' hands as quickly as possible. This has traditionally been done through usability testing. However, usability testing has a well-known deficiency: it uses a small number of users in an artificial environment performing artificial tasks. This method has great value for informing design decisions, but it cannot replicate having customers use the software to perform real tasks in their actual business environments. A challenge to making quick experiments work is to clearly define what the team needs to learn and what hypothesis they are trying to test. Building only what needs to be built to test the hypothesis enables the team to rapidly deploy a potential solution. Using a constrained set of users, the solution can be tested in the real world and the team can quickly learn what does and doesn't work. By setting up a rapidly iterating process to improve the solution and redeploy it, the team gets to a better solution faster and for less development expense than more traditional processes. It's also very empowering for the team to own the decision making about when to deploy, when to improve, and when to abandon the solution and try another one, without having invested too much time or resources in the experiment.

One example of a quick experiment at Intuit was the development of a new service. A small team of five members used the techniques described earlier in this article. To quickly experiment, they identified multiple hypotheses to test and then structured several variations of the service to test the hypotheses. The key to the quick experimentation was to not invest in any infrastructure; they leveraged internal systems that were imperfect for what was needed but were good enough. This required more human resources to run the service, but this was a quicker, less expensive alternative to building a process to support a service that had not yet been proven. They quickly identified that their assumptions about two of the hypotheses were wrong and were able to change the service variations to reflect the learning and create a better experience. Their ability to test the service design and assumptions about what would make the service successful saved Intuit both time and money in investment and systems development.

While the service described was new, it has taken longer to figure out how to experiment in areas that are embedded in already successful products, where users pay money and expect our high standard of release quality within the product. But Intuit has successfully leveraged the small experiments process even within these products by controlling who sees the new piece of functionality and inviting them to participate, thus setting their expectations and giving them control over the experience. This involves some amount of infrastructure work in our web products so that selected users can be isolated from non-participating users, but that work then enables many teams to experiment, and we feel it is worth the investment.

How the Development Process Has Improved

So how do all the processes we've outlined affect the development process, specifically the interaction between experience design and engineering? When we compare how we work now with the way we used to work (a typical "waterfall" model of development, where product management drafts requirements, then design creates and documents the design, and then engineering implements it), it is a radical departure. Like many other companies, Intuit now uses agile-like processes, and that, combined with the new methods just described, mean that the development process has changed in important ways.

Increased Speed in Development Processes

As many design practitioners have noted, agile has made us rethink how design interacts with development. It is widely acknowledged that for significant features and products, design needs to get ahead of the engineering in the agile stages, utilizing a sprint 0. A *sprint 0* is a time-boxed period prior to the first sprint in an agile project. The sprint allows product managers to determine requirements and designers to establish the design direction. This is not to say that the design is fixed after sprint 0, but it is a phase where serious thought is put into solving customer problems and getting some design down on paper. Without a sprint 0, the team risks creating a design that is incomprehensible to users at the end. But utilizing the design-thinking processes detailed previously enables teams to do that design thinking and experimenting together during stage 0, resulting in a team with a shared understanding of the user and his or her needs. Design thinking gives structure and goals for sprint 0 that were unclear in our organization before we embraced design thinking methodology.

Once a project has been defined using these methods, implementation is much faster since the engineers participate in the definition phases and, ideally, have already done some preliminary engineering through their experiments. One caveat here is that sometimes there is pressure to ship the "small experiments" code, which can be counterproductive. If engineers can develop the prototype without any expectation of shipping the code, they can work more quickly with a bias for speed rather than for supportability or scalable architecture.

Increased Efficiency in Development Processes

The emphasis on design thinking also creates more focus to ensure the right problem is being solved. Thus engineering is less likely to spend time building a product that does not meet a customer need, failing either partway through the development process or, even worse, once it's released. We don't claim that design thinking completely cures the mismatch between user need and product idea, but it does improve the odds of releasing a product that solves a real user need in a way that will resonate with customers.

Increased Role for Engineering

A benefit to both designer and engineer is a closer working relationship between the two functions that leverages each group's strengths. We have long felt that great design ideas are not limited to designers; they come from everyone. Engineering participates and sometimes leads the activities to understand the customer and their problems; as a result, they are better able to participate in the design process and contribute valuable ideas that are grounded in the customer's needs. In fact, in some of our organizations, engineering drives these processes and leads all the activities we have described. For those engineers who want to play a larger role than implementing a vision given to them by other functions, this empowers them to really drive new thinking and design in ways that are not possible using more traditional processes.

What Design Thinking Means for User Experience

We've discussed what design thinking means for development, but how does it affect User Experience practitioners?

Strategic Role for Design

Within the groups that were the early adopters of the design-thinking approach at Intuit, design thinking has fundamentally changed the focus of what designers do. While we are still responsible for the product and service designs, we now influence product strategy. This is empowering but also requires new skills. There is a new emphasis on designers needing business acumen and leadership to facilitate design thinking throughout the organization. Although designers are all trained in traditional design-thinking methodology, they are not necessarily skilled at leading others in strategic thinking or at having the business acumen necessary to play this new strategic role. Training and mentorship needs to be undertaken for designers to gain or hone their business knowledge and skills, gaining the ability to judge success not only in design terms, but also in business outcomes for the company. This need is recognized by the California College of the Arts; they have created a new MBA in Design Strategy program. But this addition to the designer's toolkit has a potential downside. Designers can become more enablers of design rather than creators of design, facilitators instead of doers, which can be a difficult transition for an organization and the designers.

This tension is recognized by others in the field. Kevin McCullagh states that, "The concern was that too much time has been spent trying to outsmart the MBAs, and that design managers had lost their focus on delivering great design. The most common response to this feeling of over-stretch was to regroup and get back to basics, with many design managers pining just to roll up their sleeves and get back to designing."[9] But we feel this is a pessimistic view and that there is room for multiple roles for designers at a company. Recognizing that this expanded role is not right for all designers will allow design thinking to flourish while still maintaining the quality of design in all its detail, which is required for creating a successful experience. Regardless of the individual's role, all designers are expected to be role models for design-thinking practices in their own work and within the organization.

Keep Designing

The ability to facilitate groups is more in the traditional skill set of designers and comes naturally to many. But again, there is a tradeoff here; many designers, including the authors, thrive by creating. Their job satisfaction is directly derived from creating something from nothing, whether it's a physical product, software, or an experience. Many designers will not thrive in an environment where that need to create is not supported. This can be remedied by the power of cross-functional teams. For example, although the original group of design thinkers (called "catalysts" at Intuit) were virtually all designers, as we broadened the group, we included all functions—we looked for potential, not necessarily for already developed design thinking skills. This means that the whole structure of design thinking does not have to be created or maintained solely by designers, allowing designers to balance the strategic, facilitative work with maintaining their own design work. This balance is not easy, but the payoff for both design and other functions in what they gain is well worth the complexity.

Open the Design Black Box

Finally, a surprising benefit to design thinking is a deeper understanding of the design *black box*. Those of you who are designers will recognize this concept: requirements, or an understanding of the customer go into the box, and wireframes and high-fidelity mockups come out the other side of the box. Many who are not in design are often mystified at the design process and despite regular attempts throughout our careers to demystify it, the ability to communicate the design process has never been entirely successful. But applying participatory design thinking has helped with that challenge. Because others now participate in some of the most mysterious design processes, they are able to see why designers need time to think about a problem, or why it often seems like designers don't seem to do anything for a while, and then within a day, create a design for a whole feature.

As much as many designers might feel that this aura of mystery might be to their benefit, we have found that our coworkers have more respect for the design craft when they learn more about it, and that respect for designers has increased, not decreased.

What Design Thinking Means for the Business

It is easy to see why design thinking is a successful user-centered approach. In order to be a truly viable method, however, it must benefit the business. The benefits of design thinking for business fall into several classes.

Improved Ideation

As employees went through the activities described in this chapter, they became more comfortable and familiar with the design-thinking methodology. Frequency and positive reinforcement in a safe environment were the keys to getting people, particularly engineers, to feel more comfortable with the progression. This, in turn, freed them up to focus less on the mechanics of design thinking and more on the ideas. We saw a noticeable increase in both the number and quality of the ideas that teams generated for a project as time went on.

New Markets Generated

Most ideas generated through the ideation process directly relate to solving a problem for a given project. Sometimes teams can discover new problems or unseen opportunities that are outside the scope of their current project. It is the ideas that initially seem odd that often turn into new markets. These new market ideas do require further investigation and subsequent ideation sessions but can turn out to be lucrative products. Here is a simple example from *BusinessWeek* on how a company grew in a new market using interior design as a catalyst:

> British Airways had built a business strategy around increasing its long-haul international flights. So the company looked to see how the interior design of its planes could be improved to offer more comfort to customers. What resulted was the first seat in the industry that could lie completely flat, allowing customers to sleep prone, rather than slouch as in conventional airline seats. The result was a significant increase in sales and profitability for long-haul international flights. Design alone made the difference because everything else remained the same.[10]

Intellectual Property Created

Some ideas generated don't really have a home with a product team but can still serve a purpose for a company. In these cases, a company can use the discoveries and inventions as exclusive rights. These rights often manifest themselves as patents. The intellectual property that the company gains from design thinking allows it to increase the return on investment by either increasing its footprint in a market thereby keeping someone else out or avoiding new competition through direct revenue obtained by negotiating usage rights. Intellectual property is extremely valuable in today's market and a company's intellectual property assets are now considered more valuable than its physical assets.[10]

Decreased Time to Market

Today's world requires companies to move as fast as possible. Getting a product out before a competitor is vital to a company's survival. The design-thinking methodology has helped Intuit deliver more products more quickly for several reasons. First, the common understanding gained from the processes allowed our teams to spend less time on assigning responsibility and more time on implementation of ideas. Second, we saw that the teams trusted each other more because they had more shared understanding. Finally, because the teams were comfortable with the processes and the artifacts generated during the process, team members were much more willing to accept lower fidelity deliverables from the User Experience team. Since these lower fidelity deliverables were more accepted, User Experience members could spend less time on generating deliverables, thereby shortening their phase of the project and the overall schedule. Thomas Lockwood, Design Management Institutes (DMI) President and design industry analyst, has his own story of time-to-market benefits:

When I was responsible for design at StorageTek/Sun Microsystems (JAVA), we established a design platform approach and simple guidelines. Brand guidelines included interface principles, typography, color, photography style, diagram style, and iconography. Product guidelines included a common platform for computer hardware and a standardized chassis and interface, as well as other shared components. In this way, our engineers didn't have to design components, only functions; development time was greatly reduced. The cost and time savings based on platform design, guidelines, or even standards can be easily evaluated; just watch your project costs rise without them.[10]

Decreased Costs

As the economy picks up, every company is going to be faced with employee turnover. Employee turnover is expensive for companies because of the loss of knowledge and diminished performance. Design thinking is one way that Intuit enables employees to be more engaged and invested in the company's success, which is demonstrated by Intuit's inclusion in *Fortune* magazine's "100 Best Companies to Work For" list. The value that employees feel will go a long way toward keeping them at a company.

Because part of the design-thinking method is generative, project teams can create a lot of ideas very quickly. These ideas are then rapidly explored and evaluated with enough detail to make decisions about them but without investing a lot of time and energy. This sound investment of idea generation decreases development costs by reducing throwaway work. Additionally, because teams have spent the time to generate lots of ideas, they are more willing to give up a weaker idea for a stronger one because they have so many to choose from.

Influencing the Bottom Line

Good design comes from design thinking, and good design is proving to be a way for companies to increase their bottom line:

> Julie Hertenstein and Marjorie Platt, from Northeastern University's School of Business, have conducted research in conjunction with DMI, the Design Management Institute, on the financial performance of design since the mid-1990s. They evaluated financial performance by using traditional financial ratios, such as return on assets and net cash flow to sales, for the sample period. They found that firms rated as having good design were stronger on virtually all financial measures from a practical and managerial perspective, as well as from a statistical perspective.[10]

The usability of a product is becoming easier to measure as technology improves. Web tools like Omniture enable you to quantify page views, fall-out rates, browser stats, and aggregate user locations. These tools help pinpoint where design changes need to be made, and then what happens as a result of those design changes. *BusinessWeek's* article "Ten Ways to Measure Design's Success" identified design adjustments as a way to increase user performance and thus the bottom line:

> Very often, the usability of an interface design is measured by analyzing the efficiency of user navigation through observation, click-through, or interviews. Web sites are constantly monitored for user performance, and most web marketers watch our behavior closely and make design adjustments to improve performance. All manner of design-based usability issues can be isolated and evaluated.[10]

How to Start Design Thinking in Your Own Organization

We've covered a lot of information in this chapter, but we haven't answered where an organization should begin. We have three recommendations that worked well in our organization and contributed to the program's success.

Recognize and Leverage Natural Design Talent in Your Organization

Designers are a natural first choice to start a design-thinking initiative. But they are not the only ones: who in your company do you consider innovative? Who is an out-of-the-box thinker? Are there employees who hold patents or people others seek out to help generate new ideas and to solve big problems? All of these characteristics can indicate a design-thinker who can be leveraged. Look for the characteristics listed at the beginning of this article, such as being collaborative, curious, empathetic, and comfortable with ambiguity.

Start Small

Despite the high-level executive involvement, design thinking was deliberately started as a small initiative; approximately 15 employees recognized as having design-thinking expertise (many of them were designers, but not all) were asked to spend a few hours each month developing a pilot program. Over time, the group documented the process of design thinking. We found that the illustrations of design thinking evolved: the simpler the illustration, the more successful it seemed to be. For example, a diagram was originally created that showed several phases of design thinking that were distributed in poster form throughout several buildings. But a much simpler form of the diagram done quickly finally got a natural viral effect because it was easy to understand (see Figure 11-1). Creating an understandable representation and illustrating the key concepts of design thinking rather than the process and how those concepts support Intuit's core mission were instrumental to the communication of our ideas.

FIGURE 11-1 The Three Key Concepts of Design for Delight, Intuit's design thinking program (drawing by Suzanne Pellican and Kaaren Hanson)

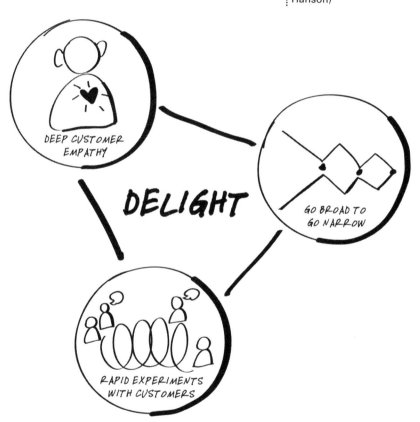

DEEP CUSTOMER EMPATHY

DELIGHT

GO BROAD TO GO NARROW

RAPID EXPERIMENTS WITH CUSTOMERS

Show, Don't Tell

Although these representations encouraged some interest, the group found that the most effective technique for disseminating design-thinking methods was to participate directly with teams at key points in their development cycle. In other words: show, don't tell. Volunteering as a facilitator for strategy and brainstorming sessions is an easy way to influence cross-functional teams.

At Intuit, a broader set of employees embraced and iterated the processes originally advocated by the catalyst group, improving and creating their own processes based on these practices to work for each organization's needs and goals. As the design-thinking practices took hold, the team expanded by training others to facilitate. The program continues to grow, and the design thinkers continue to facilitate sessions in different parts of the organization.

We believe that including design-thinking practices can benefit many organizations, broadening their ability to respond to business pressures in an innovative and efficient way. We hope that our experience with design thinking will help you implement it in your organization, and that you will see the same benefits that we have.

Summary

- **What is the business context (e.g., product, customers)?**
  Intuit Inc. is a leading provider of financial management, tax, and online banking solutions for consumers, small- and mid-sized businesses, accountants, and financial institutions.

- **Which (business) problems did you address with your UX practice?**
  Design thinking has enabled Intuit to speed up the process of defining customer problems as well as imagining a broader range of solutions for our small business customers.

- **What were constraints and prerequisites?**
  Intuit has a customer-centric culture, which was the foundation for adopting design thinking. Our constraints are similar to others in the software industry: development time, efficient use of resources, and maintaining a competitive edge.

- **In which development context did you apply your UX practice?**
  Most of our development teams work in a modified agile development context.

- **What compelling events supported you in applying your UX practice successfully?**
  At Intuit, several executives initiated, sponsored, and promoted the design-thinking initiatives. Due to this high-level sponsorship, design thinking rapidly gained visibility throughout Inuit.

- **What was the achieved product impact?**
  Improved ideation (better quantity and quality of ideas) and decreased time to market for the projects that utilized design thinking were two key benefits.

- **How did you apply the UX practice?**
  Inspirational talks, workshops, hackathons, and quick experiments were some of the key events that helped make design thinking ubiquitous at Intuit.

- **Which recommendations do you have for our readers?**
  Recognize and leverage natural design talent in your organizations. Start small, and show, don't tell to demonstrate the benefits of design thinking.

References

1. Design Council. 2007. "Value of design: Design Council." http://www.designcouncil.org.uk/our-work/Insight/Research/How-businesses-use-design/Added-Value-2007/.

2. Simon, Herbert A. 1996. *The Sciences of the Artificial.* Boston: MIT Press.

3. Brown, T. 2008. *Design Thinking. Harvard Business Review.* http://harvardbusinessonline.hbsp.harvard.edu/hbsp/hbr/articles/article.jsp;jsessionid=NG00FBJJBIPOGAKRGWCB5VQBKE0YOISW?ml_action=get-article&articleID=R0806E&ml_page=1&ml_subscriber=true (accessed June 2008).

4. Brown, Tim, and Jocelyn Wyatt. 2010. "Design Thinking for Social Innovation." *Stanford Social Innovation Review* (Winter).

5. 2010. "Vincent Van Gogh Quotes." http://thinkexist.com/quotation/for_my_part_i_know_nothing_with_any_certainty-but/254951.html.

6. Brown, Tim. 2005 "Strategy by Design." *Fast Company.* (June 1). http://www.fastcompany.com/magazine/95/design-strategy.html.

7. Neumeier, Marty. 2008. "Designing the Future of Business." *BusinessWeek* (August 13). http://www.businessweek.com/innovate/content/aug2008/id20080813_677771.htm.

8. Rae, Jeneanne. 2008. "P&G Changes Its Game." *BusinessWeek* (July 28). http://www.businessweek.com/innovate/content/jul2008/id20080728_623527.htm.

9. McCullagh, Kevin. 1st August 2009. New Challenges for Design Managers. http://www.plan.bz/plan-views/2009/august/new-challenges-for-design-managers.

10. Lockwood, Thomas. 2009. "Ten Ways to Measure Design's Success" *BusinessWeek* (October 5). http://www.businessweek.com/innovate/content/oct2009/id2009105_225354.htm.

Further Reading

Hagel, J., and J. Seely. 2008. "How SAP Seeds Innovation." *BusinessWeek.* http://www.businessweek.com/innovate/content/jul2008/id20080723_353753.htm?link_position=link3 (accessed August 21, 2008).

Lombardi, V. nd. "What Is Design Thinking?" *Noise Between Stations.* http://noisebetweenstations.com/personal/weblogs/?page_id=1688 (accessed August 21, 2008).

Maddock, G., and R. Vitón. 2008. "Believe in Innovation to Win." *BusinessWeek.* http://www.businessweek.com/managing/content/may2008/ca20080520_060268.htm?campaign_id=alerts (accessed August 21, 2008).

Vossoughi, S. 2008. "It's All About Experience." *BusinessWeek.* http://www.businessweek.com/innovate/content/apr2008/id20080411_491286.htm (accessed August 21, 2008).

Wladawsky-Berger I. 2008. "The Challenges of Innovation." *BusinessWeek.* http://www.businessweek.com/innovate/content/aug2008/id20080822_832405.htm?campaign_id=alerts (accessed August 21, 2008).

Index